Princess Marg
y Diana Mitzah vucard
n Cotillard Maria Félix
co Princess of Hanover
ntess Jacqueline de Ribes
e Dietrich Rihanna
Francine Weisweiller
Portman Geneviève Page
ess Charlene of Monaco
Pahlavi Rita Hayworth

WOMEN IN DIOR
PORTRAITS OF ELEGANCE

Women in Dior: Portraits of Elegance
© 2016 Rizzoli International Publications, Inc.
300 Park Avenue South, New York, NY 10010
www.rizzoliusa.com

© 2016 Christian Dior

Texts: Laurence Benaïm
Foreword: Florence Müller

Photography of dresses: Laziz Hamani,
assisted by Nicolas Guérin

Cover: *Angélique* dress by Mats Gustafson, 2016

Publisher: Charles Miers
Editorial Direction: Catherine Bonifassi
Art Direction: Daniel Baer
Production: Maria Pia Gramaglia
Editor: Daniel Melamud
Copy Editor: Victorine Lamothe-Maurin

Editorial Coordination:
CASSI EDITION, Audrey Gregorczyk

Translation:
Gail de Courcy-Ireland

All rights reserved. No part of this publication may be reproduced, stored in a retrieval system, or transmitted in any form or by any means, electronic, mechanical, photocopying, recording or otherwise, without prior consent of the author.

Library of Congress Control Number: 2016934771
ISBN: 978-0-8478-4933-8
2016 2017 2018 2019 / 10 9 8 7 6 5 4 3 2 1
Printed in Italy

WOMEN IN DIOR
PORTRAITS OF ELEGANCE

Text by Laurence Benaïm
Foreword by Florence Müller

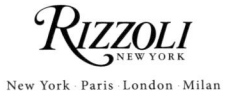

New York · Paris · London · Milan

Patricia López-Willshaw

Edmonde Charles-Roux Lad

Suzanne Luling Mai

Princess Grace of Mon

Margot Fonteyn Co

Sophia Loren Mule

Carla Bruni-Sarkozy

Zizi Jeanmaire Natali

Carmen Colle Prin

Duchess of Windsor Fara

PHOTOGRAPH CREDITS

p. 6: © Cecil Beaton/Camera Press/Gamma; p. 9: © 2013 Mark Shaw/mptvimages; p. 11: © Association Willy Maywald/ADAGP, Paris 2016; p. 12: © Willy Rizzo/*Paris Match*/Scoop; p. 15: © Patrick Demarchelier; p. 16: Courtesy the John F. Kennedy Library and Museum; p. 18: © Laziz Hamani; p. 21: © 1989 Center for Creative Photography, Arizona Board of Regents; p. 22: Personal archives of the family of Claire Newman; p. 25: Arik Nepo, *Vogue* Paris, February 1949: © Condé Nast Publications; p. 26: © Gérard Uféras; p. 27: © Laziz Hamani; p. 29: © 2013 Mark Shaw/mptvimages; p. 30: Photo André Ostier, © The estate of André Ostier; p. 31: © Jack Nisberg/Roger-Viollet; p. 32, 33: © Laziz Hamani; p. 35: Photo André Ostier, © The estate of André Ostier; p. 36, 37: © Laziz Hamani; p. 39: Photo André Ostier, © The estate of André Ostier; p. 40: © Robert Doisneau/Rapho; p. 41: © Laziz Hamani; p. 43: Henry Clarke, *Vogue* Paris, December–January 1957, © Henry Clarke, musée Galliera/ADAGP, Paris 2016; p. 44-45: Arik Nepo, *Vogue*, August 15, 1952, © Condé Nast; p. 47: © Cecil Beaton/Condé Nast via Getty Images; p. 48, 49: Photos André Ostier, © The estate of André Ostier; p. 50: © Laziz Hamani; p. 53: © Association Willy Maywald/ADAGP, Paris 2016; p. 54: © Jack Garofalo/*Paris Match*/Scoop; p. 57: © The Richard Avedon Foundation; p. 58, 59: © Laziz Hamani; p. 61: Guy Arsac, *Vogue* Paris, May 1958, © Condé Nast Publications; p. 62: © TCD; p. 63: © Robert Doisneau/Rapho; p. 65: © Association Willy Maywald/ADAGP, Paris 2016; p. 66, 67: © Laziz Hamani; p. 69: © Association Willy Maywald/ADAGP, Paris 2016; p. 71: © Keystone/Getty Images; p. 72: © TopFoto/Roger-Viollet; p. 73 : © Laziz Hamani; p. 75: © Willy Rizzo/*Paris Match*/Scoop; p. 76: © Keystone-France; p. 77: © Rue des Archives/AGIP; p. 79 : © Eugène Kammerman/Rapho; p. 80: © 2013 Mark Shaw/mptvimages; p. 81: Henry Clarke, *Vogue*, March 15, 1957, © Condé Nast; p. 82: © Laziz Hamani; p. 85: Courtesy the John F. Kennedy Library and Museum; p. 86: Cecil Beaton, *Vogue* Paris, February 1951, © Condé Nast Publications; p. 89: © API/Gamma Rapho; p. 91: © Rue des Archives/AGIP; p. 92: © Keystone-France; p. 93 : © Association Willy Maywald/ADAGP, Paris, 2016; p. 95: © Marilyn Silverstone/Magnum Photos; p. 97: © Tim Graham/Getty Images; p. 98: © Villard/Sipa Press; p. 99: © Laziz Hamani; p. 100: © Steve Parsons/PA Photos/Abacapress.com; p. 102-103: Annie Leibovitz, *Vanity Fair*, September 2008, © Annie Leibovitz/Trunk Archive; p. 105 : © Pascal Le Segretain/Getty Images for the Princess Grace Foundation-USA; p. 106: © The Andy Warhol Foundation for the Visual Arts, Inc./ADAGP, Paris 2016 – Cliché: Banque d'Images de l'ADAGP; p. 107: © Yousuf Karsh/Camera Press/Gamma; p. 109: © Bettmann/Corbis; p. 110: © Pool Simon/Uzan/Gamma; p. 111: © Keystone-France/Getty Images; p. 112 : © Laziz Hamani; p. 115: © Christopher Polk/Getty Images; p. 116: © Bert Stern; p. 119: © mptvimages; p. 120-121: © The Richard Avedon Foundation; p. 123: photo Horst P. Horst, © Condé Nast; © Victoria and Albert Museum, London; p. 124: All rights reserved; p. 125: © Laziz Hamani; p. 127: Photo André Ostier, © The estate of André Ostier; p. 128, 129: © Laziz Hamani; p. 131: © Dan MacMedan/WireImage; p. 132-133: © Paolo Roversi; p. 135 : © Pascal Le Segretain/Getty Images; p. 136-137: © Mario Sorrenti/Art Partner; p. 139: © Rindoff/Le Segretain/Getty Images for Dior; p. 140-141 : © Annie Leibovitz/Trunk Archive; p. 143: All rights reserved; p. 144: © Maurice Zalewski/adoc-photos; p. 145: All rights reserved; p. 147, 148, 149: © Christian Dior. Cover: © Mats Gustafson.

Designs created by Christian Dior (1947-1957): p. 6, 21, 22, 25, 27, 35-49, 58, 59, 62, 66, 67, 71, 75-81, 86, 89, 91, 107, 109, 110, 119, 123, 125, 129, 131, 144.
Christian Dior designs created by Yves Saint Laurent (1958-1960): p. 29, 30, 60, 63, 127, 128.
Christian Dior designs created by Marc Bohan (1961-1989): p. 9, 16, 31-33, 57, 72, 73, 95, 106, 111, 116.
Christian Dior designs created by John Galliano (1997-2011): p. 15, 98, 101-103, 105, 112.
Christian Dior designs created by Raf Simons (2012-2015): p. 115, 132-133, 135, 139, 140-141, 147-149.

This exhibition has been supported by:
The City of Granville
in particular the Mayor, Mrs. Dominique Baudry,
Mireille Deniau, Deputy of Culture and the Rights of Women,
Florence Lequin, Deputy of the Tourist and Communication Office,
Virginie Frouin, Director of Communication,
Jérôme Robin, and the Municipal Workshop of the City of Granville.
Ministère de la Culture, DRAC Basse-Normandie
Conseil général de la Manche
Conseil régional de Basse-Normandie
LVMH / Moët Hennessy • Louis Vuitton
Christian Dior Couture and Parfums Christian Dior

We would like to thank the institutions who loaned their works to the exhibition:
Palais Galliera – City of Paris Museum of Fashion,
and in particular Olivier Saillard, Véronique Belloir, Corinne Dom,
Marie-Laure Gutton, and Alexandre Samson.
Musée des Arts décoratifs,
and in particular Olivier Gabet, Pamela Golbin, Éric Pujalet-Plaà, Joséphine Pellas,
Emmanuelle Garcin, and Myriam Tessier.
Bibliothèque Historique de la Ville de Paris,
and in particular Alain Durel, Bérengère de l'Épine, and Pauline Girard.
Josée and René de Chambrun Foundation,
and in particular Georges Renand, Marie-Alpais Torchebœuf, Jeanine de Cardaillac, and Juliette Jestaz.
The Prince's Palace of Monaco,
and in particular Hervé Irien and Christian Selvatico.

Private Collections:
Collection Didier Ludot, Paris and in particular Didier Ludot and François Hurteau-Flamand,
Bernadette Castel and Constance Riou, Béatrice Colle-Saalsburg, Thomas Gunther, Elizabeth Kirchner,
Jeanine Malclès, Charlotte Mosley, Mr. and Mrs. Adrien Ostier, Sylvie Richez-Gabay and Shaïna Gabay,
Mr. and Mrs. Pierre Rosenberg, Michèle Thouvenin, and Frédérique Véran.

We would like to thank:
Patrick Demarchelier, Mats Gustafson, Laziz Hamani,
Annie Leibovitz, Paolo Roversi, Mario Sorrenti, and Gérard Uféras.

Particular thanks to:
H.S.H. the Princess Charlene of Monaco, H.R.H. the Princess of Hanover, H.I.M. Empress Farah Pahlavi,
the Countess de Ribes, Carla Bruni-Sarkozy, Geneviève Page, Marion Cotillard, Jennifer Lawrence,
Natalie Portman, Rihanna, and Charlize Theron as well as Véronique Simian, Lotfi Maktouf, Françoise Dumas,
Stéphane Goriau, Véronique Rampazzo, Bastien Duval, Liz Mahoney, Jay Brown, and Ciarra Pardo.

*We thank everyone who brought their support to the preparation, organization,
and promotion of the exhibition and book* Women in Dior: Portraits of Elegance:
Macha Belanger and Philippe Meyssat (Sipa Press), Caroline Berton and Vanessa Bernard (Condé Nast
Publications), Daniel Bouteiller (Télé Ciné Documentation), Denis Canguilhem and Clément Kachelhoffer
(adoc-photos), Tammy Carter (Center for Creative Photography), Nelly Dhoutaut (Hachette Filipacchi
Associés - La Scoop), Michel Donval, Adeline Grolleau and Julie Legrand (ADAGP), Jacqueline Gertner (JFK
Presidential Library), Martine Guillemain (Getty Images), Thomas Michael Gunther, Erin Harris (The Richard
Avedon Foundation), Andy Howick (mptvimages), Hannah Kadah and Gregory Spencer (Art Partner), Nikandré
Koukoulioti (Magnum Photos), Estelle Leeds, Karine Mahiout (Abaca Press), Michaela McMahon-Dunphy,
Philippe Brutus and Michael Van Horne (Art+Commerce), Barbara Mazza (Roger-Viollet), Julien Mellone
(Corbis), Mrs. Tina G. Newman, Jutta Niemann (Association Willy Maywald), Laetitia Payen and
Isabelle Sadys (Gamma Rapho), Celine Smith (V&A Images), Sonja Spies-Orlowski (Trunk Archive),
Gabrielle Pintér (Rue des Archives), and Kyle Tannler (Condé Nast).

Clémentine Bollard, Laurent Chrétien, Angélique Durif,
Carolina Hall, Marie-Flore Levoir, David Richard, and Olivier Tavoso.

Laurence Benaïm would like to thank:
H.I.M. Empress Farah Pahlavi, Catherine Rivière, Timothy Lloyd Pope, Sophie Gins, Patricia Astric-Blanc,
Monique Bailly, Florence Chehet, and Florence Leonetti for their anecdotes,
as well as Kambiz Atabai and Karine Porret.

ACKNOWLEDGMENTS

This publication accompanies the *Women in Dior: Portraits of Elegance* exhibition
organized by the Association Présence de Christian Dior at the
Musée Christian Dior in Granville from May 5 to September 25, 2016,
and presented with the Normandy Impressionist Festival.

This project has been completed thanks to:
Bernard Arnault, President of LVMH / Moët Hennessy • Louis Vuitton,
Sidney Toledano, Chief Executive Officer of Christian Dior Couture,
Claude Martinez, Chief Executive Officer of Christian Dior Parfums.

President of the Association Présence de Christian Dior
Jean-Paul Claverie

General Curator
Florence Müller

Scenography
Simon Jaffrot, Noémie Bourgeois,
assisted by Marie Docquiert and Mathilde Peterlini.

Musée Christian Dior in Granville
Brigitte Richart, Curator,
Barbara Jeauffroy-Mairet, Associate Curator,
as well as Laura Hamonic, Ophélie Verstavel,
Paule Gilles, Audrey Barbero,
Eleonore Filice, and Gilles Hamel.

Christian Dior Couture
Olivier Bialobos as well as Solène Auréal, Camille Bidouze, Séverine Breton,
Sylvain Carré, Cécile Chamouard-Aykanat, Gérald Chevalier, Bernard Danillon de Cazella,
Anne de Dieuleveult, Mathilde Favier, Jérôme Gautier, Sandra Georges, Justine Lasgi, Philippe Le Moult,
Alexander Lopez, Soizic Pfaff, Hélène Poirier, Solenn Roggeman, Perrine Scherrer,
Alessandro Sellaretti, Hélène Starkman, Joana Tosta, and Jennifer Walheim.

Christian Dior Parfums
Jérôme Pulis as well as Frédéric Bourdelier,
Fanny Bourdette-Donon, Lorraine Fagot,
and Vincent Leret.

LVMH / Moët Hennessy • Louis Vuitton
Loïc Bégard

Christian Dior
COUTURE

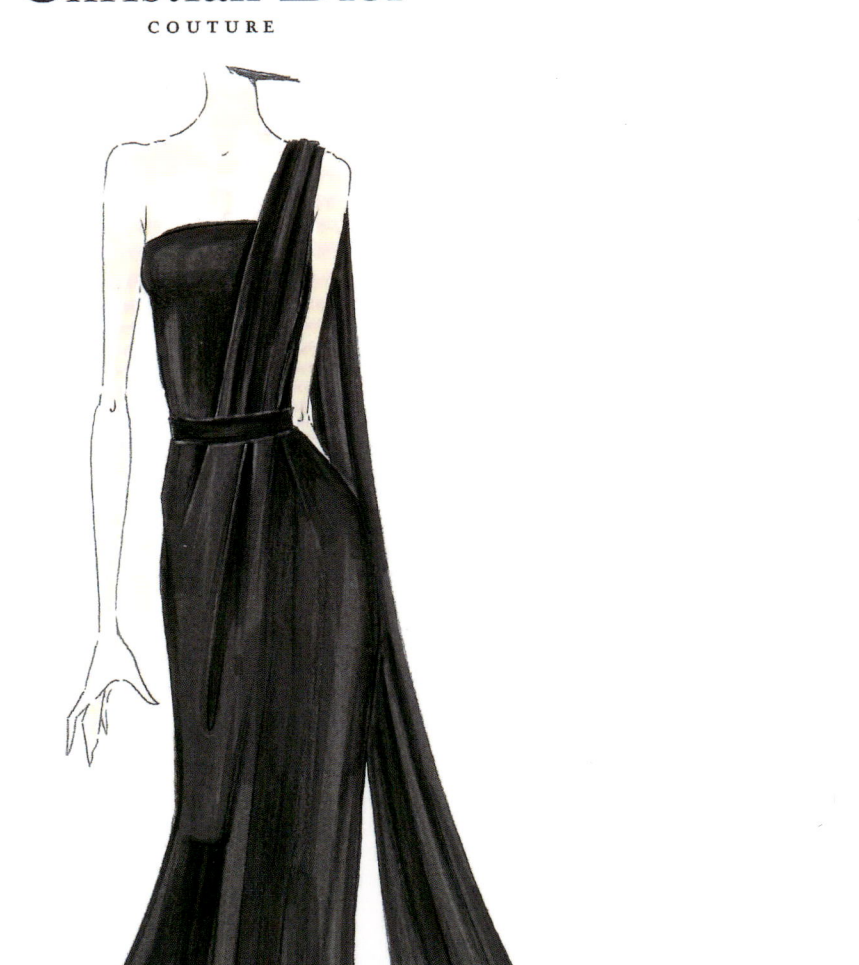

Sketch for a black silk crepe dress, a special haute couture creation worn by Amal Clooney during the 2015 Golden Globes.

Christian Dior
COUTURE

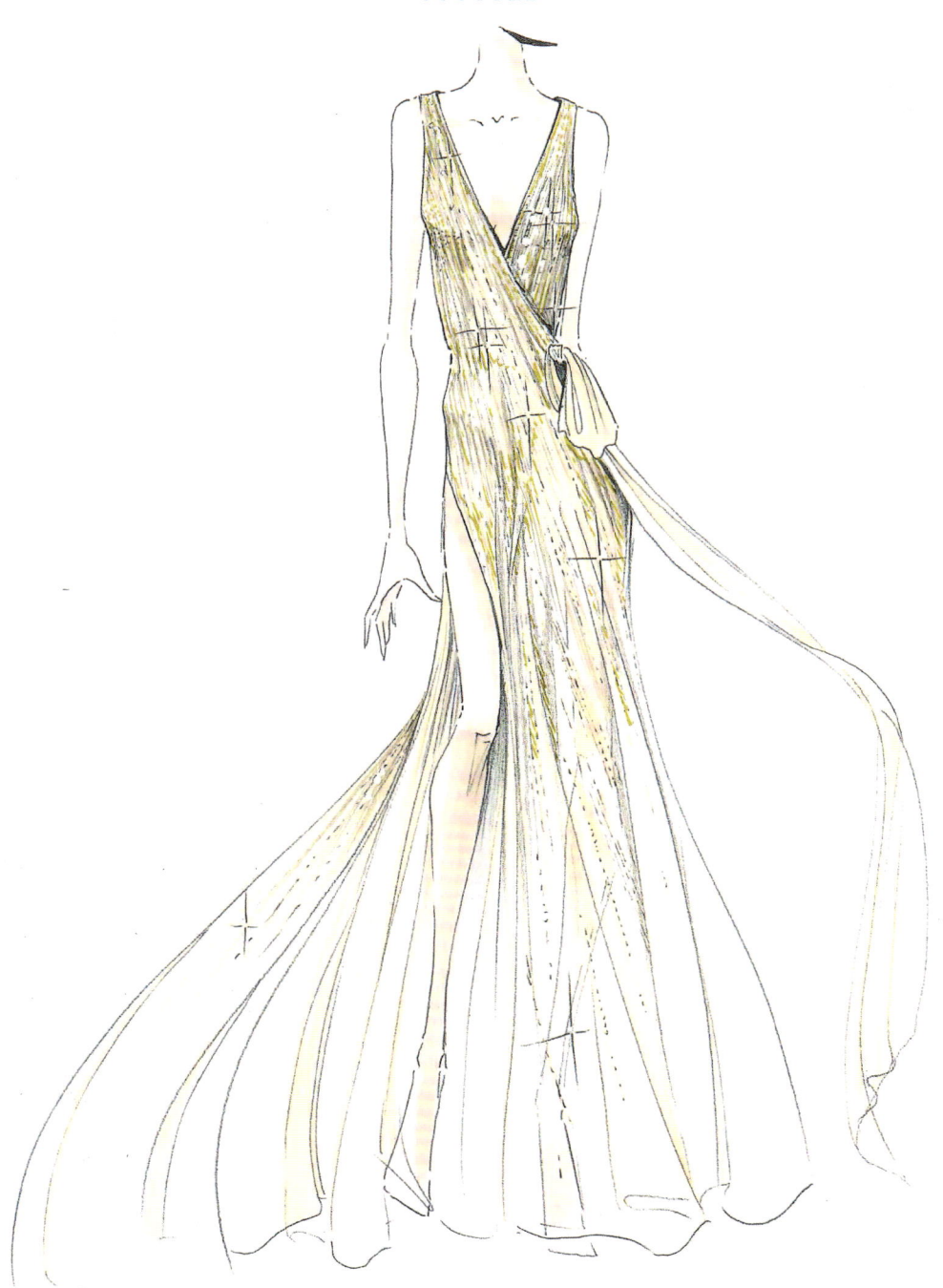

Christian Dior
COUTURE

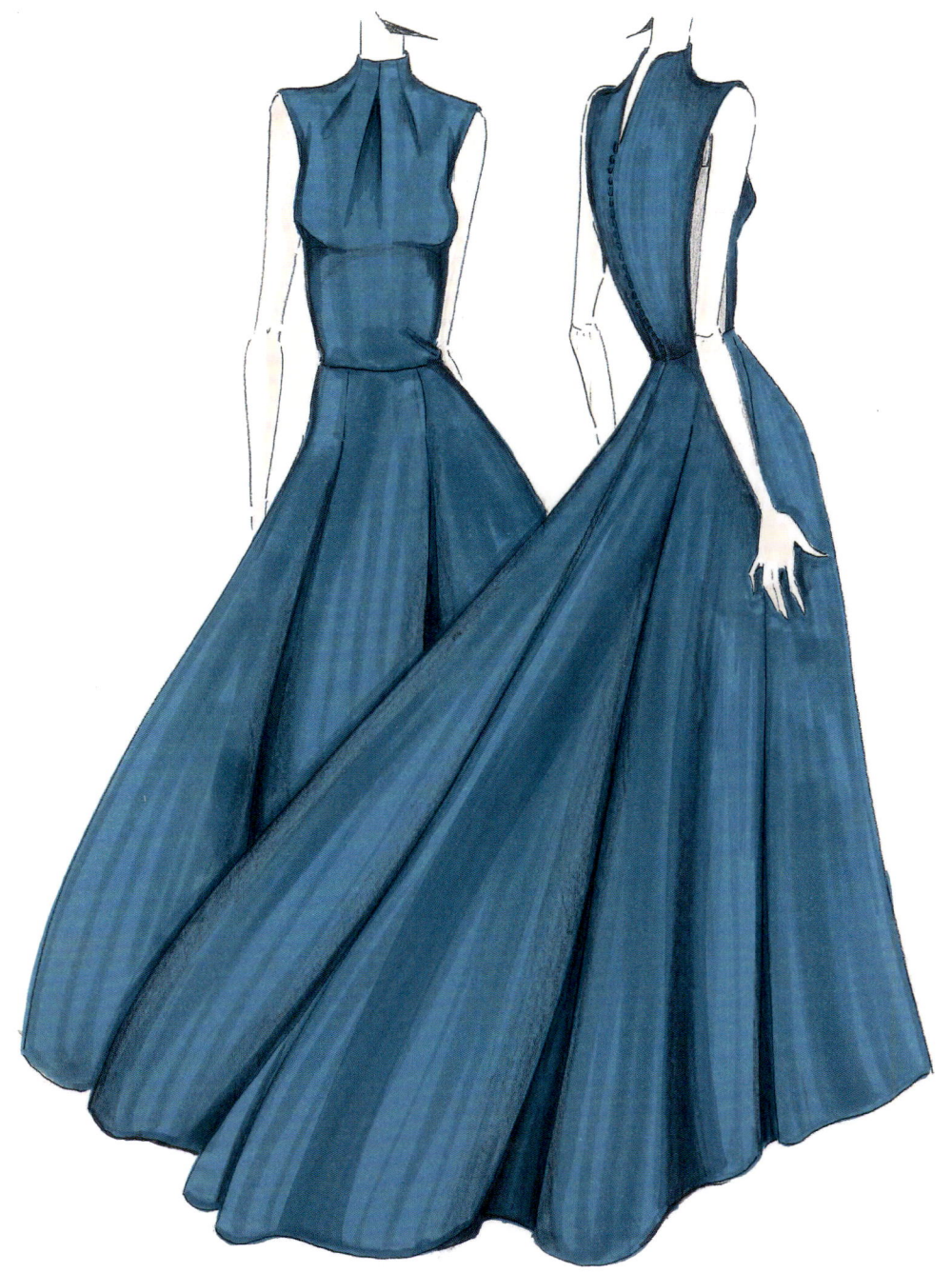

The Special Creations

The list is impressive: a parade of stars and luminous dresses, a collection of thousands of likes and followers clicking their applause on the Web. Some dresses are inspired by archival designs, like the ones chosen by Marion Cotillard (Academy Awards in 2014) or Rihanna in 2015, with a sheath dress reproducing the lines of a garment designed by Christian Dior in 1951. Others are brand-new creations throughout. "I love it!" said Jennifer Lawrence on discovering her dress made for the 2013 Oscars by the Dior ateliers.

As far as execution of the dresses is concerned, everything takes place on the inside, a question of structure and support that is the mainstay of the Dior tradition: grosgrain ribbon placed under the bust and again at the waist, a "marguerite" cotton tulle to provide extra support, to avoid the danger that it might "sag and slump with the heat." Everything is considered in advance, from the hours that can be spent waiting on the red carpet to diverse production constraints. The art behind the illusion is never visible to the naked eye. In this vein, Natalie Portman's *Miss Dior* dress, adorned with five thousand embroidered flowers, makes way for a simple black sheath dress in which the star takes off . . . in a helicopter! In 2015, the two dresses made for Charlize Theron to shoot the *J'adore* film in the Hall of Mirrors in Versailles necessitated 150 hours of handiwork, not to mention two hundred hours of embroidery for the see-through sequins, fragments pierced and sprayed with gold to achieve the simultaneously "discreet and shimmering" effect.

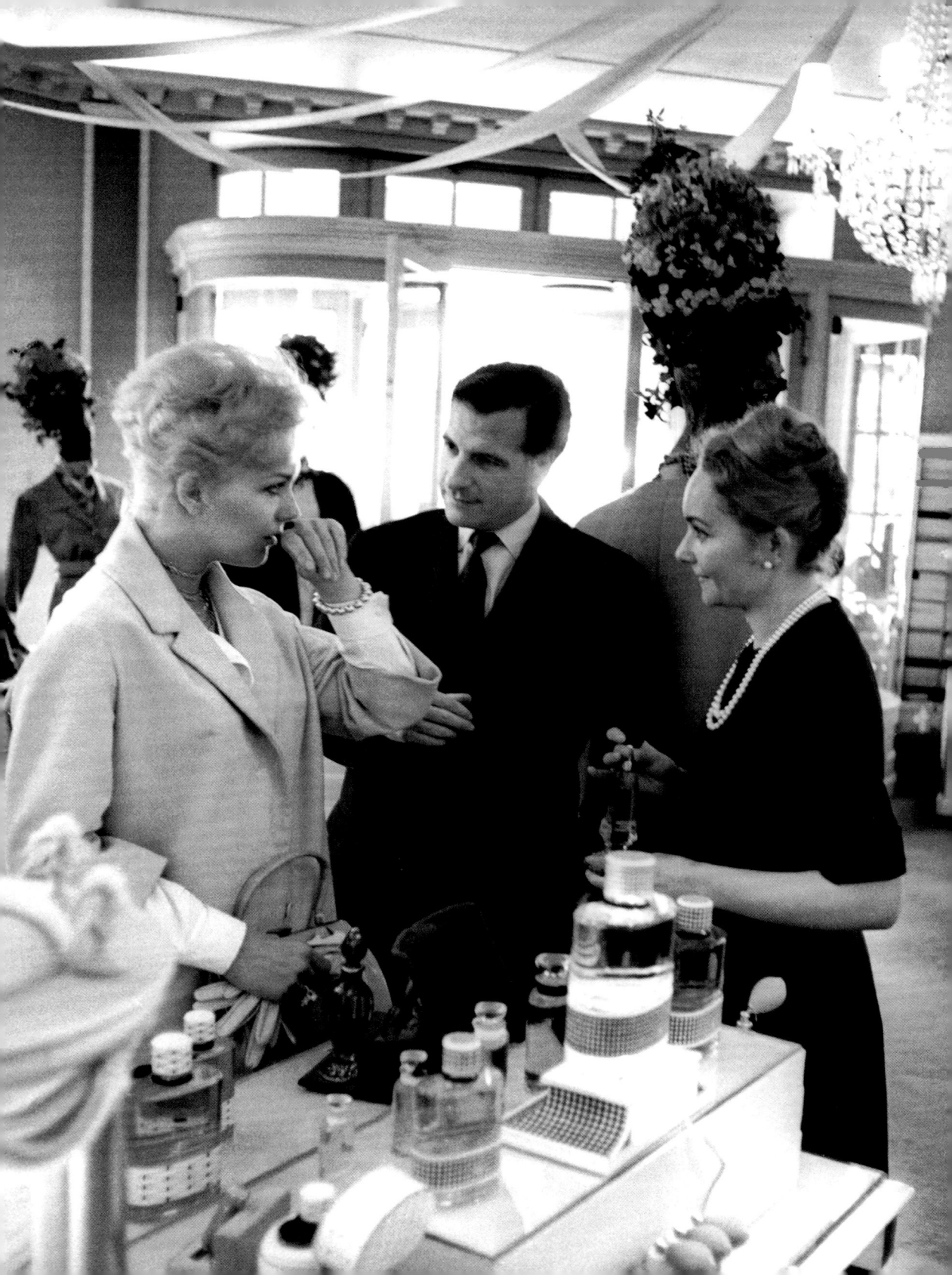

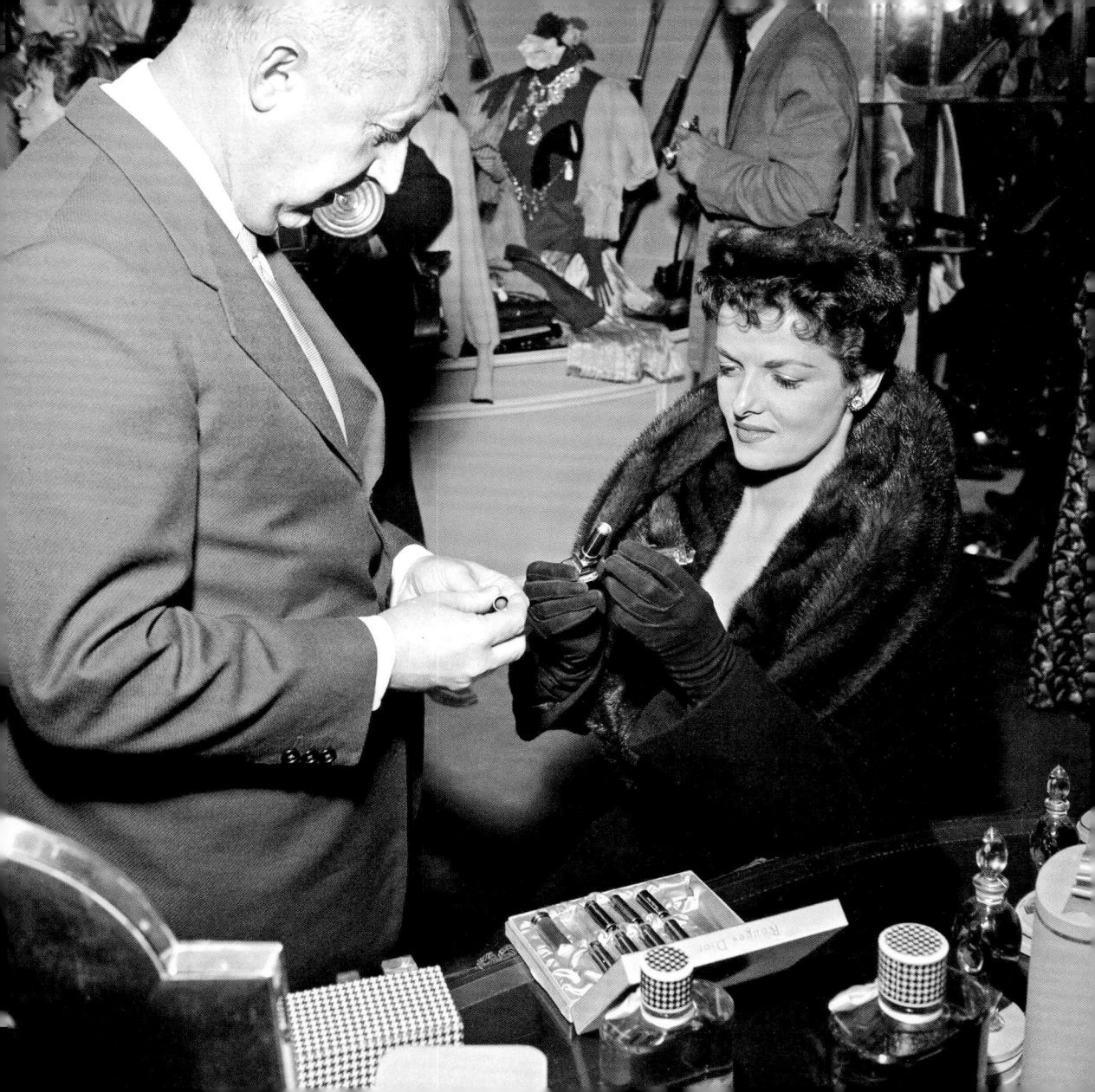

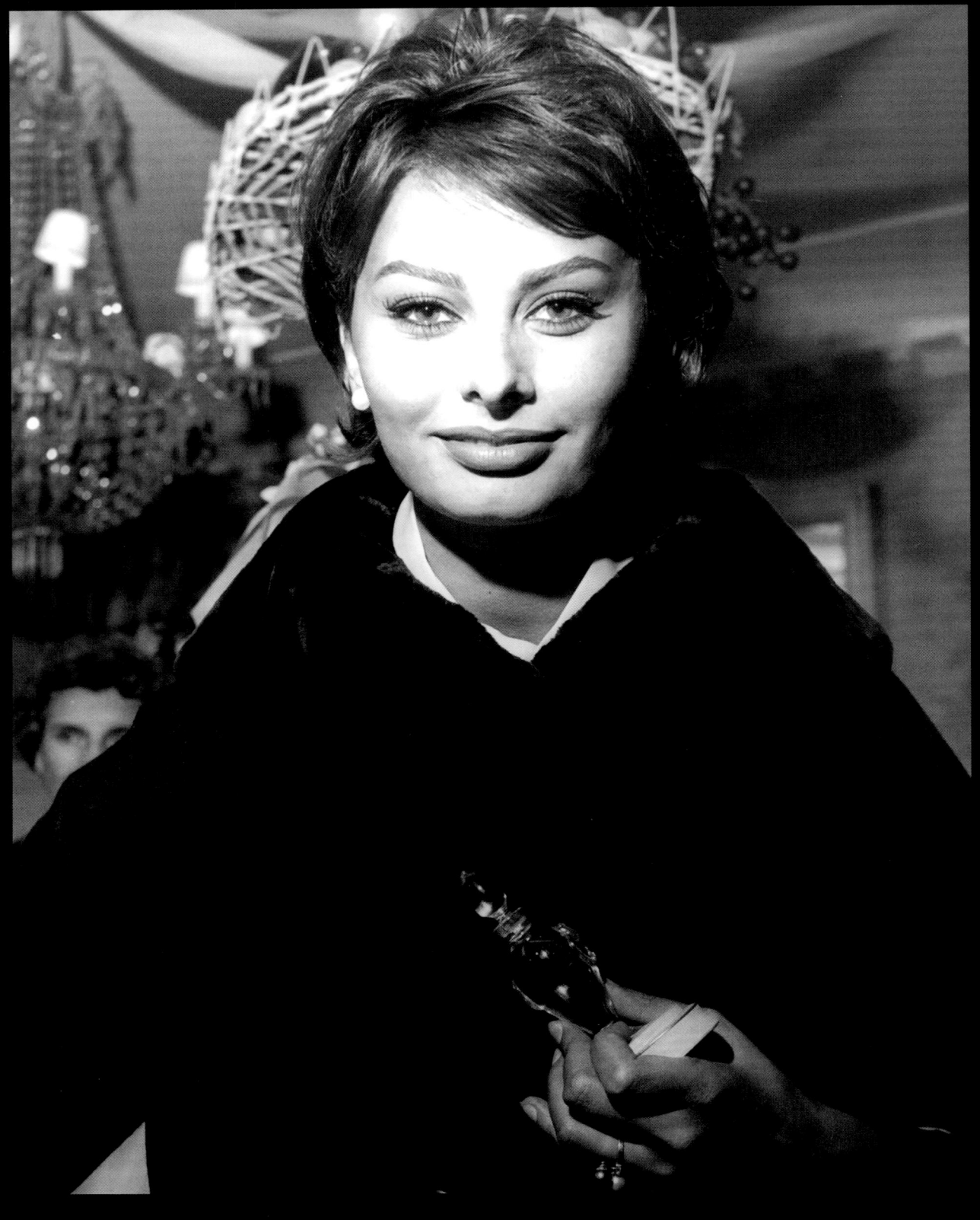

Sophia Loren in the Avenue Montaigne Dior boutique, where she just received a bottle of *Miss Dior* in clear Baccarat crystal, around 1961.

Dior Perfumes the Stars

"Perfume is the indispensable complement to the personality of women, the finishing touch on a dress, the rose with which Lancret signed his canvases." On February 12, 1947, the day of his first collection, Christian Dior sprayed *Miss Dior* around the Trianon gray salons of the couture house he had just founded. The perfume was still a prototype, but already it entered the Dior legend. A pink and gray *Miss Dior* dress would even be created in 1949: Covered with embroidered silk flowers, this cocktail dress design with six petticoats opened an endless chapter of *Miss Dior* allusions. Wearing Dior fragrance is about being punch-drunk on optimism and love, magnifying an image that goes hand-in-hand with Paris—the elegance immortalized by Gruau in 1949 in a picture of a swan wearing a pearl necklace and a black bow around its neck. The trail would be represented by a black tulle negligée and a pair of white gloves placed on a neo-Louis XVI chair. The bow and the houndstooth motif engraved on the bottle are part of this enchantment of the senses for which Dior held the secret. Josephine Baker, Marlene Dietrich, and Margot Fonteyn all wore *Miss Dior*, revealing their loyalty to the Dior spirit as much as the scent. From Kim Novak and Princess Grace, who were faithful to *Eau Fraîche*, to Giulietta Masina and Olivia de Havilland, who loved *Diorissimo*, society ladies and celebrities added the discreet charm of a fragrant ritual to their public appearances. Dior had defined fashion as "the art of renewing the feeling of being in love." In a play on endless echoes, Dior perfumes express this ideal of beauty and become one with their time: Launched in 1999, *J'adore*, embodied by the sculptural actress Charlize Theron and housed in a bottle that stands out from all the rest with its solar, feminine curves, ranks top of the best-selling perfumes in the world.

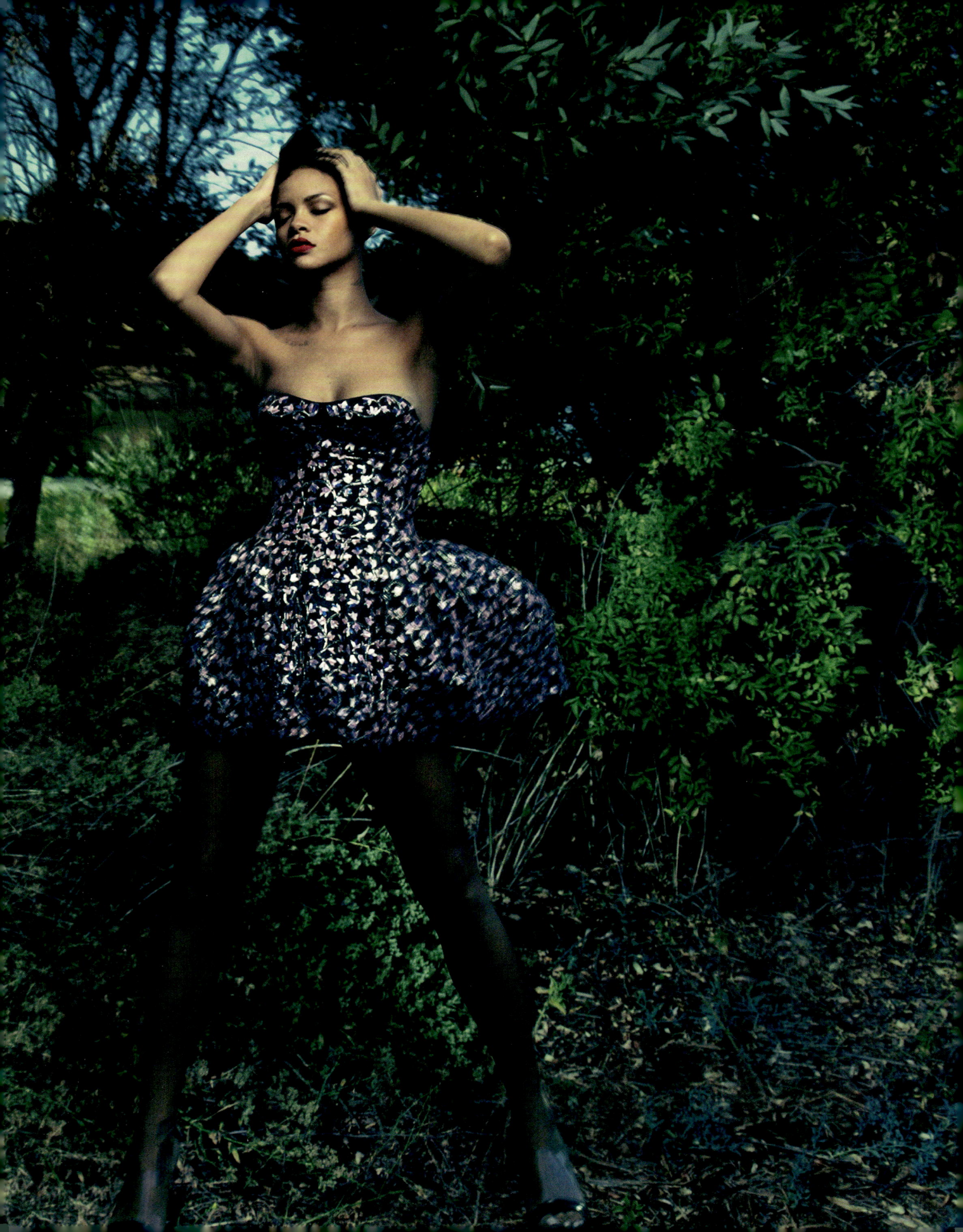

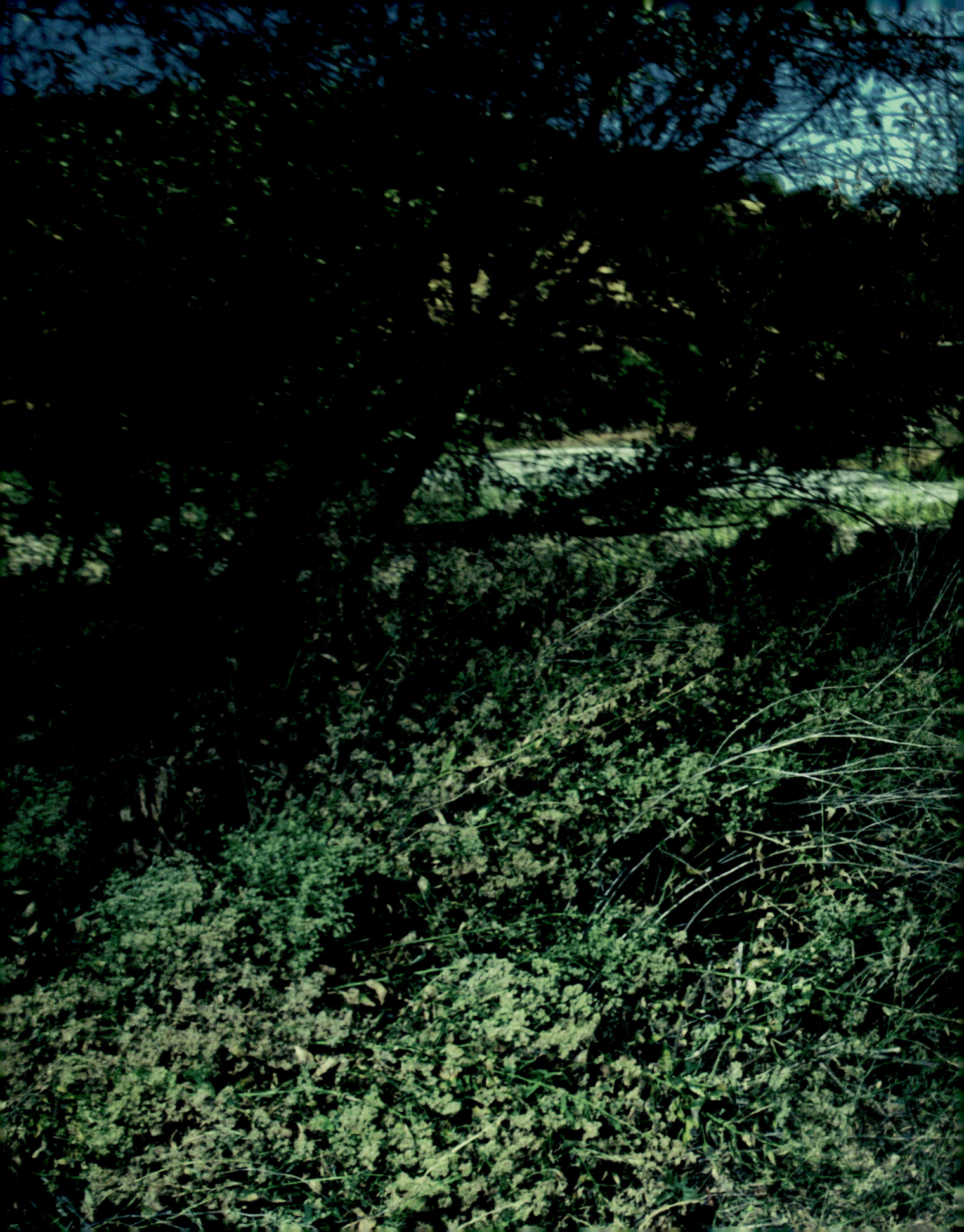

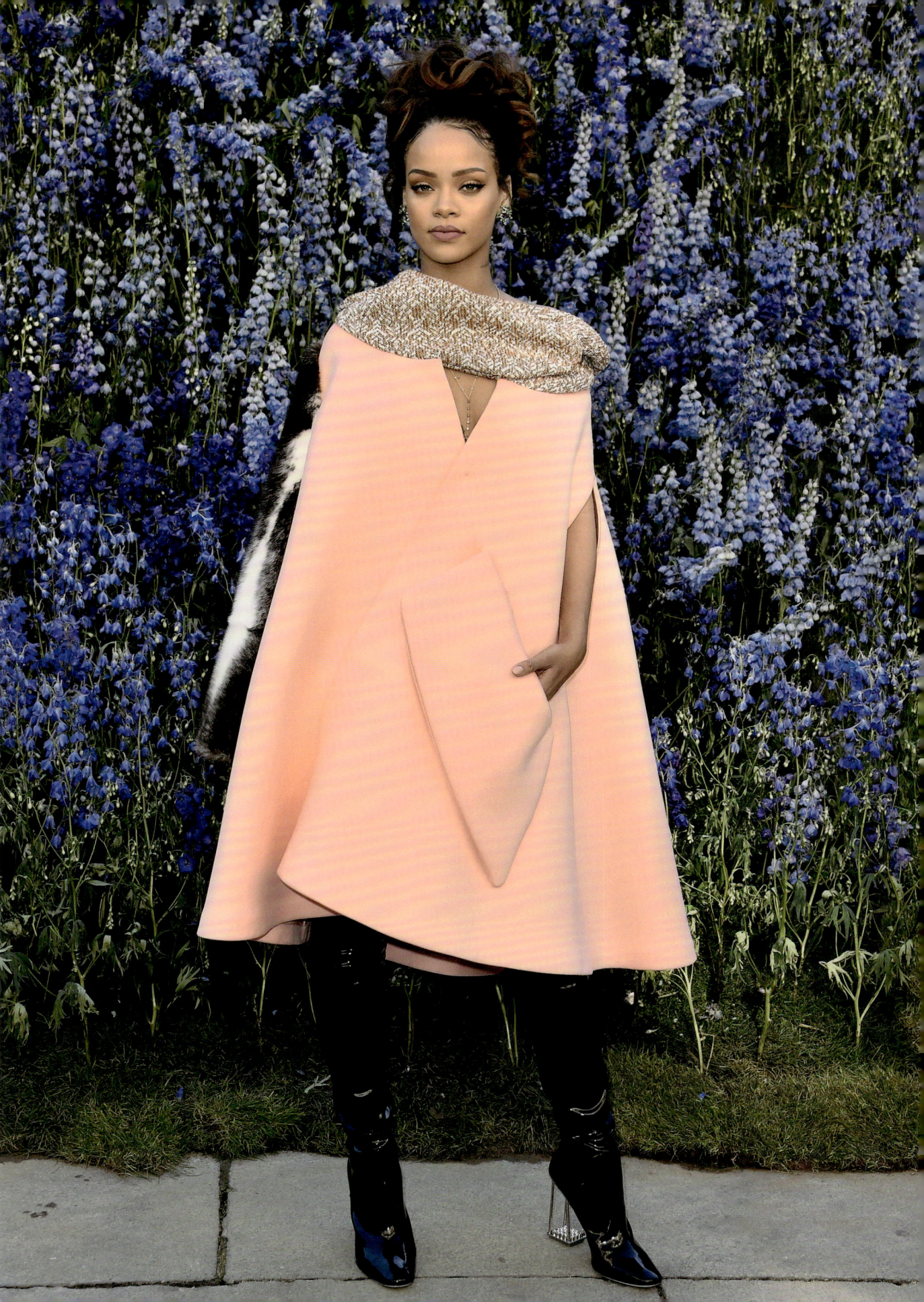

Rihanna

Rihanna is the face of the *Secret Garden* campaign shot at Versailles by Steven Klein. The first black face of the house of Dior, she is also the third most influential personality in the world on Facebook: Every one of her appearances triggers hundreds of thousands of likes on social networks. Rihanna appeared at the Diamond Ball charity gala (Los Angeles, December 2015) in a champagne satin bustier dress and cape by Dior Haute Couture, celebrating with panache the union between R&B and great French tradition. With Dior, one of today's greatest pop icons—she has sold approximately twenty-five million albums and 140 million singles—adopts multiple looks and roles: She chose a chaste, immaculate chiffon dress for the ninety-fifth anniversary of *Vogue* Paris (October 2015) and a salmon-pink neoprene coat, a *Diorama* handbag, black vinyl thigh-high boots by Dior, and Milly Carnivora earrings for Paris Fashion Week in Autumn 2015. . . . "Make sure you can walk in stiletto heels if you want to rock them like Rihanna," one blogger recommends. Whether strutting through the Hall of Mirrors in a glittering dress or posing for *Dior Magazine* in a fishnet number (shot by Craig McDean in Autumn 2015), her strength of character, underscored by *Rouge Dior* lips, seems to know no bounds. "She is a goddess, but she is accessible," states Sidney Toledano, President of Dior Couture. The sumptuous singer from Barbados knew how to transform herself from brunette to redhead at the 2011 Grammy Awards, wowing the audience in her hand-painted taffeta and tulle Dior Haute Couture ball gown. Rihanna, the heroine of *Anti*, her eighth album (2016), tells it as she is and has no qualms about tweeting: "I'm crazy and I don't pretend to be anything else."

OPPOSITE Rihanna chose a design from the Autumn-Winter 2015 haute couture collection to attend the Spring-Summer 2016 ready-to-wear collection's runway show in Paris, October 2, 2015.

FOLLOWING PAGES Rihanna photographed by Annie Leibovitz for *Vogue*, November 2012. She wears a design from the Autumn-Winter 2012 haute couture collection.

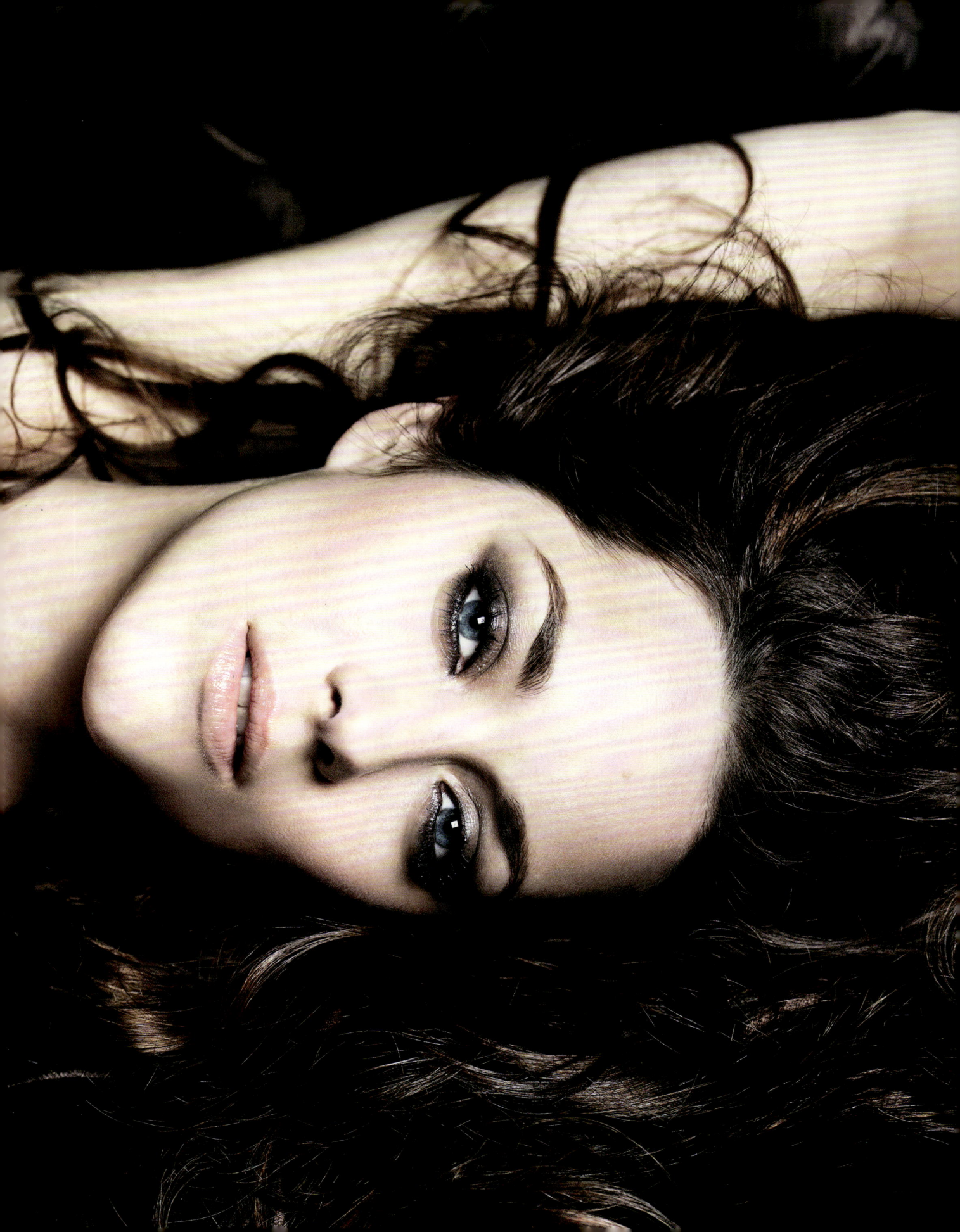

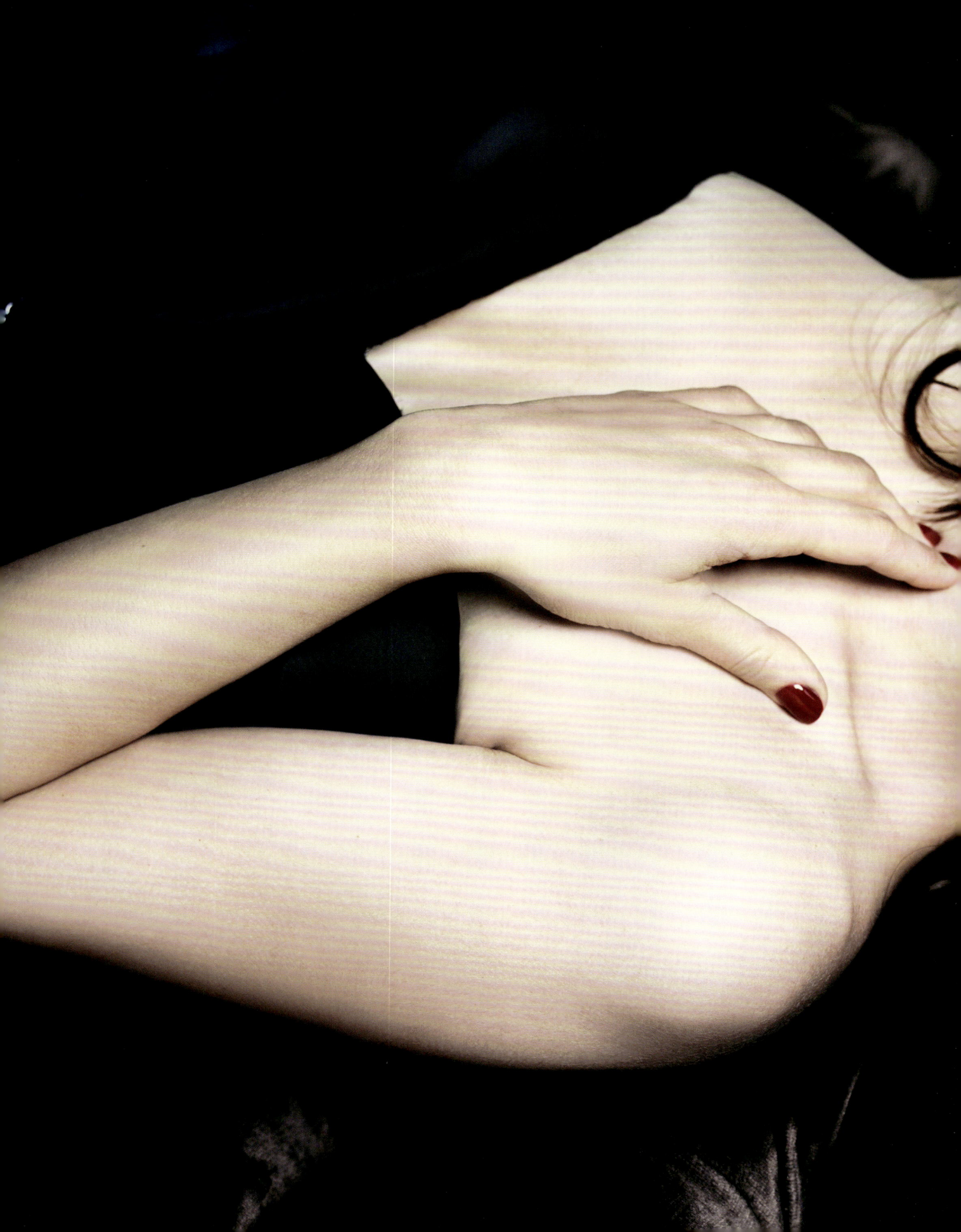

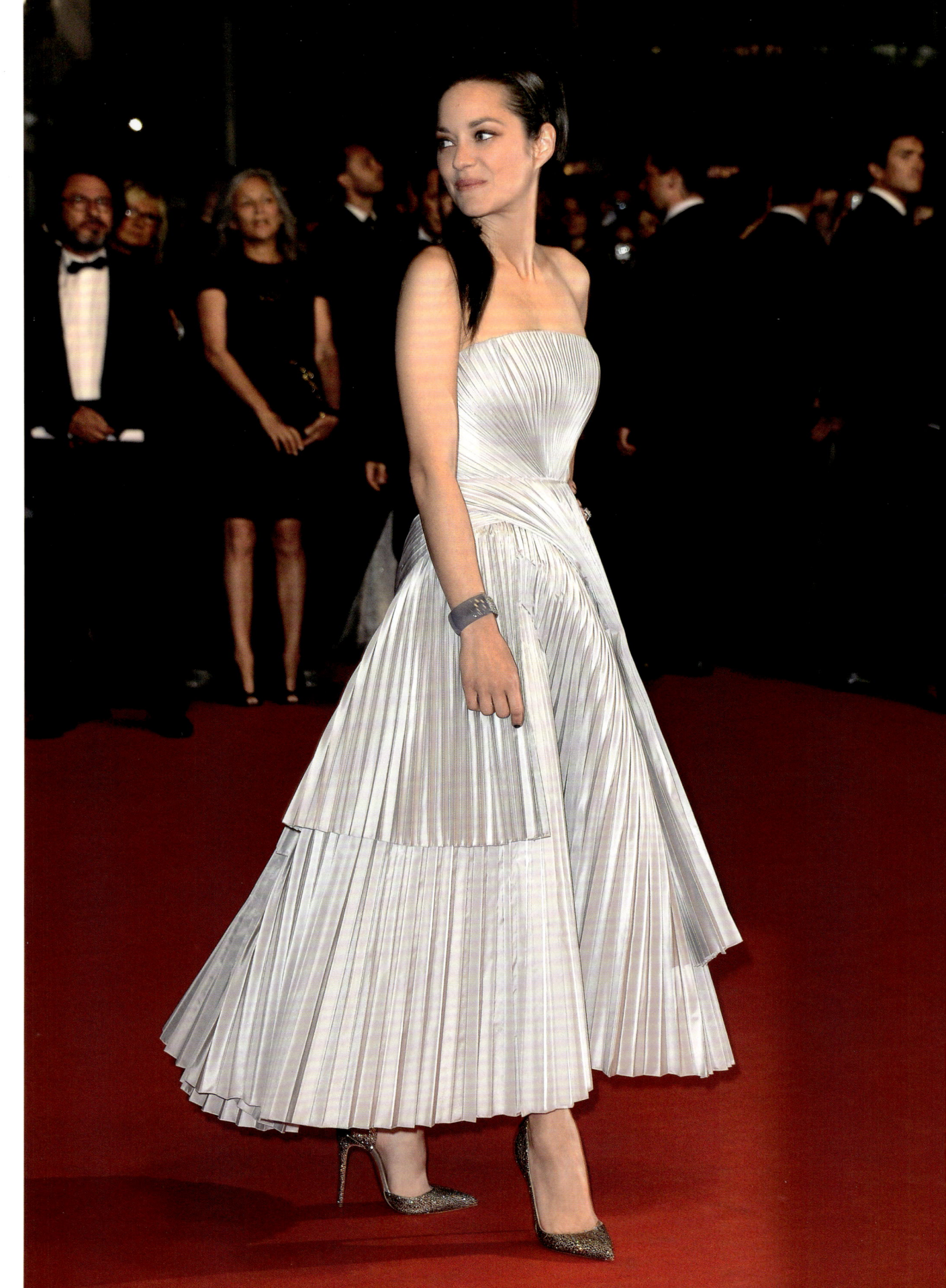

Marion Cotillard

Marion Cotillard has turned fashion into a unique expression, a way for her to play with the many facets of her personality. With *La Vie en Rose*, which opened the Berlin Film Festival in 2007, Cotillard won a Golden Globe for her performance in 2008, the Best Actress BAFTA, the César for Best Actress, and the Academy Award for Best Actress. Just one year later, she starred as the heroine in *The Lady Noire Affair*, shot by Olivier Dahan. She says that as a face of Dior she has discovered that fashion is "an art that is infinitely rich. An art that magnifies, provokes, and questions as well."[1]

This is proved in pictures, starting with the short advertising films for Dior shot by other directors, such as John Cameron Mitchell or David Lynch: Whether playing a Hitchcock heroine or a cabaret dancer in a silver sheath dress, or dressed in an entirely re-embroidered long ecru silk evening gown or an ensemble decorated with multi-colored ribbons (at the Césars in 2015), Cotillard shows that she is unique and multiple at the apex of her art. With her hair slicked back or flowing in the wind, wearing an *Aurore* mini-dress, wedge sandals, and a *Lady Dior* handbag in the sunny Hamptons, in the United States, one of the most sought-after French actresses in the world is nicknamed the "French mermaid." Nude silk chiffon (Costume Institute Gala, May 2009) or sea-green re-embroidered crepe (Cannes Film Festival, 2009) gave her a spidery appearance, sharpened by a graphic, ultra-contemporary silhouette. "Comfort is my only criterion. It's just a question of feeling."[2] She confesses to having a passion for Dior, "a poetic creator full of imagination, who invented, reinvented and was constantly in tune with his time."

[1] *Madame Figaro*, May 14, 2014.
[2] *L'Express Styles*, May 9, 2012.

OPPOSITE Marion Cotillard wears a special Christian Dior design during the Cannes Film Festival, May 21, 2014.

FOLLOWING PAGES Marion Cotillard photographed by Mario Sorrenti for *Vogue* Paris, August 2012.

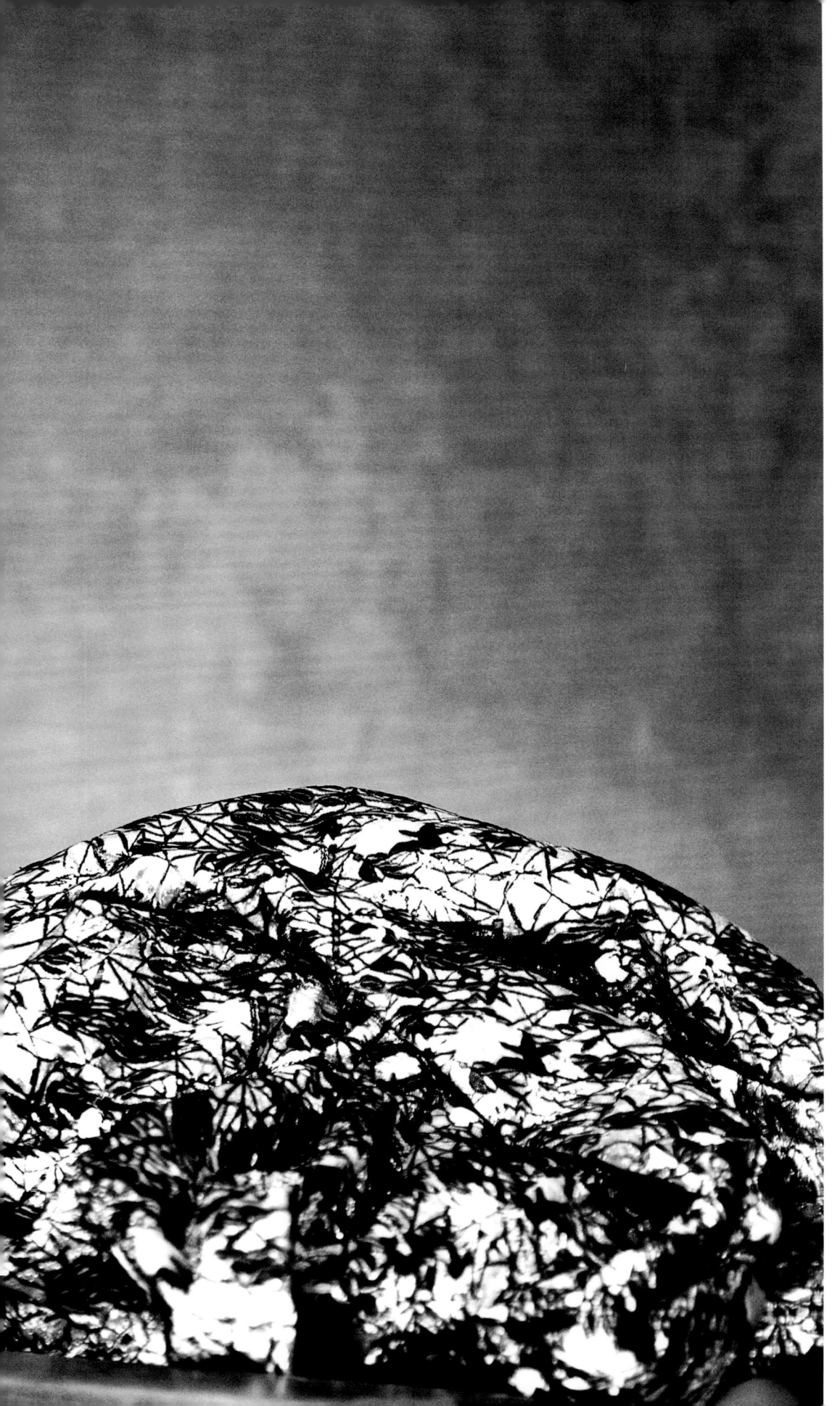

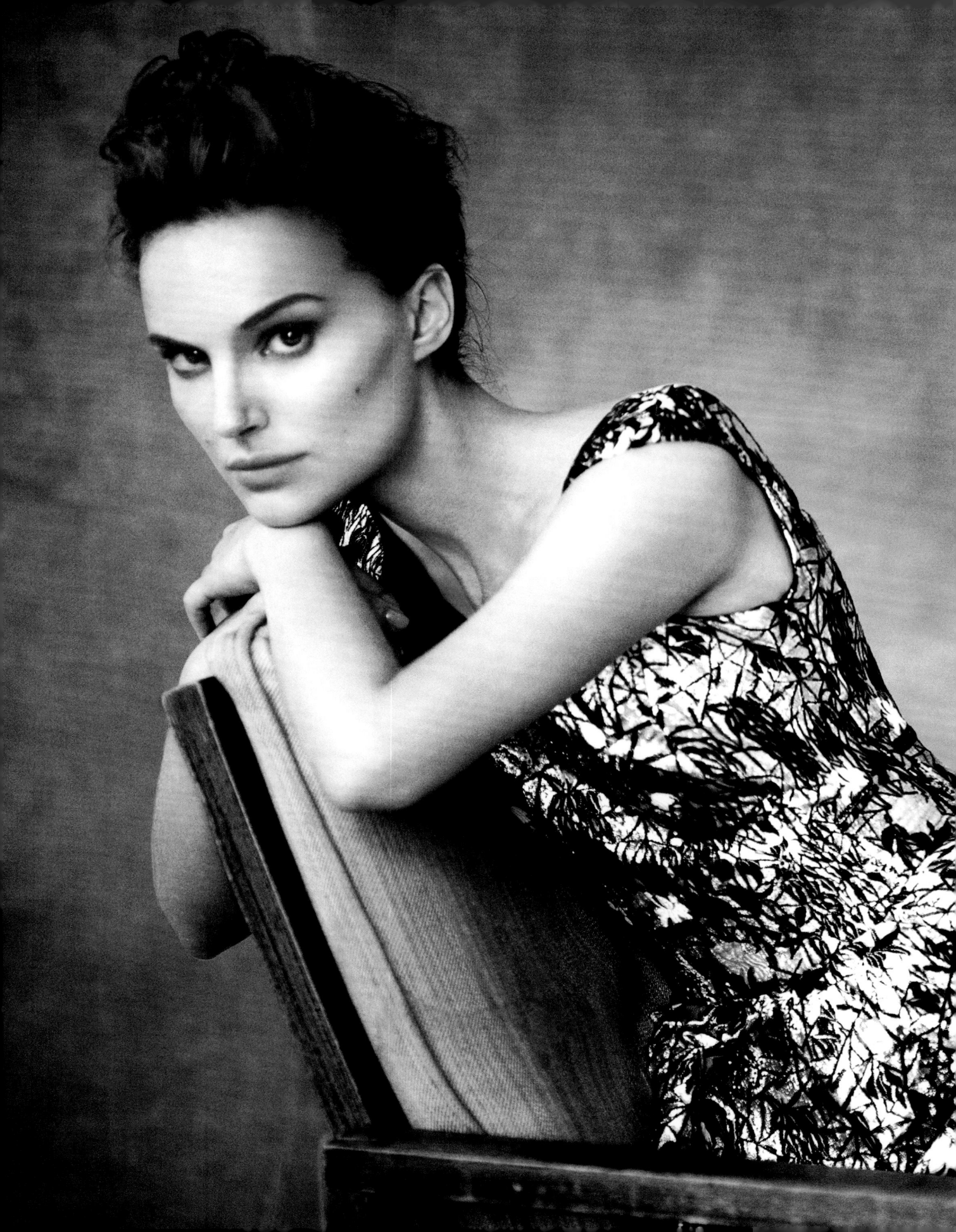

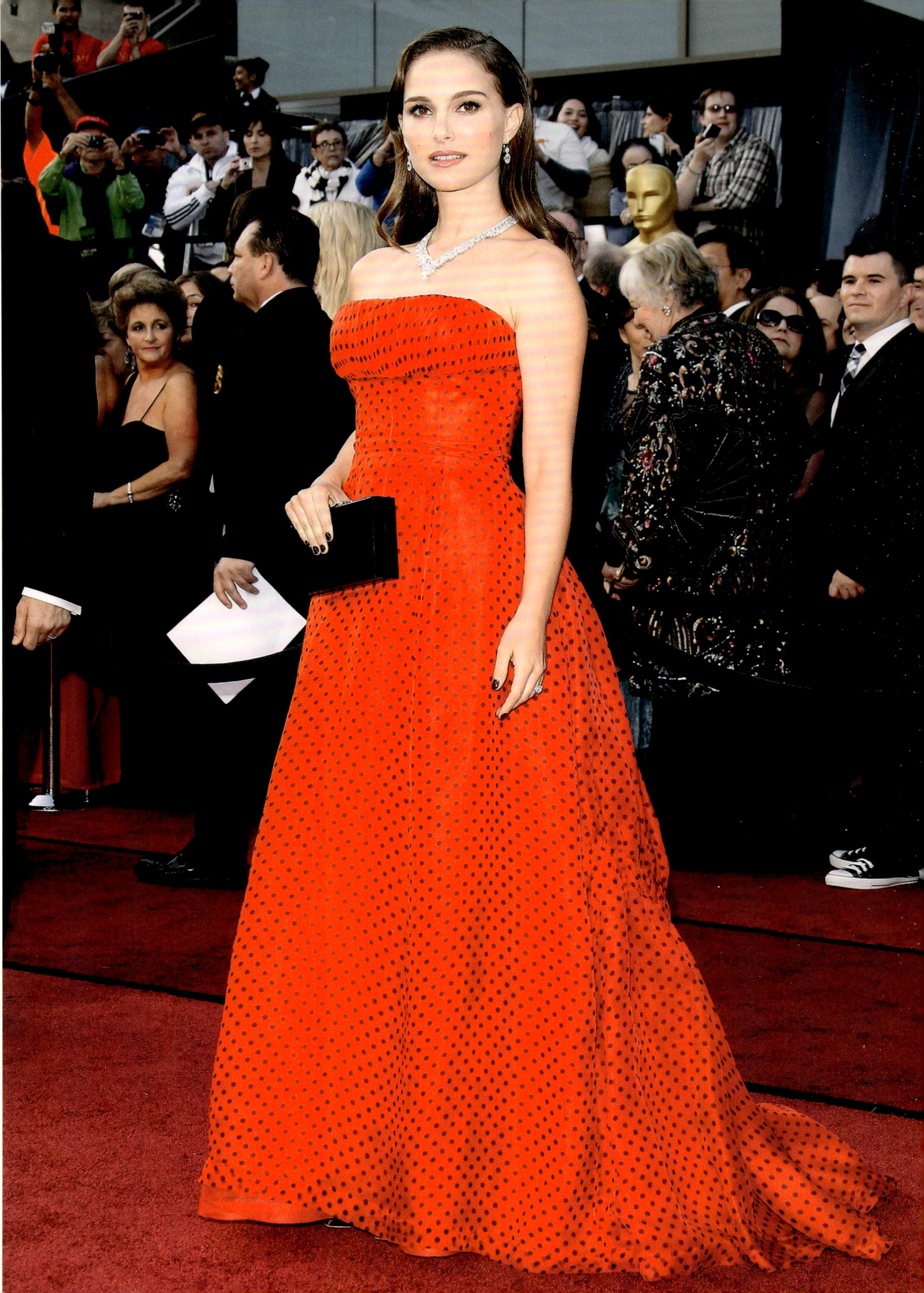

Natalie Portman

"In America, they say I'm European," states Natalie Portman, whose father chose her first name in tribute to the song by Gilbert Bécaud. She has been the heroine of *Miss Dior* since 2010 and in 2011 won the Academy Award for Best Actress for her role as Nina Sayers in *Black Swan*. Since then she has become the face of the iconic *Rouge Dior* lipstick, first launched by Dior in 1953. Red was one of the couturier's favorite colors, often associated with the shocking "Trafalgar" moments with which he peppered his presentations, a bright red that Natalie Portman chose for the red carpet at the Cannes Film Festival in May 2015. The star has a host of performances to her credit, from *Star Wars* to *Jane Got a Gun*, which she partly produced, to a forthcoming role as Jackie Kennedy in autumn 2016, but has entrusted her most glamorous role to the house of Dior. She never fails to point out that Dior is "a true symbol of elegance in the United States."

The former Harvard psychology student asserts that the house of Dior is "elegant and completely responsible. I have met people there who are extremely committed, open, and generous, the guardians of a creative savoir-faire as well as an ethic."[1] The house of Dior supports her humanitarian involvement—notably for the Foundation for International Community Assistance (FINCA International) for which she is "Ambassador of Hope"—and also represents her happy times in France, when she starred in her first film at the age of thirteen (*Léon* by Luc Besson). For Portman, Dior is the romance of Paris, where she likes to stroll and dance: "Between you and me, don't all girls dream of being Parisian, of having that effortlessly chic look and being as cool as a jazz tune?"[2] There have been many artistic matches over the years, such as being chosen by her friend Shirin Neshat to star in a video for the *Miss Dior* exhibition inaugurated at the Grand Palais in Paris in 2013. First there was the pale pink dress adorned with chiffon—reinvented by Raf Simons in a contemporary nod to the *Miss Dior* dress from 1949—that she wore in the first highly romantic advertising film directed by Sofia Coppola (2013). Then came the sheath dress re-embroidered with white flowers that she cheekily strips off to a Janis Joplin soundtrack in the *Miss Dior* film by Anton Corbijn (2015), the director of *Control* and *A Most Wanted Man*: "Having played with her fiancé's bow tie, danced fully clothed in a fountain, fled in an open-top car, and ended up lying on a bed of roses, the intrepid Miss Dior gets married, bringing the adventure to an end . . . or almost. The sublime Natalie Portman arrives at the altar in a white dress but ends up running away, leaving her shoes behind her like a modern Cinderella."[3] A way for this Hollywood feminist to embody the Dior message, to encourage women "in their quest for freedom, independence, and individuality."[4]

[1] *Madame Figaro*, July 12, 2012.
[2] *L'Express Styles*, February 2011.
[3] *Vanity Fair* France, February 2015.
[4] Ibid.

OPPOSITE Natalie Portman in the *Nuit de feu* dress, Spring-Summer 1954 haute couture collection, *Muguet* line, during the Oscars ceremony in Los Angeles, February 26, 2012.

FOLLOWING PAGES Natalie Portman photographed by Paolo Roversi in 2014. She wears a dress from the Spring-Summer 2014 ready-to-wear collection.

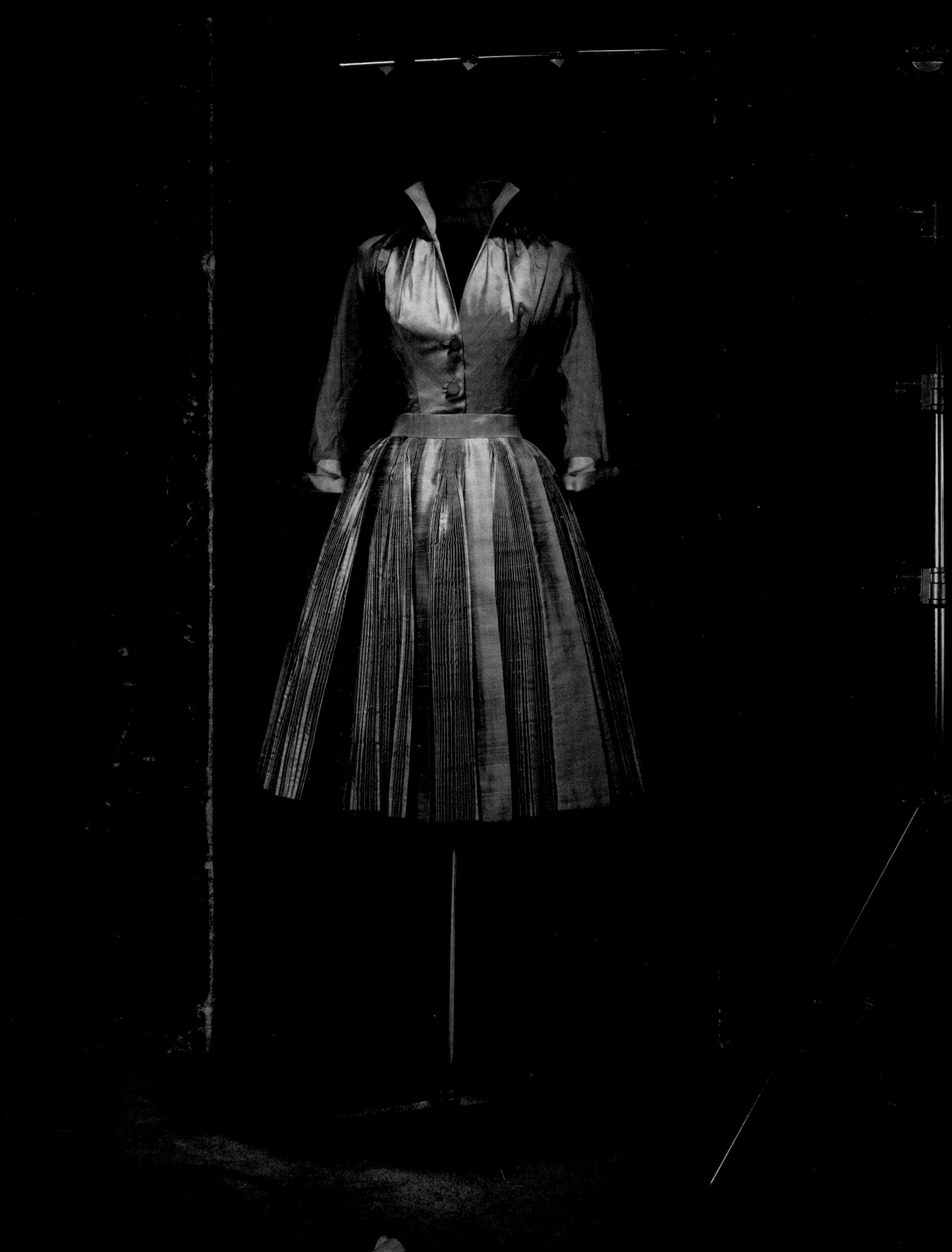

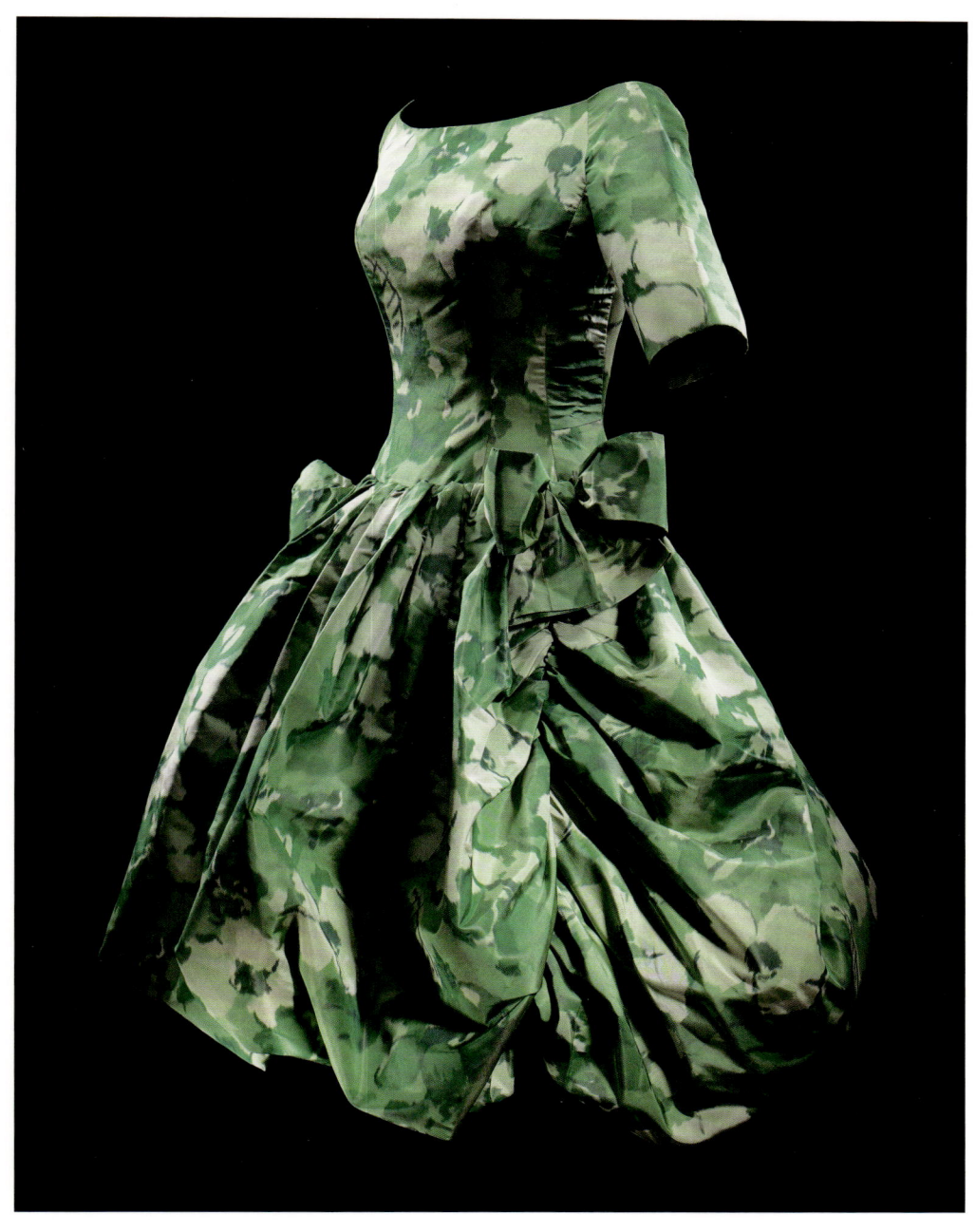

ABOVE The short *Salade* evening dress in stem and dark green–printed taffeta, Spring-Summer 1960 haute couture collection, *Silhouette de demain* line.

OPPOSITE The formal *Topaze* afternoon dress in Aleutian gray ordered by María Félix, Autumn-Winter 1951 haute couture collection, *Longue* line.

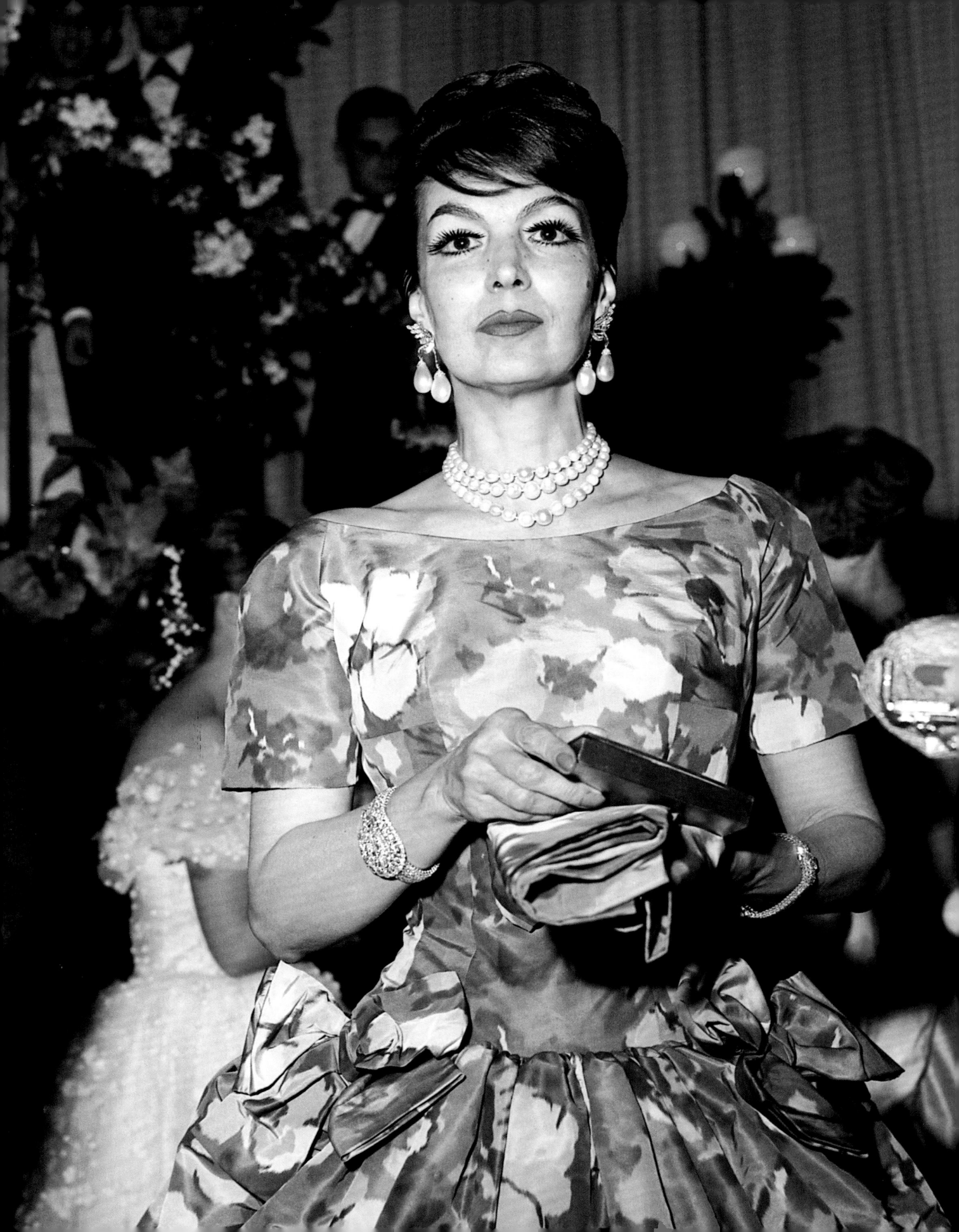

María Félix

"You will be beautiful, famous, and elegant" a gypsy-woman had told the youngest of twelve children. *La Belle Otero, Faustina, French Cancan* by Jean Renoir, from 1942 to 1971 she starred in over forty-five films in Mexico, France, and Italy before retiring from the spotlight. A faithful Dior client, María Félix wore numerous designs, from *Bateleur*, the half-black-wool, half-leopard-skin coat (Autumn-Winter 1949), to the *Bruxelles* evening dress in pink tulle entirely re-embroidered with pearls that gave her a Goyesque air (Autumn-Winter 1959): "It is the only collection whose style is completely different from the others," she said about Yves Saint Laurent's break with the past when he took over the couture house. "The skirts are varied and portray a flexible, supple woman. For evening, the fabrics are taffeta, satin, or faille; for afternoon, crepe; for daytime, mohair in particular. This fashion demands sophisticated women and violent makeup."

At cocktail parties, grand dinners, and balls the Doña set off her attire with extraordinary jewels. Her Dior saleswoman, Sophie Gins, recalls: "She was mad about jewelry and dresses. She ordered five or six items every season!" The highly coveted double fitting room was reserved for her at 30 Avenue Montaigne. For daytime, the former convent girl from Pico Heights liked to underscore her slim waist with belts (*Riviera* ensemble, Winter 1957). For evening, she turned herself into a goddess with dancing dresses that always highlighted the bust. She was particularly fond of *Zenaïde* in 1959, an anthracite black taffeta evening gown that was characteristic of designs "that flowed down the body with their vague waist, then puffed out above the knee, which gave the figure complete freedom." María Félix particularly loved furs and ordered several pieces by Frédéric Castet, of whom she was an admirer as well as a close friend. Having joined the house of Dior in 1953, in 1968 he created the fur prêt-à-porter and high fur department at 30 Avenue Montaigne.

Maria Félix at a ball organized by Francine Weisweiller for her daughter Carole in her private mansion at the Place des États-Unis, June 24, 1960. The actress wears the *Salade* dress, Spring-Summer 1960 haute couture collection, *Silhouette de demain* line.

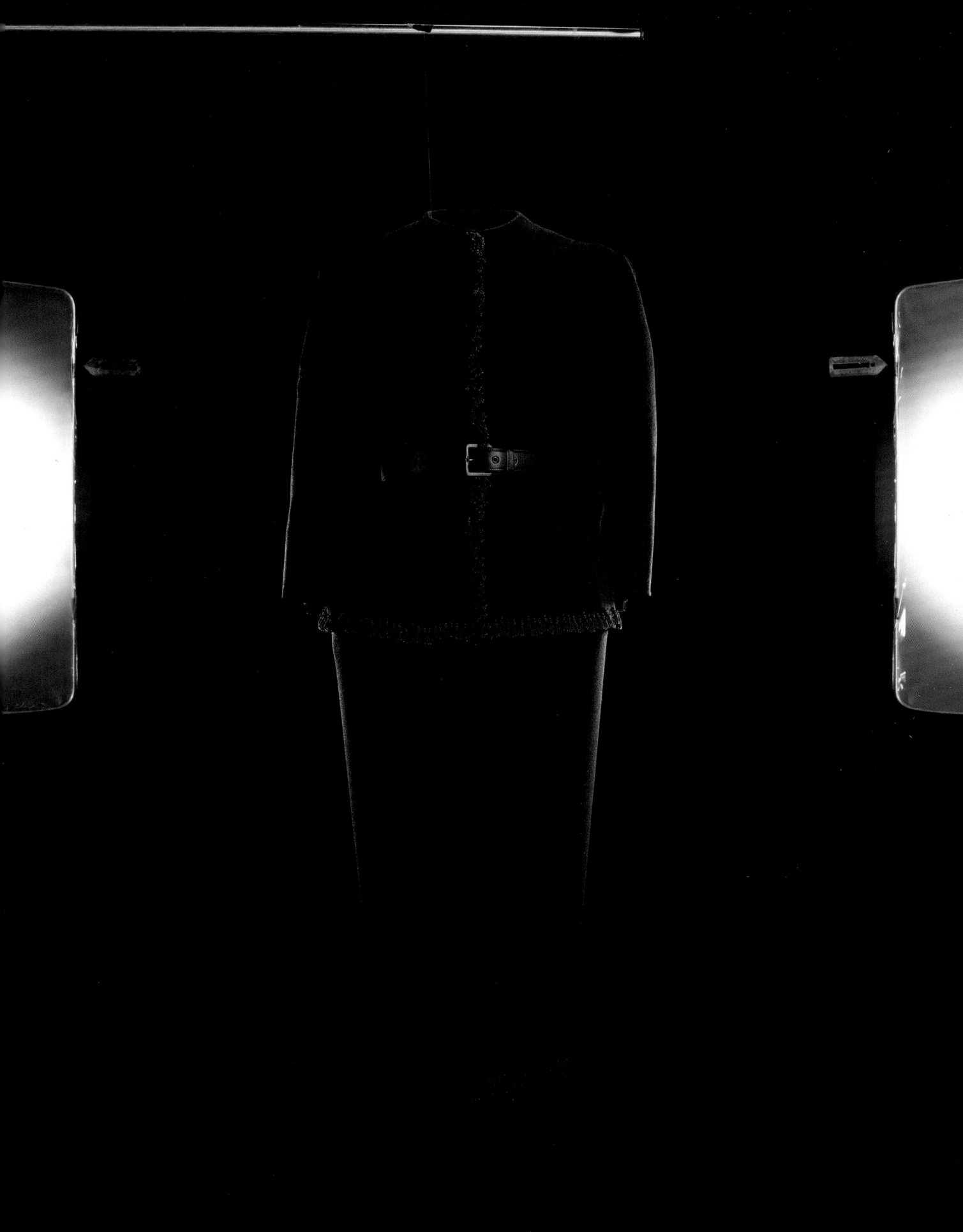

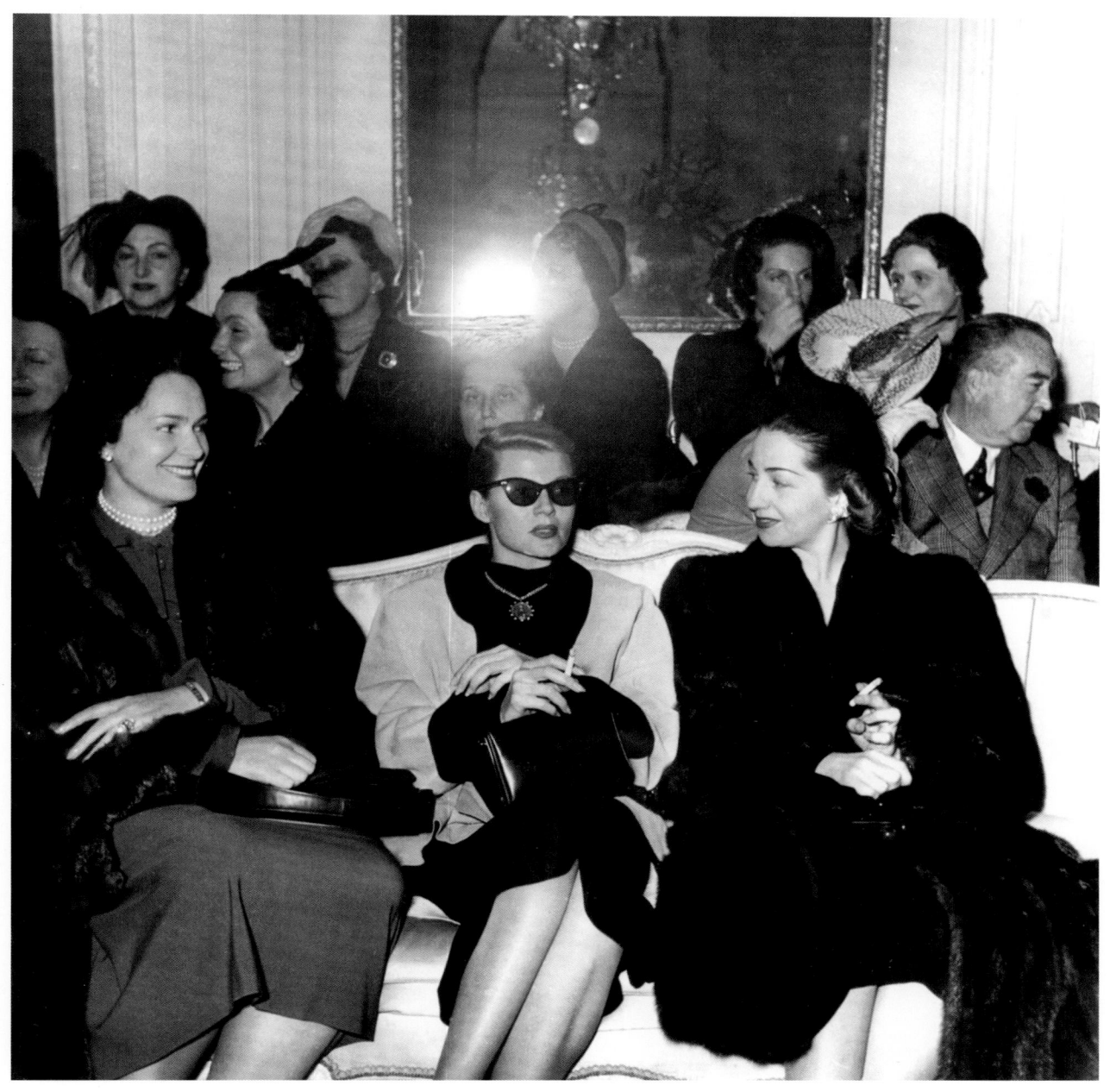

ABOVE Rita Hayworth next to Begum Aga Khan III, née Yvette Labrousse (left), who attended the Spring–Summer 1956 collection presentation at Christian Dior.

OPPOSITE The *Pompon* suit in black wool lined with a fringe of small pompoms and lace, is part of seven designs from Christian Dior's first collection, Spring–Summer 1947 haute couture, ordered by Rita Hayworth.

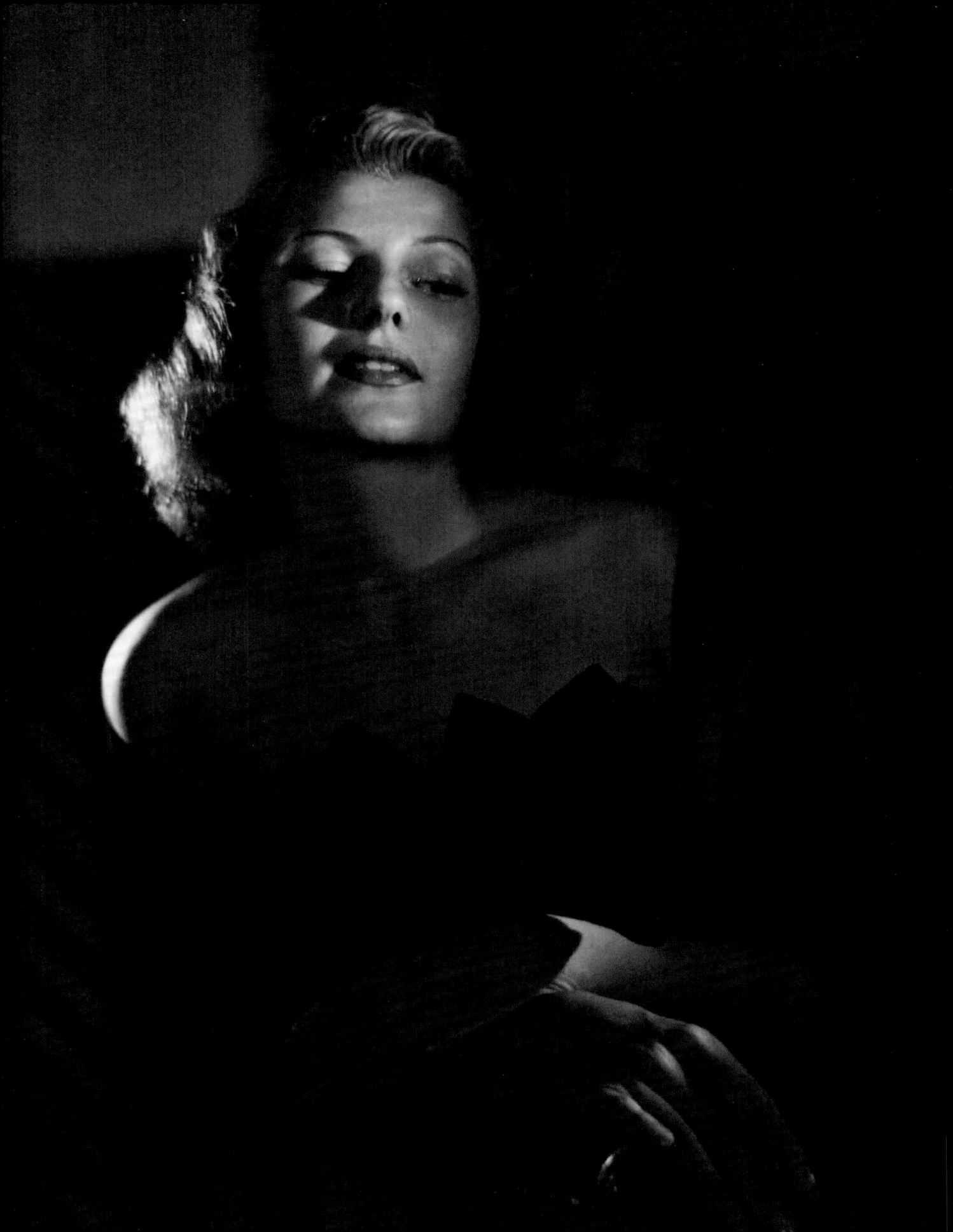

Rita Hayworth

In February 1947, less than a year after starring in Charles Vidor's *Gilda*, the film that would turn her into every man's femme fatale, Rita Hayworth became a client at Dior. She ordered a dozen or so designs, from the *Maxim's* late afternoon dress to *Gag*, "an ensemble for outdoors in black wool lined with mattress canvas," or *Amour*, a restaurant dress in fine black wool. She was obsessive about black—the black of the famous black wool *Pompon* suit fringed with braid or the black of the *Femina* sheath dress. In Paris she wore *1947*, a blue marocain afternoon dress with white polka dots. She could no longer stroll peacefully in the French capital, where she was constantly stopped and bombarded with questions: What does she eat? What does she read? Who dresses her? Who does her hair? Hayworth had cut-and-dried ideas and knew what suited her. She had her day suits shortened and wore the original *Soirée* dress in blue organza with white polka dots. This was what the "Love Goddess" wore in 1947 when she attended the avant-première of *Gilda* in Paris. "She will wear these clothes in New York and Hollywood, and next season all the American women will be dressed like her," noted *Elle* magazine.[1]

[1] *Elle*, June 24, 1947.

Rita Hayworth poses for Horst P. Horst in her *Maxim's* dress, Spring-Summer 1947 haute couture collection, *Corolle* line.

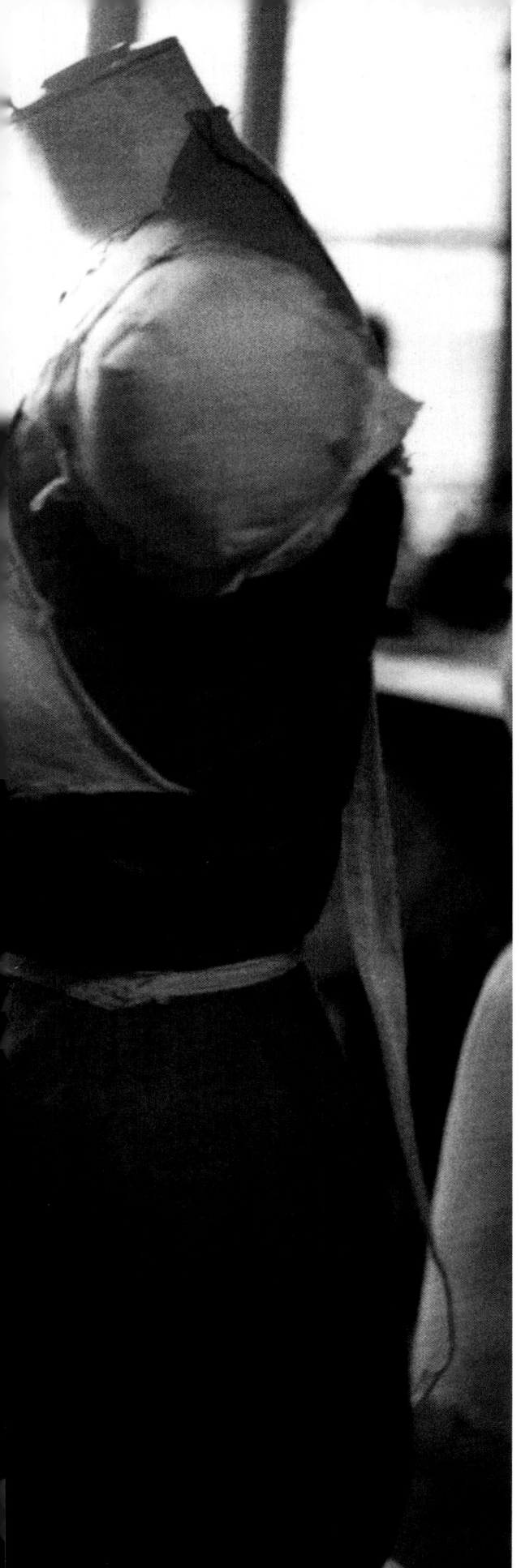

Marlene Dietrich's couture mannequin, the Dior atelier, August 1952. Photograph by Richard Avedon.

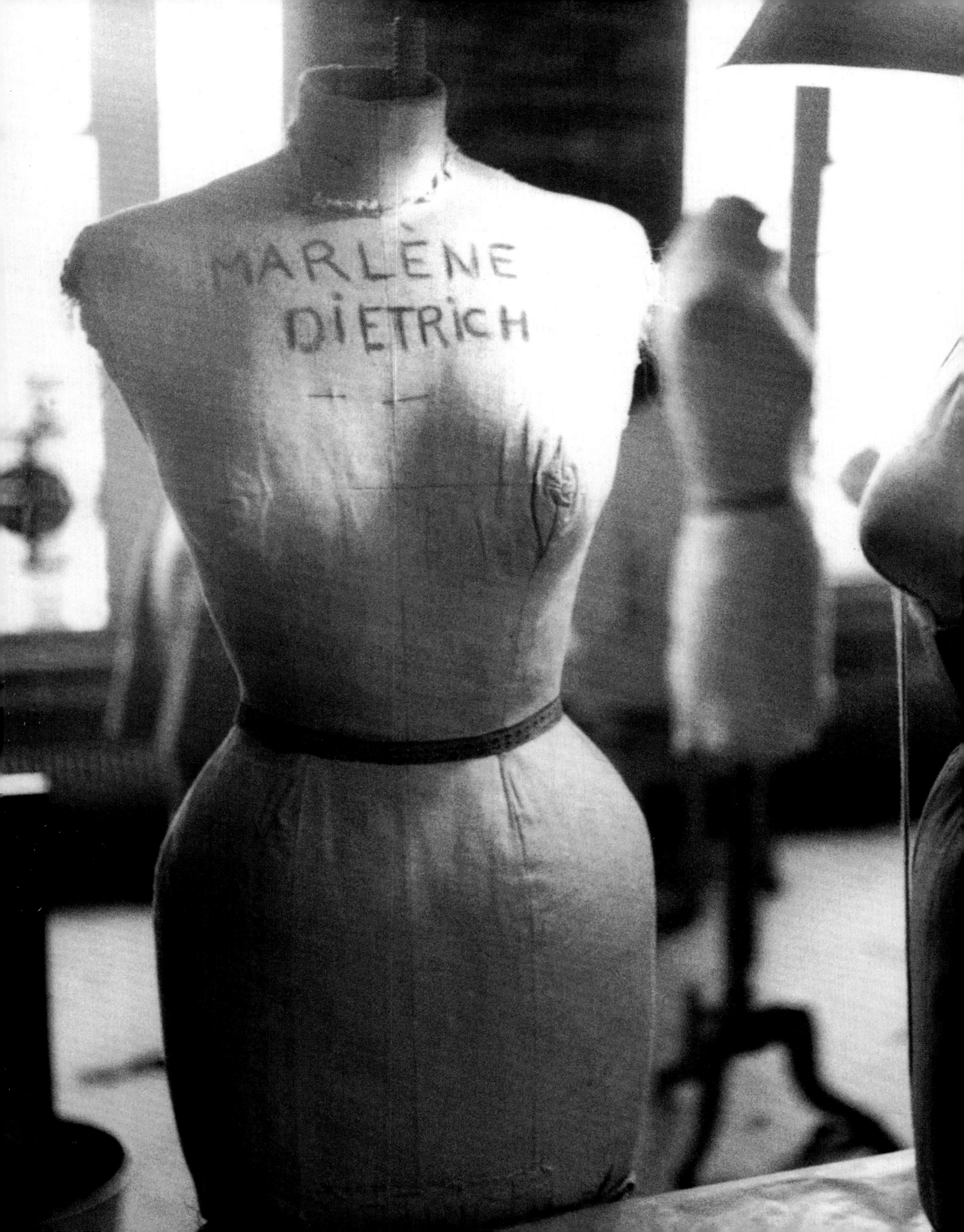

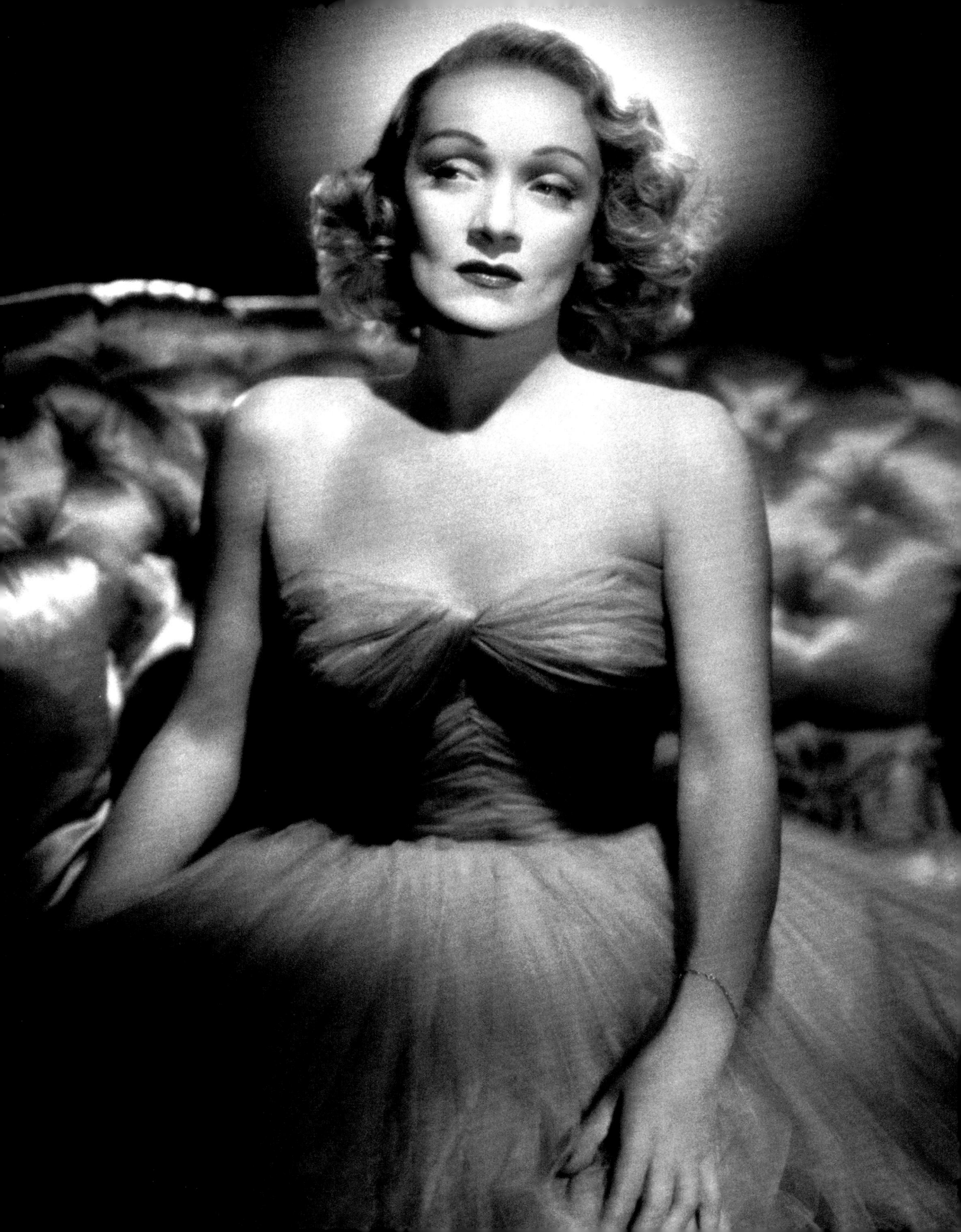

Marlene Dietrich

In the eyes of her daughter, Maria Riva, Marlene Dietrich was one of those women who imagined her acting through her costumes. "She might not know a character's name and have only a vague idea about the plot, but what she wore was always very precisely defined."[1] She fell head over heels for Dior very early on, ordering designs from the second collection, Autumn-Winter 1947, including the *Chandernagor* dress, which was presented in July 1947. Dresses, shoes, stockings, gloves, handbags, overcoats, suits: The house of Dior was her Parisian haven. In November 1948, she attended the first summer collection presented by Dior-New York covered in diamonds.[2]

While the Dietrich style is broadly associated with masculine looks, from the pajama created by Schiaparelli for *Agent X27* to the tuxedo in *Morocco* or the officer's uniform in *Seven Sinners*, it was also enhanced by the dresses created for her by Christian Dior or the Dior suits that she wore with nothing underneath. This naturally calls to mind the *Acacia* suit and the Dior wardrobe worn by Charlotte Inwood in Alfred Hitchcock's *Stage Fright* (1950)—up to a dozen designs—but also the *Cygne noir* evening gown from the *Milieu de Siècle* line (Autumn-Winter 1949), a long skirt with velvet panels and a large bow at the waist, worn with a satin bustier cut low in the back. Dietrich had a second bodice made to go with the skirt in order to have different ways of wearing the ensemble.

Through the outfits she ordered from Dior, including the *Précieux* evening dress with a long straight skirt from the *H* line (Autumn 1954), Dietrich revealed how well she knew her own body and her desire to lengthen it further and magnify an imperceptible illusion mastered by haute couture. She had no qualms about adding a suspender belt stitched to the bottom of a batiste bodice. Beyond the Hollywood razzle-dazzle, Dior codified the postwar elegance of this "divine" actress who would become the exclusive ambassador for Christian Dior stockings in 1954... Marlene Dietrich stayed loyal to the house of Dior. She ordered an afternoon dress created by Yves Saint Laurent for Dior in 1960, as well as the *Stockholm* dress, her very last haute couture purchase from the Avenue Montaigne couture house. This was followed by a succession of assorted items—pajamas, men's sweaters, and even a cap signed "Christian Dior Monsieur, Paris," cravats, *Diorama* perfume and makeup, notably lipsticks number 8 and 25, all of which would be delivered to her apartment located near the Bar des Deux Théâtres, just yards from the house of Dior. Dior/Dietrich: a truly iconic pair.

[1] *Libération*, June 18, 2003.
[2] Marie-France Pochna, *Christian Dior* (Paris: Flammarion, 1994).

Marlene Dietrich dressed in Dior in *Stage Fright* directed by Alfred Hitchcock (1950).

all of Ava Gardner's outfits were creations inspired by the Christian Dior Spring-Summer 1956 haute couture collection (*Flèche* line): "F, the first letter of *femme* (woman) and of *flèche* (arrow), which combine curves and arcs." That season, shiny black mink, Barguzin sable, "chiaroscuro" bouquet prints, and stockings "designed for the whims of sunlight" gave their own glimpse of the dimension the film-loving couturier afforded fashion.

By making women into heroines again, Dior's tour de force was to have created close links between couture and cinema. This was the theme of the exhibition *Stars in Dior*, presented by the Musée Christian Dior in Granville in 2012. Laetitia Casta, Eva Green, Julianne Moore, Carey Mulligan, Chiara Mastroianni, Lupita Nyong'o, Emma Stone . . . But also Isabelle Adjani, who on September 17, 1985, was among the 1,200 guests gathered at Vaux-le-Vicomte under chandeliers dressed in ivy and purple flowers for the ball held to launch the perfume *Poison*. She looked absolutely sumptuous in her dress of draped emerald and amethyst satin. In 1991 she was the patron of the *Bal Dune* dressed in a pink-orange crepe silk dress. There were ten thousand champagne-colored roses blooming on the buffet and hundreds of tables laid beneath gold tulle drapes. "This shower of gold and silver shining in a bright sky in the midst of a stormy night was an extraordinary sight: Those few minutes of hypnosis were an exquisite lapse back into childhood," she later said. Thousands of branches of coral adorned the compositions of euphorbia, wild clematis, lilies, and orchids. From Cannes to Hollywood, these "personal appearances" transcend the hours of waiting to go up the red carpet or attend increasingly impressive photo calls crackling with flashes and tweets. Beyond the circumstances and constraints, the clothing has one supreme mission: to translate the fabric of a temperament. From Charlize Theron, who is the face of *J'adore*, to Jennifer Lawrence, Marion Cotillard, or Natalie Portman, who embodies *Miss Dior*, the ascendency holding sway is one of global seduction.

---

[1] Jerome Hanover, *Stars in Dior* (New York: Rizzoli, 2012).

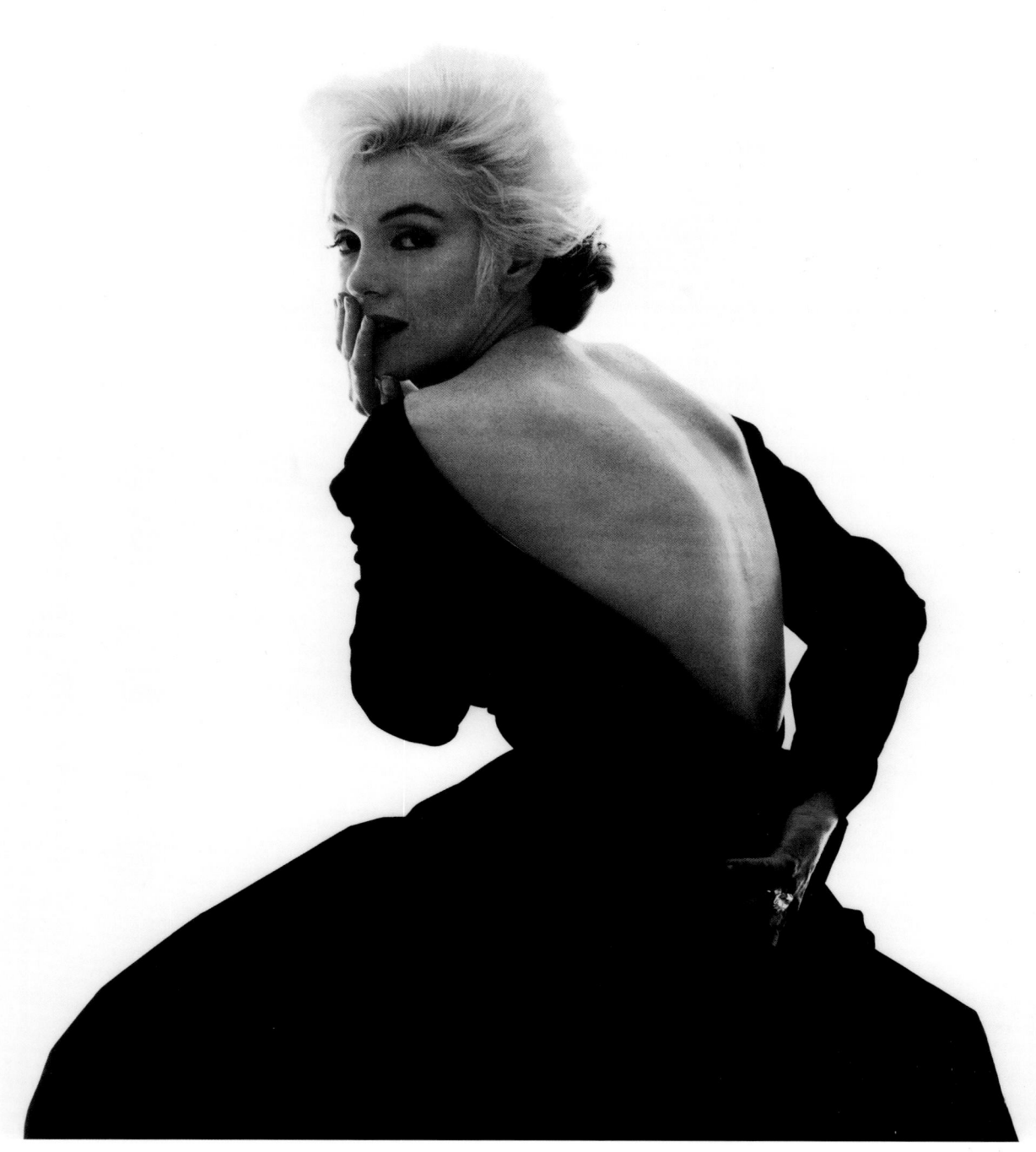

Marilyn Monroe wears a Dior design during *The Last Sitting* photographed by Bert Stern for *Vogue* at the Bel-Air Hotel in Los Angeles, June 1962.

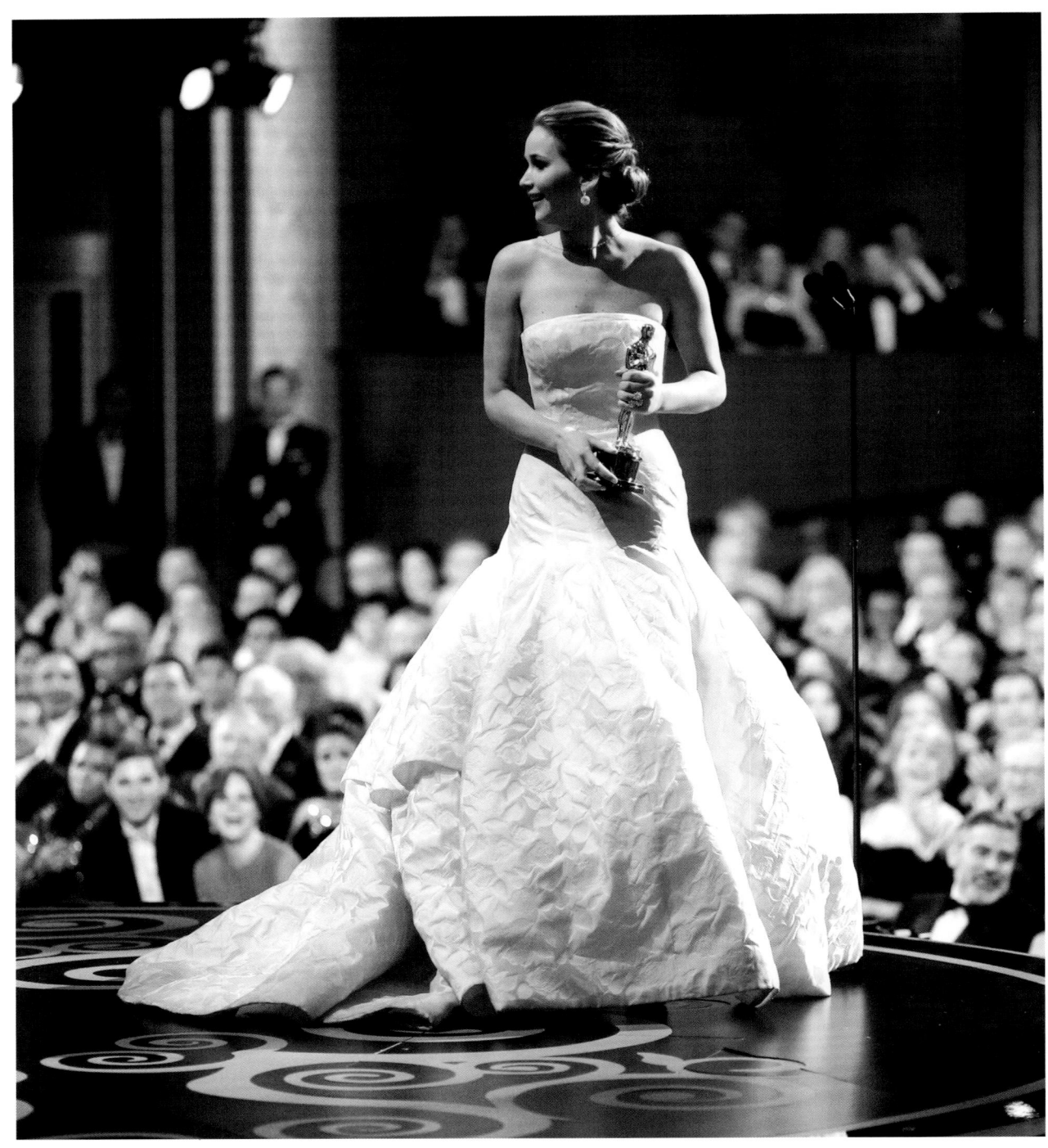

PREVIOUS PAGE A dress in embroidered black tulle (Autumn-Winter haute couture collection) worn by Marion Cotillard for the Oscars, February 22, 2009.

ABOVE Jennifer Lawrence receiving the 2013 Oscar for Best Actress for her role in *Silver Linings Playbook* at the Dolby Theatre in Los Angeles, February 24, 2013. She wears a dress from the Spring-Summer 2013 haute couture collection.

Divine Apparitions

The twentieth century managed to bring about a triumph: Celebrity went from being a singular honor to a plural incarnation. And celebrities all take off on the red carpet. Cinema is a magnet for passions and obsessions. Dior has featured on many a screen: Lauren Bacall in *How to Marry a Millionaire* (1953, Jean Negulesco), Ingrid Bergman in *Indiscreet* (1958, Stanley Donen), or *Goodbye Again* (1961, Anatole Litvak). "No Dior, no Dietrich!" Marlene Dietrich's famous words have gone down in history, directed at Alfred Hitchcock when she chose to be dressed exclusively in Dior for *Stage Fright*. Olivia de Havilland even shot scenes for *The Ambassador's Daughter* (1956, Norman Krasna) in the couture house's salons. In 1942 Christian Dior had designed Odette Joyeux's costumes for Roland Tual's *The Four-Poster*, adapted from the novel by Louise de Valmorin. The house of Dior has been associated with the silver screen ever since it was founded. Marc Bohan dressed Elizabeth Taylor and Lauren Hutton: The former ordered no less than twelve outfits from his very first collection in 1961. He forged a close relationship with her that lasted twenty years, as he did with Sophia Loren. These heroines in Dior have likewise been heroines on the big screen, from Sophia Loren starring in Charlie Chaplin's *A Countess from Hong Kong* (1967) to Elizabeth Taylor in Joseph Losey's *Secret Ceremony* (1968), Isabelle Adjani and Lauren Hutton in Jean-Paul Rappeneau's *All Fired Up* (1981), or Penelope Cruz in Pedro Almodovar's *Broken Embraces* (2009).

For commercials shot by the biggest names—from Claude Chabrol to Jean-Jacques Annaud, Wong Kar Wai or David Lynch—before the shoots the work in the Dior ateliers is always impressive, and a sine qua non condition for any star appearance. "The entire world of haute couture is founded on the idea of staging a *mise en scène*," wrote film critic Serge Toubiana. "Creators design beautiful dresses to be worn, of course, to move with the women's movements, but above all to be seen. It's no surprise that the links between haute couture and cinema have always been mysterious and captivating. They are founded on similar gestures, the same desire for beauty, a relatively similar artisanal economy."[1] Meetings, sketches, selecting fabrics, making toiles... time cannot go against the ritual needed to master personal appearance: Up to four fittings and 650 hours of work for the dress inspired by the *Diorama* model (1951) created for Mélanie Laurent hosting the sixty-fourth Cannes Film Festival ceremony in May 2012. In the film *The Little Hut* (1957, Mark Robson),

IV

RED CARPET

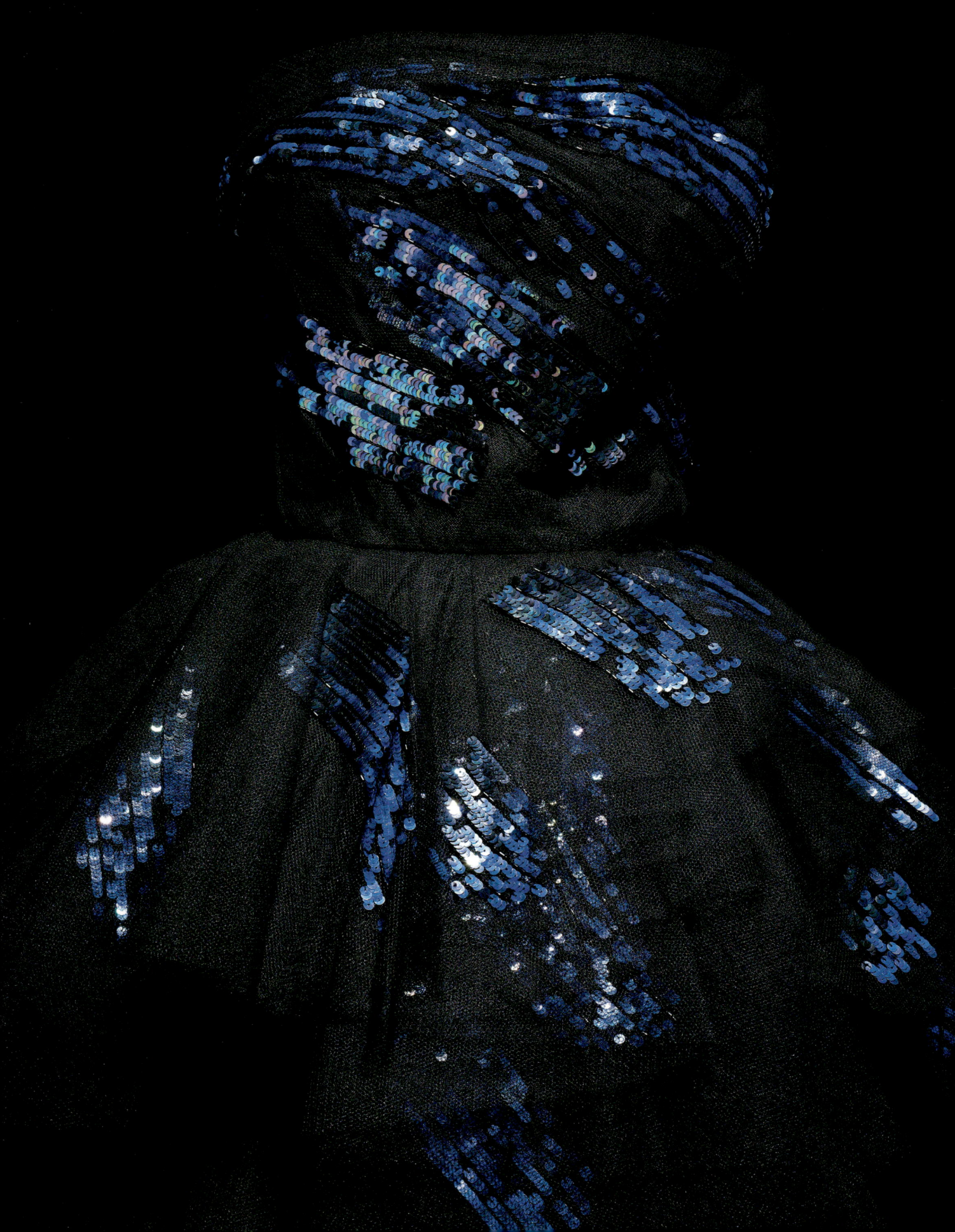

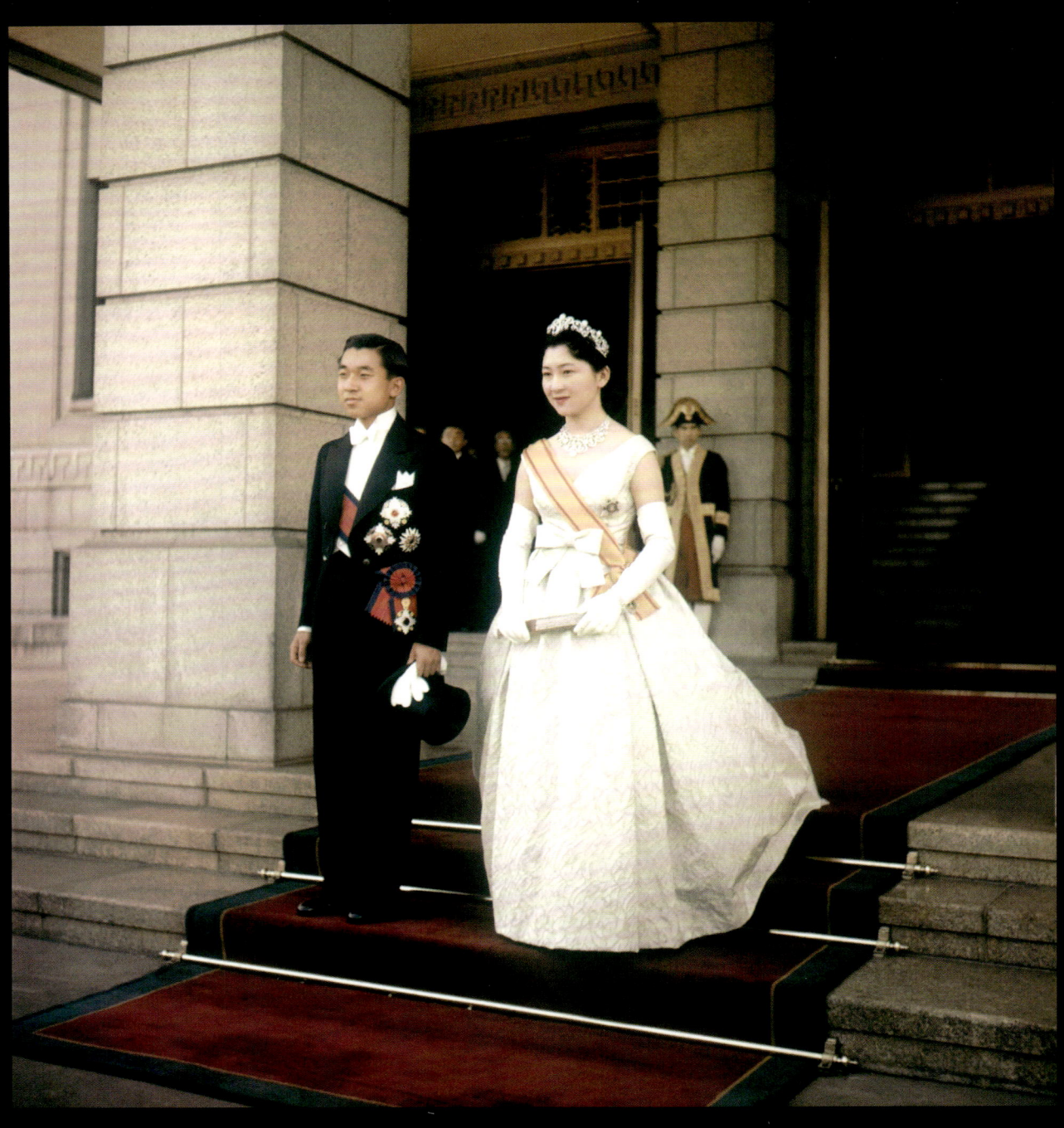

The prince successor Akihito and his wife, Princess Michiko, dressed in Yves Saint Laurent for Dior following their marriage at the imperial palace in Tokyo, April 10, 1959.

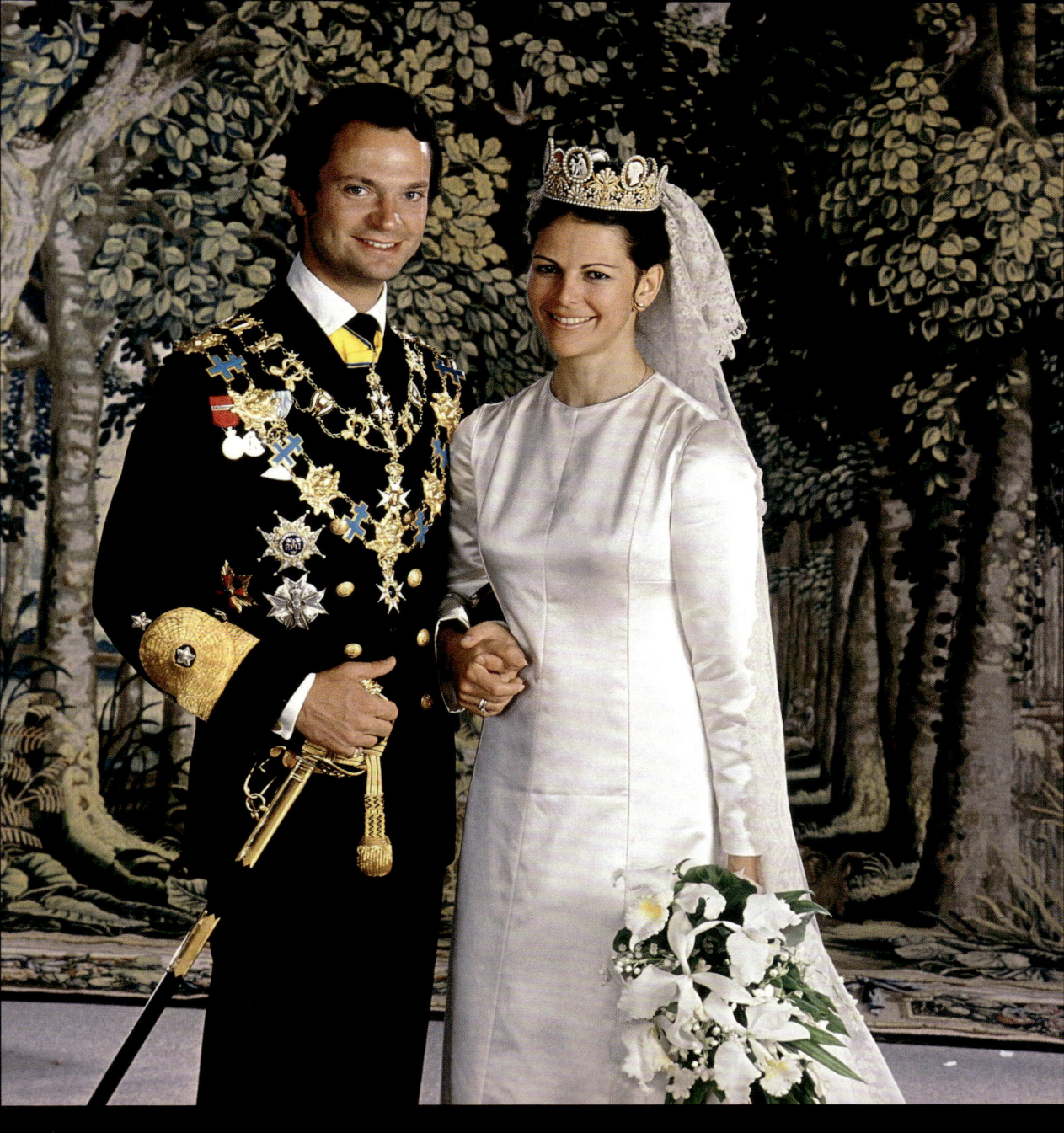

Official portrait of the Swedish King Charles XVI Gustave and Queen Silvia of Sweden, née Silvia Renate Sommerlath, at their wedding on June 19, 1976. She wears a traditional white satin dress finished with a long train created by Marc Bohan for Christian Dior.

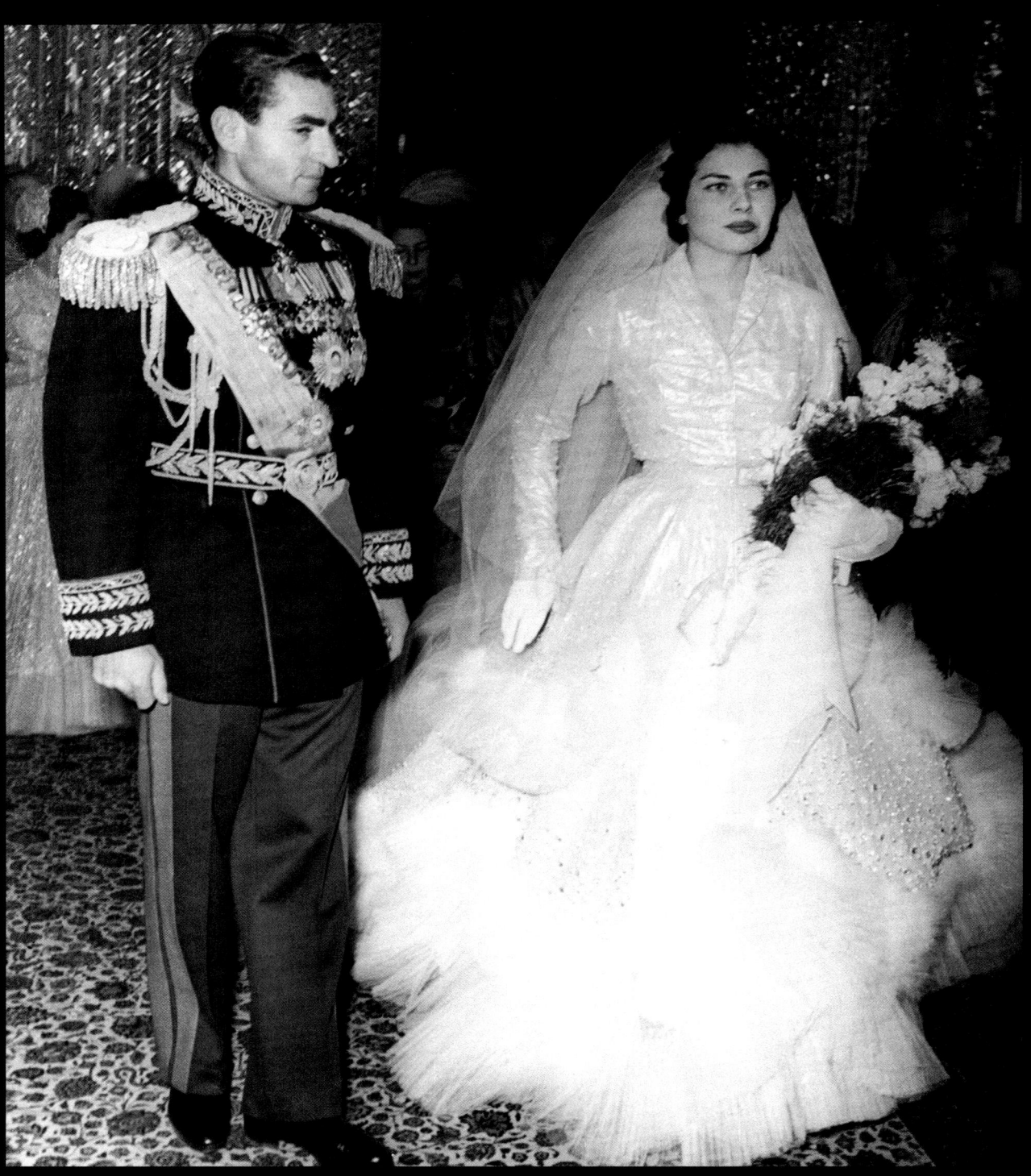

Princess Soraya at her wedding to Mohammed Reza Pahlavi, the Shah of Iran, February 12, 1951. She wears an adaptation of the *Europe* design, Autumn-Winter 1950 haute couture collection, *Oblique* line, and a white mink cape specially created by Christian Dior for the event.

Grand Weddings

In the *grand salon* at 30 Avenue Montaigne, brides-to-be admire themselves in the mirror that has seen sixteen-year-old Soraya Esfandiari Bakhtiari—whose dress was a profusion of silk, tulle, and brocade (1951)—Farah Diba, Silvia Renate Sommerlath, and Caroline of Monaco, all of whom were married in Dior. In 1959 the Empress Michiko chose the house of Dior to design the three dresses for her civil wedding. For her marriage to King Hussein of Jordan in 1978, Queen Noor chose a dress with a very bohemian inspiration, created by the house of Dior in London. Once documented by up to 150 journalists (Farah Diba's sumptuous wedding in Tehran in 1959, for instance), today grand weddings take place in the privacy of Middle Eastern palaces. The secrecy that surrounds them is matched only by their pomp and splendor, for the dresses are made to be seen by women and the groom alone. One dress even found itself preserved under glass in the owner's private apartments—a living memory of its enchantment. They are a dream come true: Delivered in a customized wooden box clad in monogrammed white card, the Dior wedding dress can require up to six hundred hours of handiwork. A princess who wanted to please her father, a keen falconer, had her dress embroidered with gold thread evoking the desert and birds of prey. . . . Another dress involved two kilometers of crumpled tulle in bronze shades. Presented in black on the catwalk, a silk taffeta crinoline dress was made in white for a wedding in Brazil. The happiest day of one's life sometimes comes with the most extravagant dreams. . . until a certain point: One bride who requested an eleven-meter train was told her request was excessive and could not be stamped with the prestigious Dior signature.

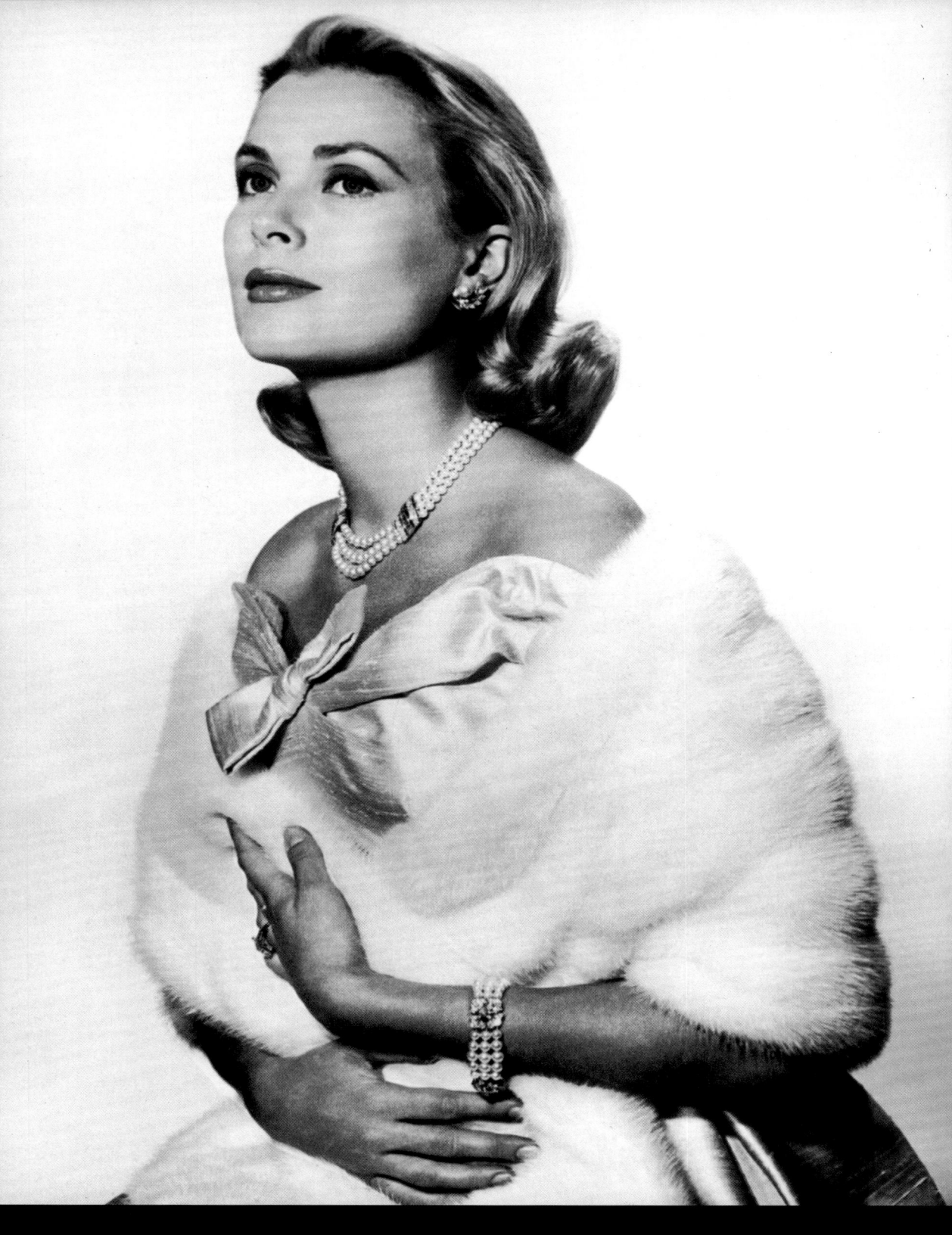

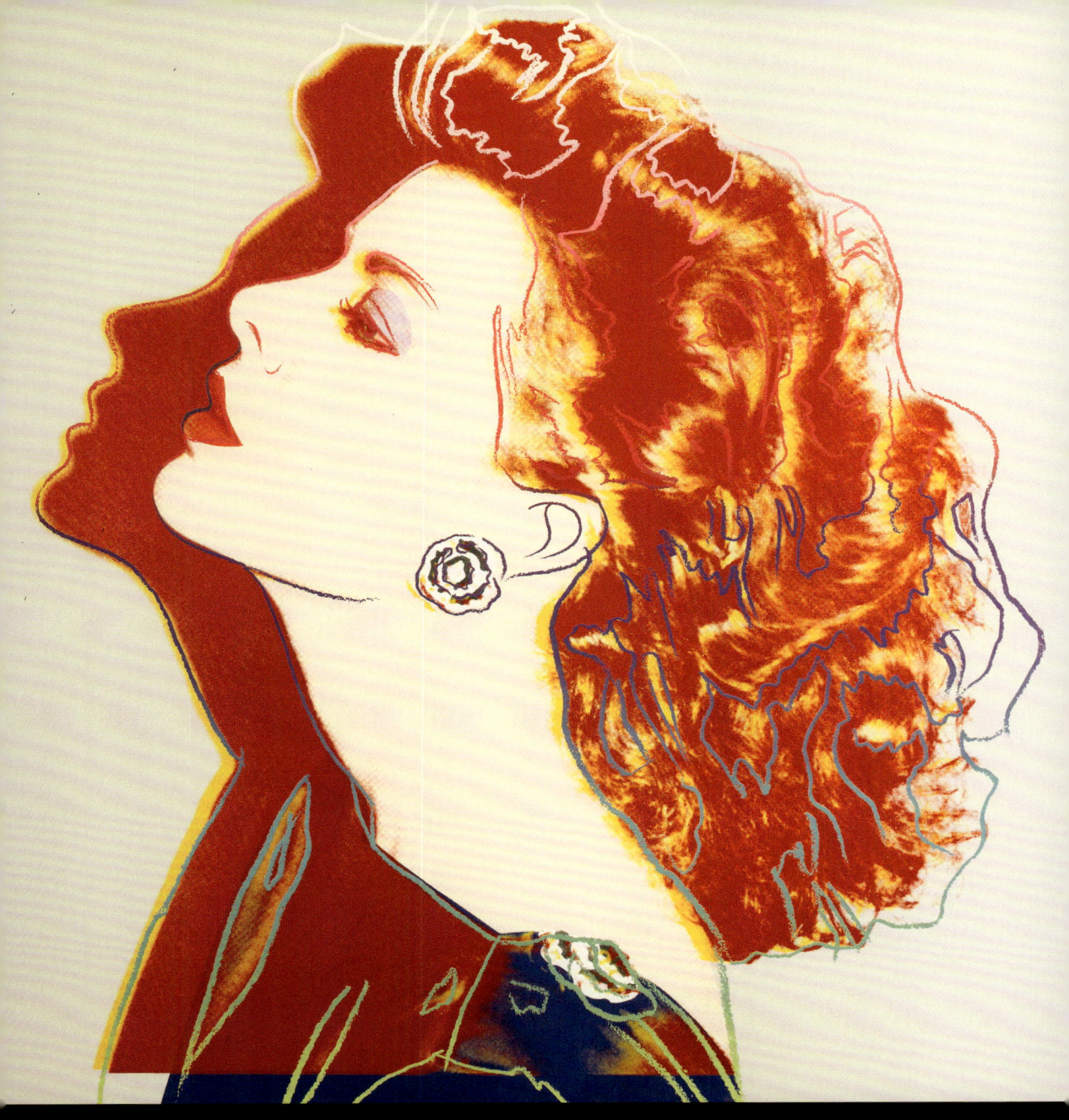

ABOVE Andy Warhol, *Princess Caroline*, 1983. Mixed media, synthetic polymer paint and silkscreen printing on canvas. 42 x 42 inches. Featured on the cover of *Vogue* Paris (December 1983–January 1984), in this portrait the Princess of Hanover wears a dress designed by Marc Bohan for Christian Dior.

OPPOSITE A portrait of Princess Grace of Monaco by Yousuf Karsh, 1956. She wears the *Colinette* dress, Autumn-Winter 1956 haute couture collection, *Aimant* line.

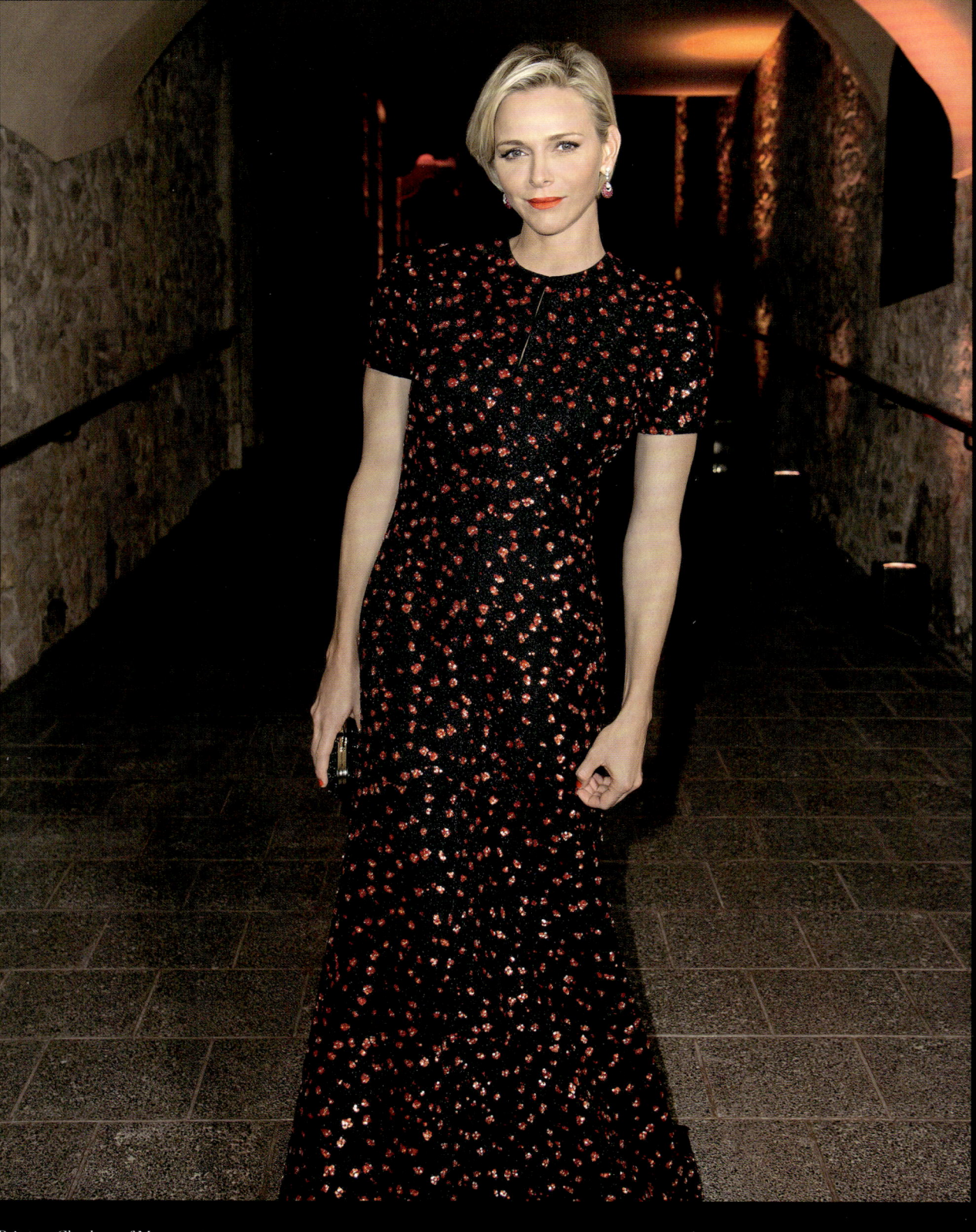

Princess Charlene of Monaco at the Princess Grace Awards gala held at the Prince's Palace of Monaco, September 5, 2015.

The Grimaldi Family

In 2016 the house of Dior celebrated half a century of special relations with the Grimaldi family: From Rainier's engagement (1956) to the official portrait of Grace in a silk ribbed dress with gold lamé leaves (1969), and from the countless suits, ensembles, and evening dresses that Grace ordered to the famous tulle dress that Caroline wore for her wedding to Philippe Junot (1978), season followed season, all held dear in Grace's heart. "Christian Dior was my entire childhood. When I was four years old I went with my mother to Avenue Montaigne, and for eighteen years Marc Bohan made all my dresses," recalls Caroline de Monaco.[1] And didn't Stephanie herself spend a year working for the Dior studio? Is it sheer coincidence that pale yellow was the favorite color of Princess Grace, who for years was dressed by Marc Bohan, creative director of Dior from 1961 to 1989? "Princess Grace suited what I was doing at Dior very well, a style that did not seek to be aggressive, but refined, feminine, and elegant. She was the greatest of my ambassadors."[2] Patron of the Baby Dior boutique in 1967, H.S.H. Princess Grace of Monaco arrived at Avenue Montaigne wearing the *San Francisco* suit.

The legacy has been passed on: Caroline's three daughters were christened in the Dior christening gown that their mother wore as a baby. Emotion reigned once again at the gala held at the Princess Grace Foundation in September 2015, when Charlene of Monaco appeared in an embroidered red and ink-blue georgette silk evening gown, continuing a history filled with glittering and luminous moments, such as the fine lace mantilla that fluttered over the dress worn by Charlene in 2013 when she visited Pope Benoit XVI at the Vatican. An ongoing history of confidence in Dior: "For the five-month anniversary of her twins, Princess Charlene of Monaco trusted in the savoir-faire of the French couture house to make her immaculate dress as well as the outfits for Gabriella and Jacques. A pretty display of cotton netting, silk crepe, and Calais lace: utterly princely."[3]

---

[1] *Le Figaro*, 1969.
[2] *Point de Vue*, September 4, 2002.
[3] *Gala*, May 10, 2015.

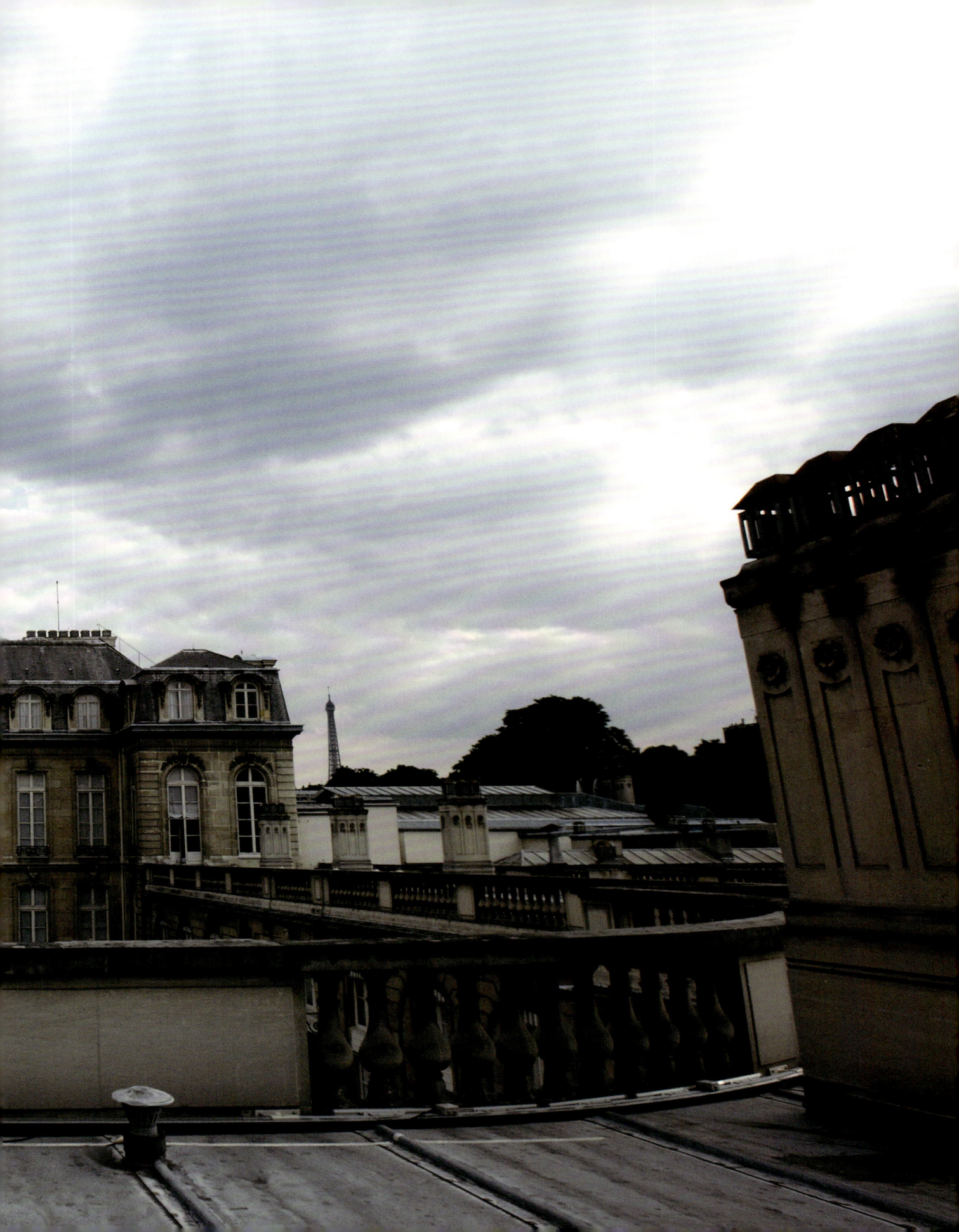

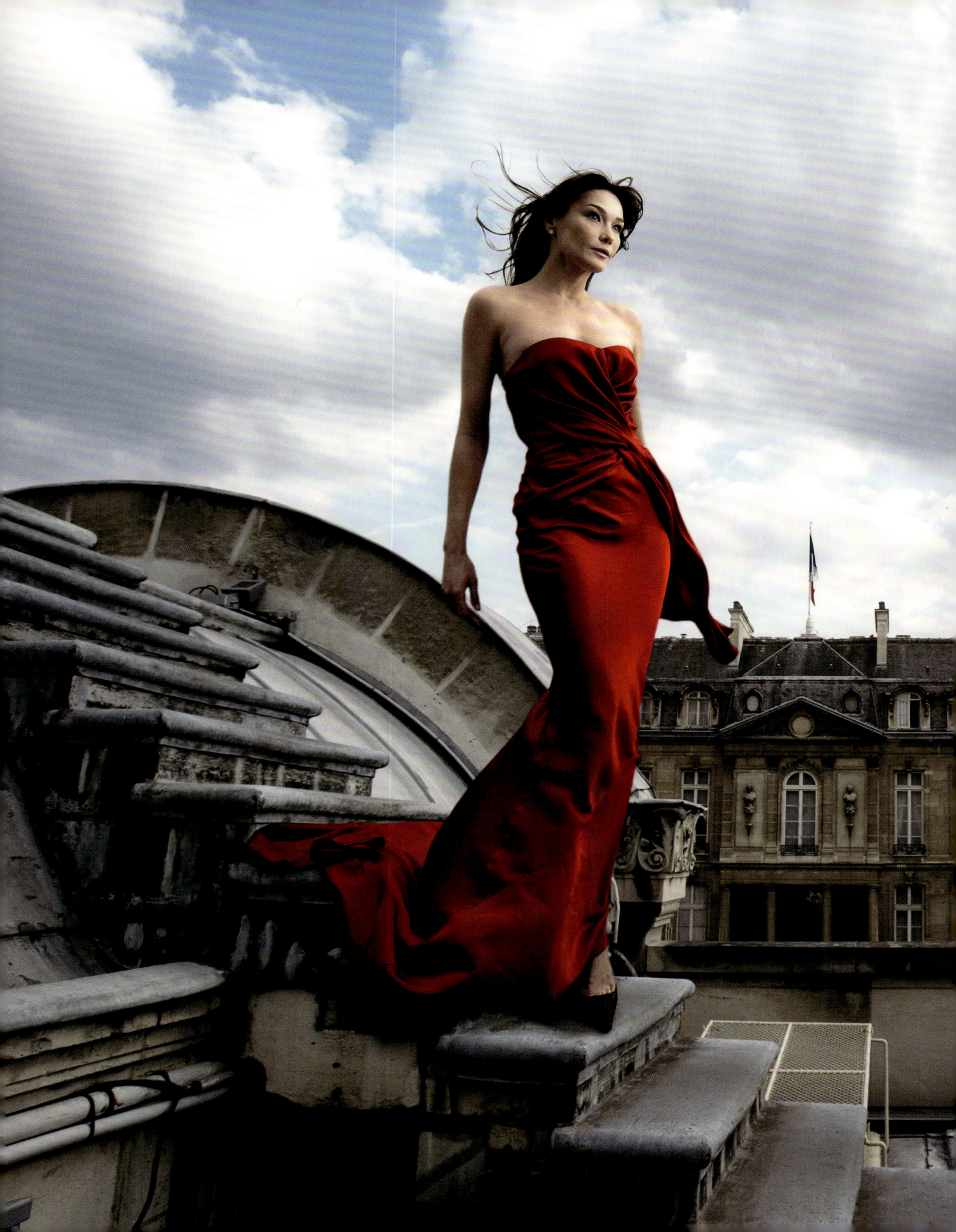

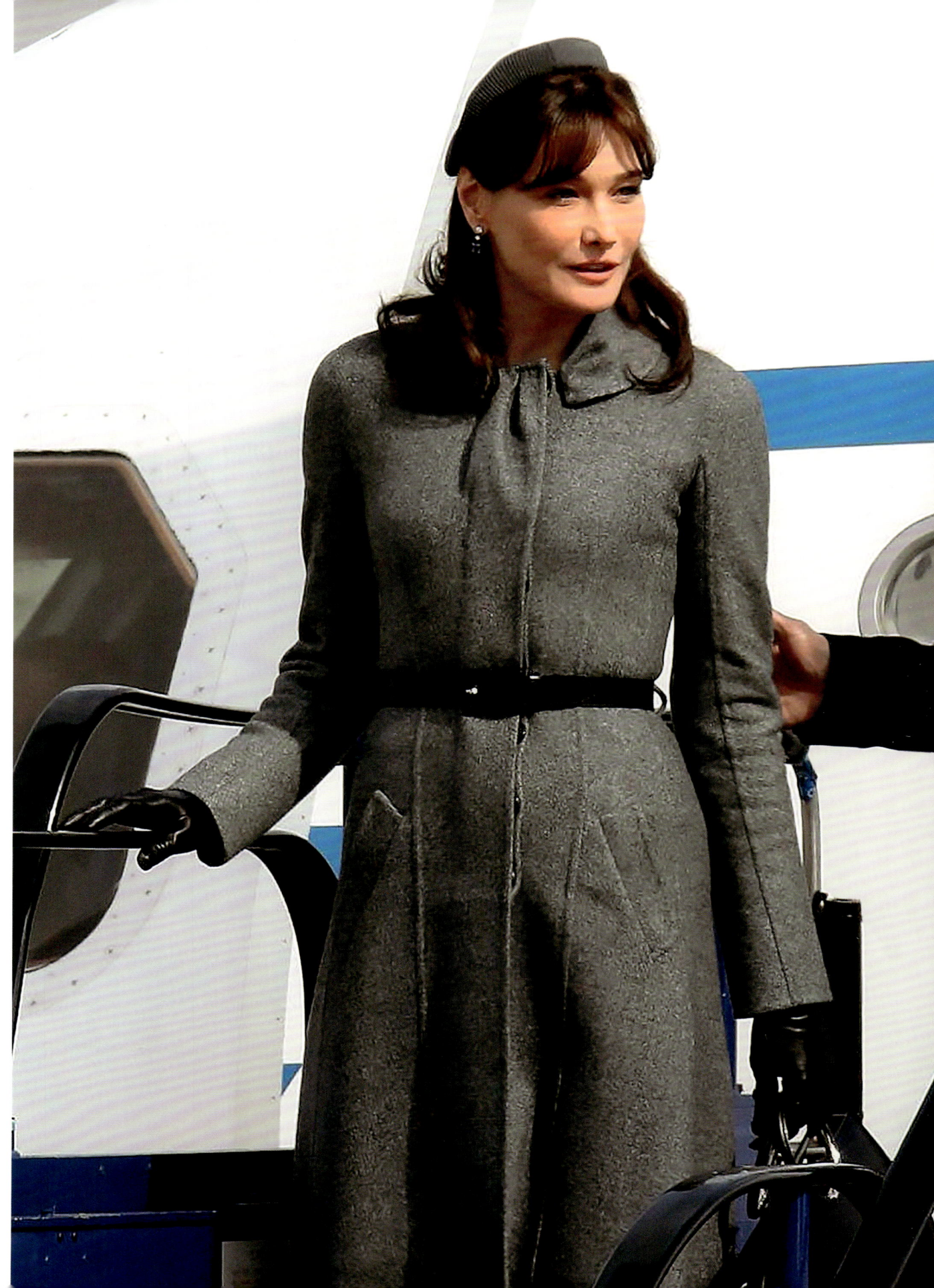

Carla Bruni-Sarkozy

On March 27, 2008, Carla Bruni-Sarkozy accompanied her husband, the French President Nicolas Sarkozy, on an official state visit to Great Britain. The former top model knew the house of Dior well, having signed her first contracts with Gianfranco Ferré and posed for the *Lady Dior* campaign. "The day I arrived, all the British tabloids published a photo of me naked taken eighteen years before. The nice thing is that they completely changed their tune when they saw me get out of the plane, all dressed up with gloves and a hat," Bruni-Sarkozy recalls.

It started with a light gray jersey coat belted at the waist and a tambourine bibi hat, whose perfectly studied lines made Bruni-Sarkozy's curtsey to Queen Elizabeth into an almost cinematographic moment: A totally Dior silhouette set off by the *Babe* handbag and black kid gloves—the climax of a ten-year friendship with John Galliano, then creative director of the couture house. "The fittings were a sheer joy," Bruni-Sarkozy recollects. "It feels like yesterday: John was tickled pink because he loves his queen." Four daywear outfits and two evening dresses formed a veritable lesson in the ultimate French touch. "John left me totally free. The looks could be separated."

Bruni-Sarkozy's appearances inspired more than one political commentator in the most unusual fashion. "Has Carla Bruni-Sarkozy invented a new diplomacy with her wardrobe?" asked *Le Monde*.[1] "I didn't rehearse. I based myself on the precious advice which the French Ambassador's wife gave me in London. Don't wear white or black. It all happened quite naturally. One certainly does feel at ease with people of good upbringing. At a certain level of education, people chase away all your fears. But you never get used to the zoo that is the media." The Dior burgundy bustier sheath dress she wore for the evening event on March 27 was a sensation. "What to wear for the Windsors?" *The Sunday Times* devoted its headline to Bruni-Sarkozy, showing her posing opposite a mirror in the famous coat.[2]

A year later, *Elle* magazine printed a long feature on "the most atypical president's wife," which looked back on this U.K. visit that revealed "Carlameleon," "regal and calm, with impressive self control."[3] This historical sequence was continued in France with the violet Dior silk suit designed by John Galliano that she wore for Bastille Day 2008, and again back in Great Britain, with the neo-60s look of the violet coat on March 27, 2009, and the gray dress she wore on June 18, 2010, to commemorate the sixtieth anniversary of General de Gaulle's radio broadcast. Despite Nicolas Sarkozy's speech in homage to Charles de Gaulle and Winston Churchill, David Cameron's response, the partisan songs, and the old aircraft parade, the press only had eyes for Carla. "The First Lady turned her marathon walk in the official stands into a delightful and even slightly cheeky catwalk show."

In 2016 Bruni-Sarkozy evoked these Dior years with a touch of emotion: "Protocol is all about customs but there are no specific references. If I was compared to Jackie Kennedy, it's probably something to do with youth, even though at the time of my husband's presidency I wasn't actually all that young anymore . . . But Jackie Kennedy came from the Bouvier family—the American establishment in a way—whereas I come from a slightly strange family of Italian industrialists and artists. I wanted to be an honor to France, to Great Britain, to my husband, to the function I held at that time. I became French the moment I got married. I knew nothing about patriotism, political engagement, and the obligations of protocol. I had to engage in a part of my life that I did not know: the honor of belonging to a country—the desire to be an honor to that country. I wanted to show the French that I would play my part, that I wanted to pay tribute to them. I had the great fortune of being dressed by a great French couture house in the hands of a great English couturier. . . . Basically, these long years of experience in fashion and humanitarian work no doubt let me mix my work as a rather 'hippie' artist with the delicate and unclear job of being First Lady of France!" she laughs.

[1] *Le Monde*, March 30–31, 2008.
[2] *Sunday Times*, April 20, 2008.
[3] *Elle*, September 2009.

OPPOSITE Carla Bruni-Sarkozy wears a Dior outfit during her arrival in London for her first official trip as France's First Lady, March 26, 2008.

FOLLOWING PAGES Carla Bruni-Sarkozy photographed by Annie Leibovitz on the Élysée Palace's rooftop for *Vanity Fair*, September 2008. She wears a red silk dress from the Spring-Summer 2009 ready-to-wear collection.

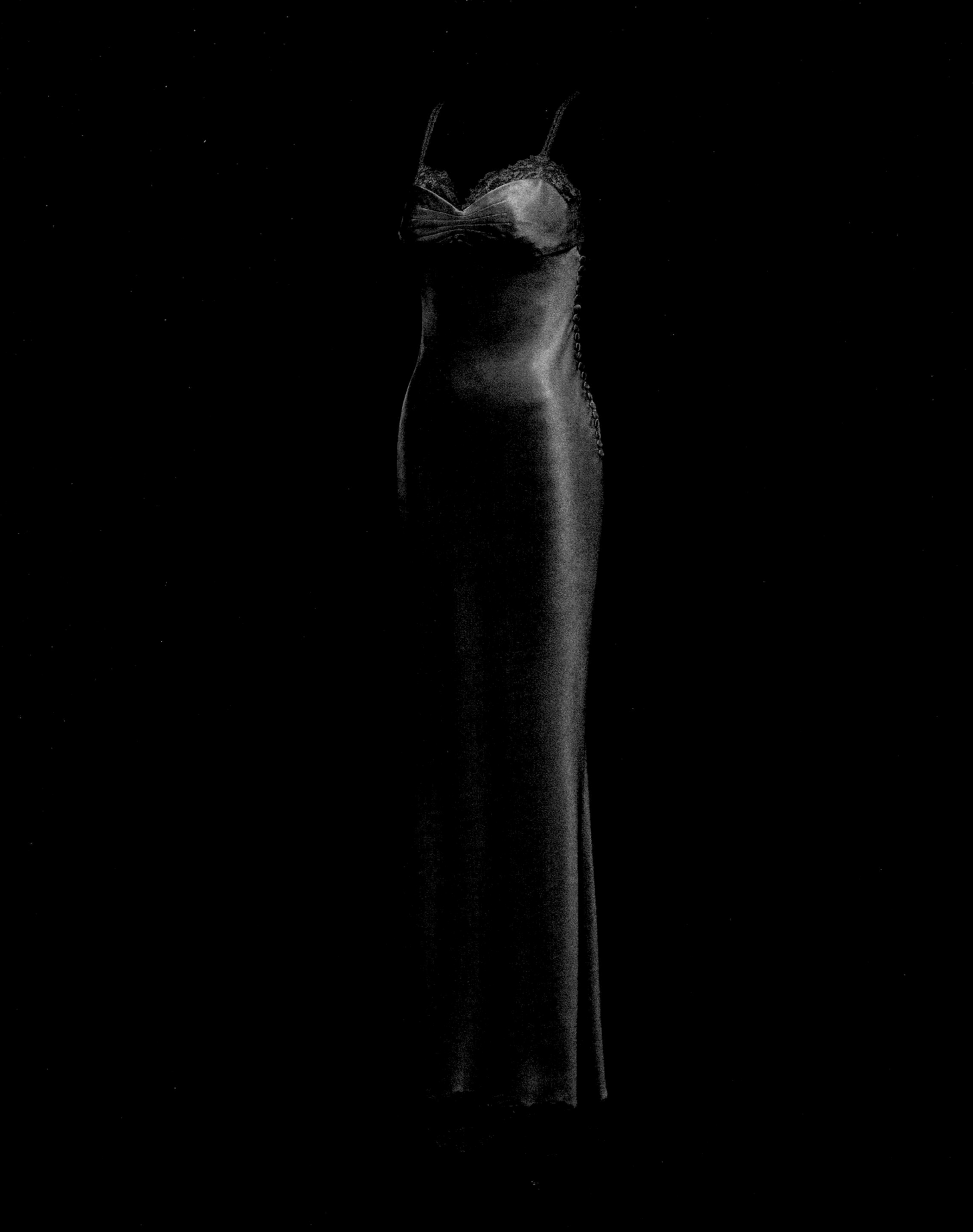

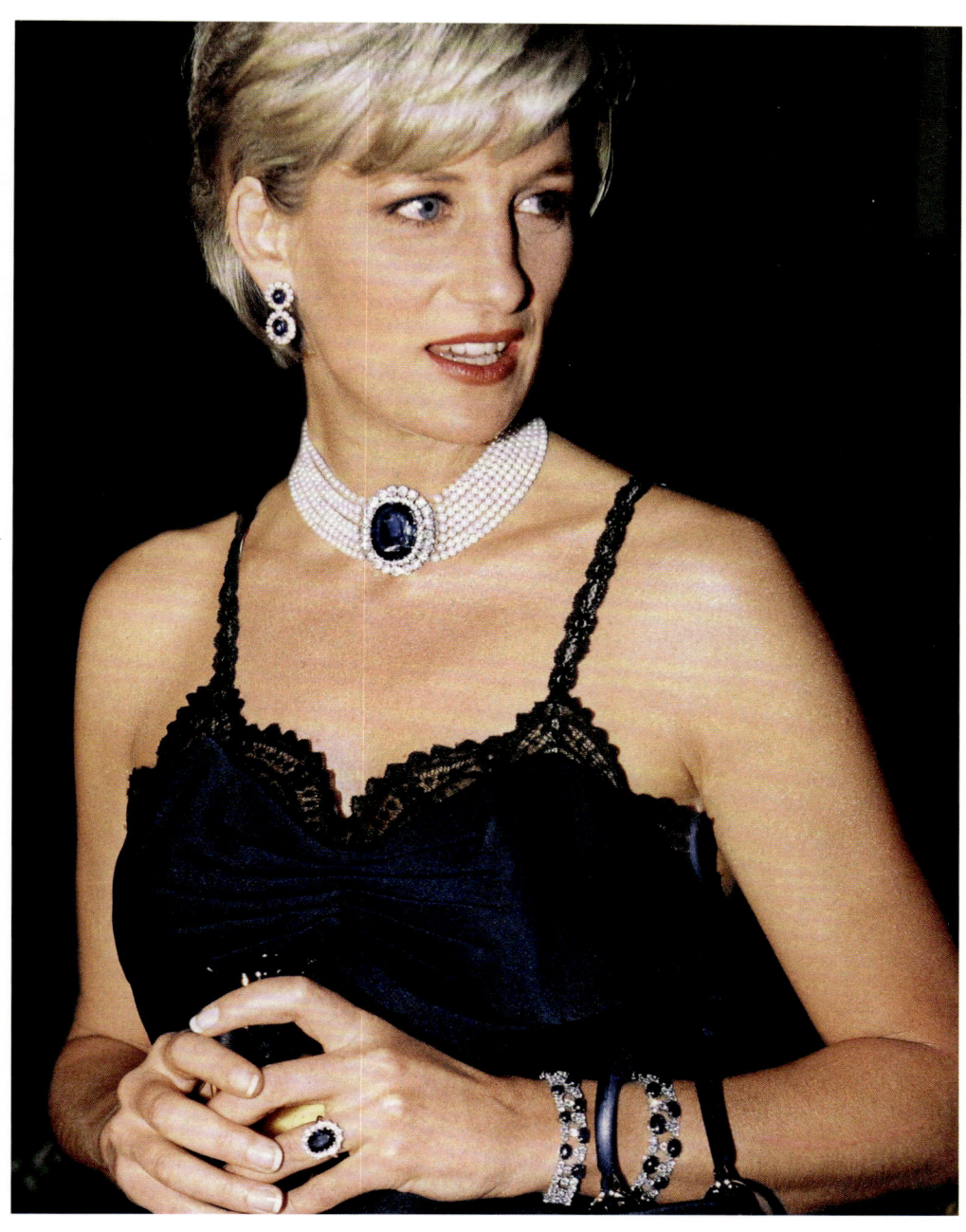

ABOVE Lady Diana wears John Galliano's very first design for the house of Dior during the Costume Institute's gala celebrating the house of Dior's fiftieth anniversary and the debut of the Dior exhibition at the Metropolitan Museum of Art in New York, December 9, 1996.

OPPOSITE A satin and midnight blue lace dress, special haute couture design, 1996.

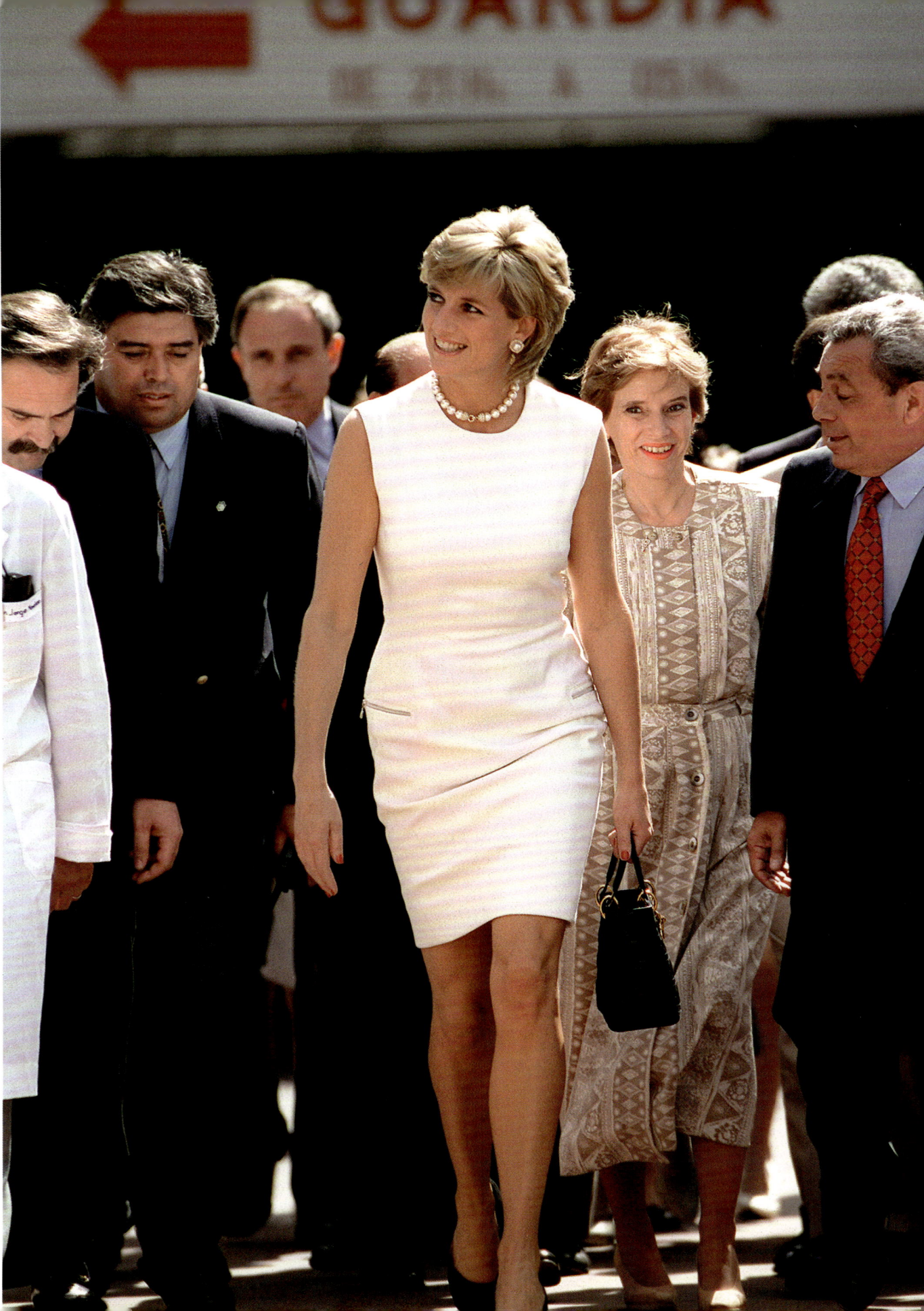

Diana, Princess of Wales

In 1995, Bernadette Chirac, who was France's First Lady at the time, gave Diana Princess of Wales a Dior handbag, a gift to mark her official visit to Paris. Princess Diana fell in love with the bag, ordered it in several colors, and wore it on numerous public occasions. . . . In tribute to the Princess, the leather handbag with its *cannage* overstitching and half-moon handles was christened *Lady Dior*. It was a worldwide success that would be made in over twenty colors in tweed, embroideries, and crocodile. . . .

Diana reinvented royal glamour. In December 1996, the freshly divorced Princess was a woman who seemed to want to declare her freedom to the world: On the occasion of the inauguration of the *Christian Dior* exhibition at the Metropolitan Museum of Art in New York, which celebrated the fiftieth anniversary of the New Look created by Dior in 1947, she wore to the Costume Institute Gala a dress designed by John Galliano for Dior: "The first dress I made was for Lady Diana, a very deep blue design," the couturier explained.[1] She wore a pearl necklace with a huge sapphire clasp around her neck, a wedding gift from the Queen Mother. "Released from boredom, the harshness of protocol, and her anxieties as a wounded woman, Diana seems to be reborn."[2]

[1] *L'Express Styles*, 2007.
[2] *Point de Vue*, 1996.

Lady Diana arrives in Buenos Aires, November 23, 1995. She carries the Dior handbag that she will eventually popularize, which will become the famous *Lady Dior*.

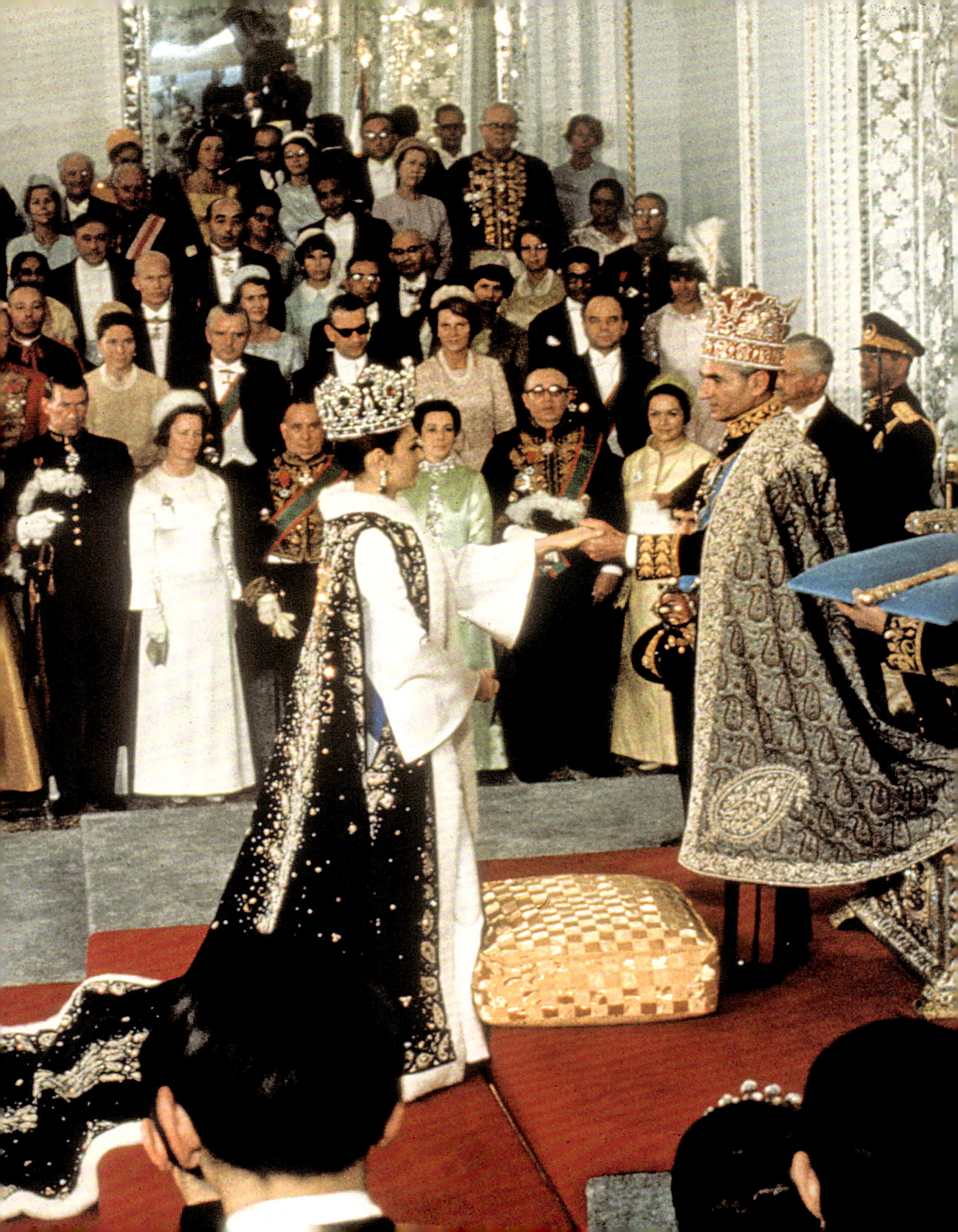

H.I.M. Empress Farah Pahlavi

"Here is Farah Diba (twenty-two years old, 5′7″), who has been chosen by the Shah to become Empress of Iran," so read the headline of *France Soir* on October 23, 1959, above the photo of the young architecture student whom Shah Mohammed Reza Pahlavi had met in Paris. It was one of the first photographs of the woman who would become the Shah of Iran's third and last wife and then stay with him until his death in exile.

An AFP dispatch stated that "the Iranians await October 26, 1959, feverishly. On this day, the Shah's birthday, he will officially announce his forthcoming marriage to Miss Farah Diba." The rumors were soon superseded by the preparations. The paparazzi waited outside the Hôtel Crillon, where Farah was staying with her uncle and aunt to prepare her trousseau. The Dior ateliers were at fever pitch. Then there was stillness. The photographer Bernard Lipnitzki captured these moments of silence bristling with whispers. In the large salon at 30 Avenue Montaigne decorated in Trianon gray, Yves Saint Laurent cut a slender figure dressed in black as he adjusted a velvet dress on the future Empress, who resembled an Ingres model in this neo-Empire garment. The two were joined in silent complicity. But the white dress that was fitted on a Stockman dummy had a much more solemn, almost mystical allure, which earned Farah the nickname "Persian Cinderella."

The wedding took place on December 21, 1959, on the first day of the Iranian calendar. Farah entered the Golestan Palace under a lucky Koran. She climbed the marble staircase laid with a red carpet for the occasion, wearing this extraordinary brocade dress with its sober décolleté, embroidered with silver thread, pearls, and crystals in Persian motifs. Her veil was held in place by an impressive tiara created by Harry Winston. "In the midst of this oriental splendor, who would recognize the young student who used to lunch on the Boulevard Saint Michel just four months ago. In the space of one hundred days she has gone through all the metamorphoses of the most precious of butterflies."[1] The memory has not faded: "Yves Saint Laurent made me the dresses I wore for the two events that transformed the life I led as an unknown student: my engagement dress and my wedding dress. He was a great artist and I had a lot of admiration for him, as well as friendship."[2] Later, in 1967, Marc Bohan designed her tunic for the coronation, when Farah became Empress.

[1] *Le Figaro*, December 22, 1959.
[2] *Point de Vue*, October 15, 2008.

Queen Farah Pahlavi wears a tunic created by the house of Dior while her husband Mohammed Reza Pahlavi crowns her *chahbanou*, the Empress of Iran, at the Golestan Palace in Tehran, October 26, 1967.

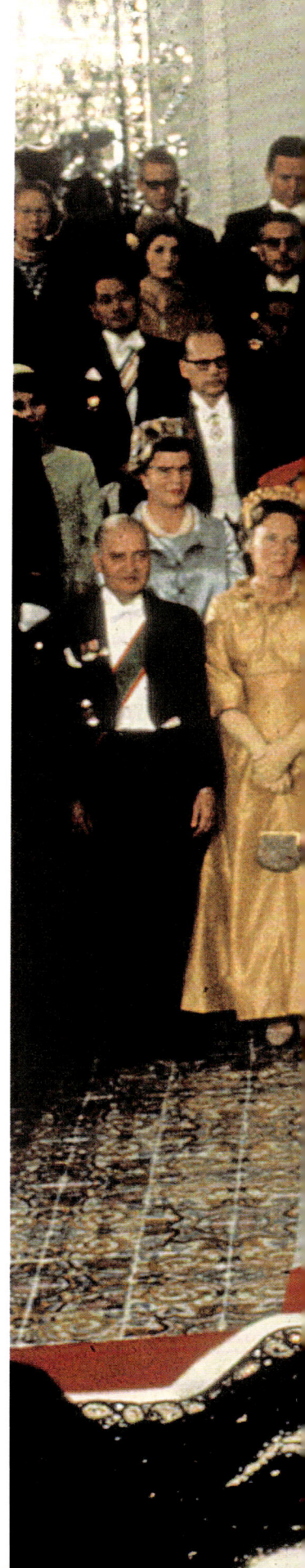

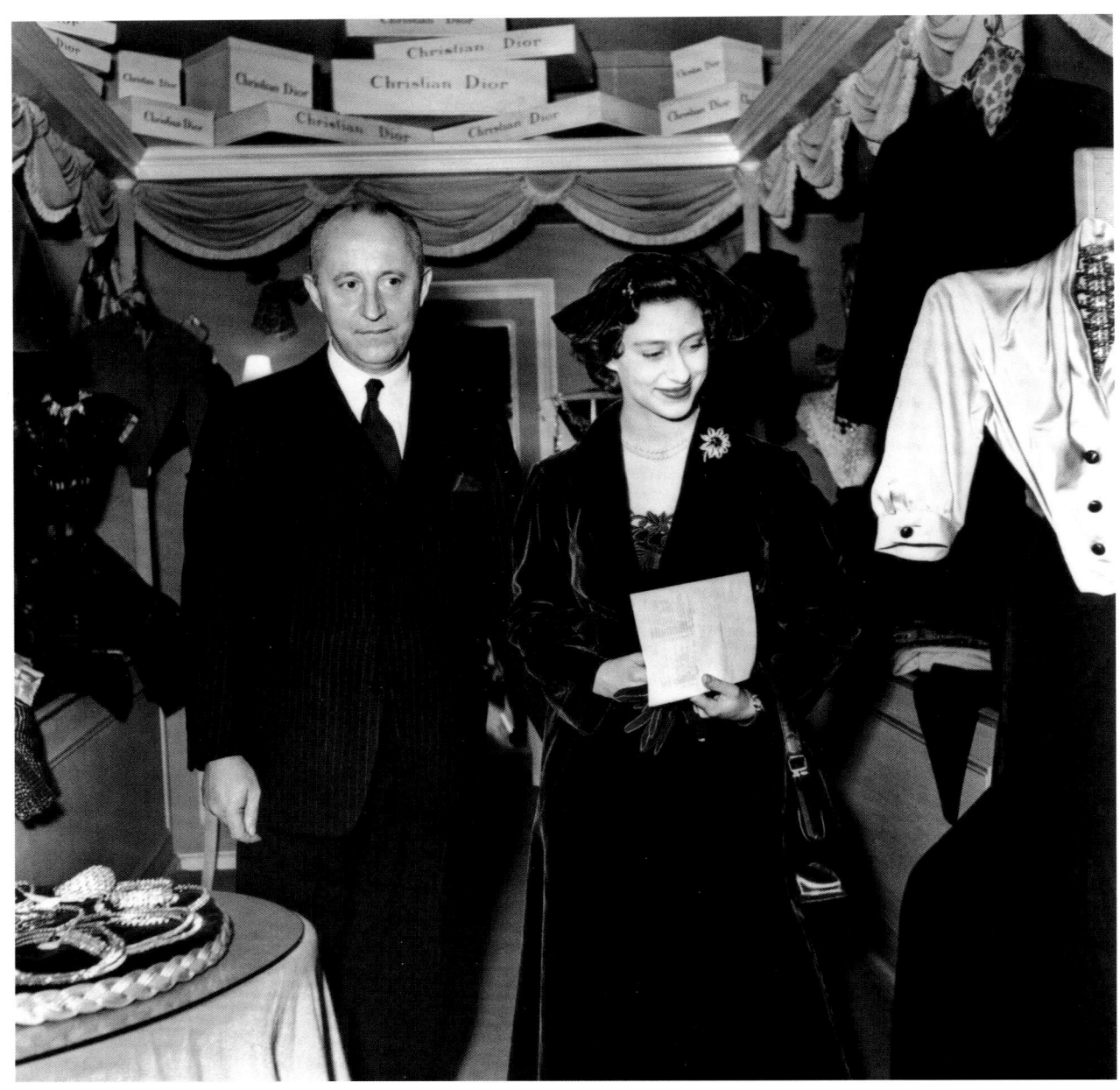

OPPOSITE The couturier Christian Dior receives a membership certificate for the Red Cross from Princess Margaret of England during a reception given at Blenheim Palace (the Duchess of Marlborough's residence, in the background), November 3, 1954. The couturier had just presented his Autumn-Winter 1954 haute couture collection before 1,600 guests.

ABOVE Christian Dior shows Princess Margaret around the Colifichets boutique during her visit to Paris on November 22, 1951.

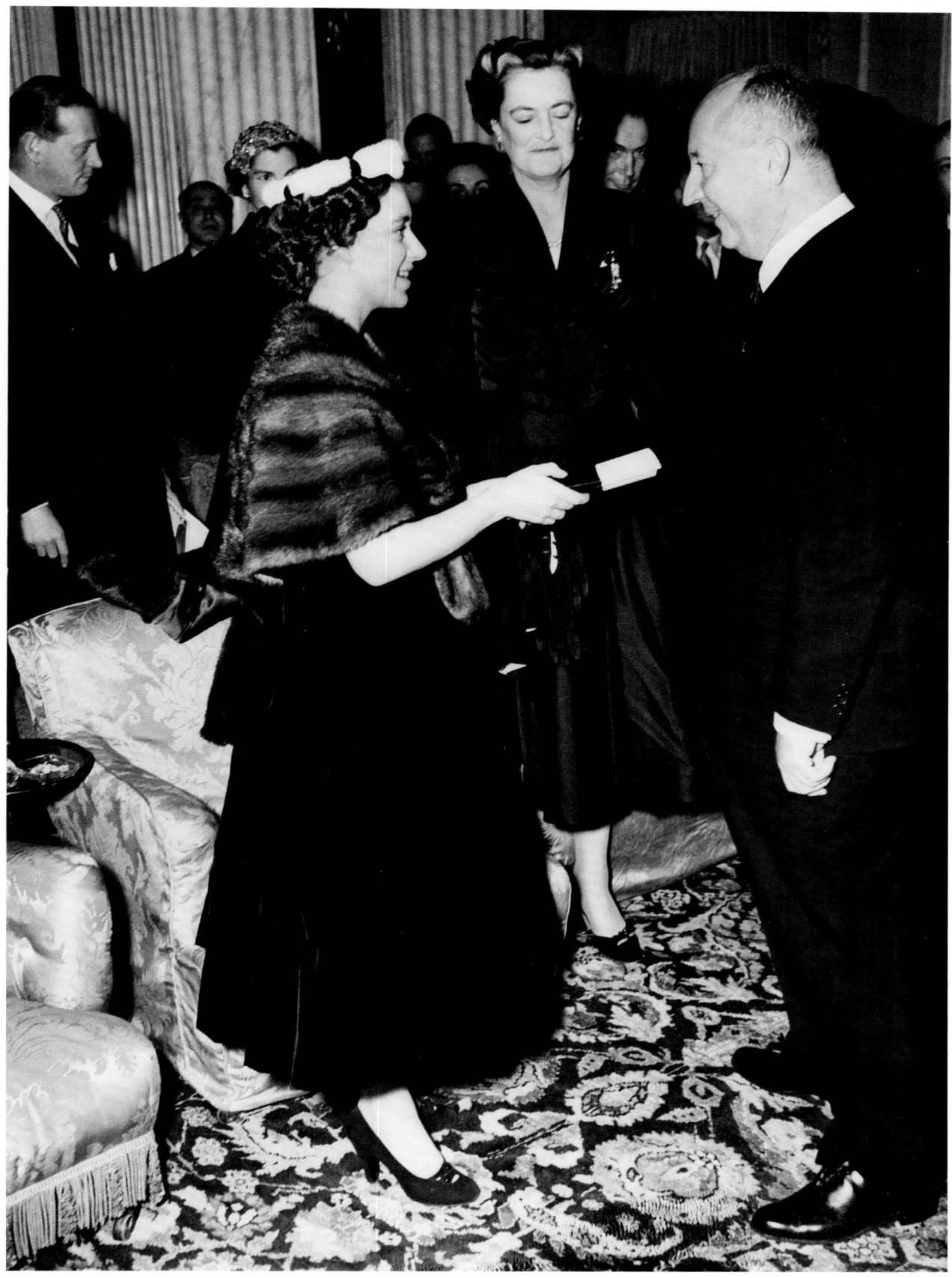

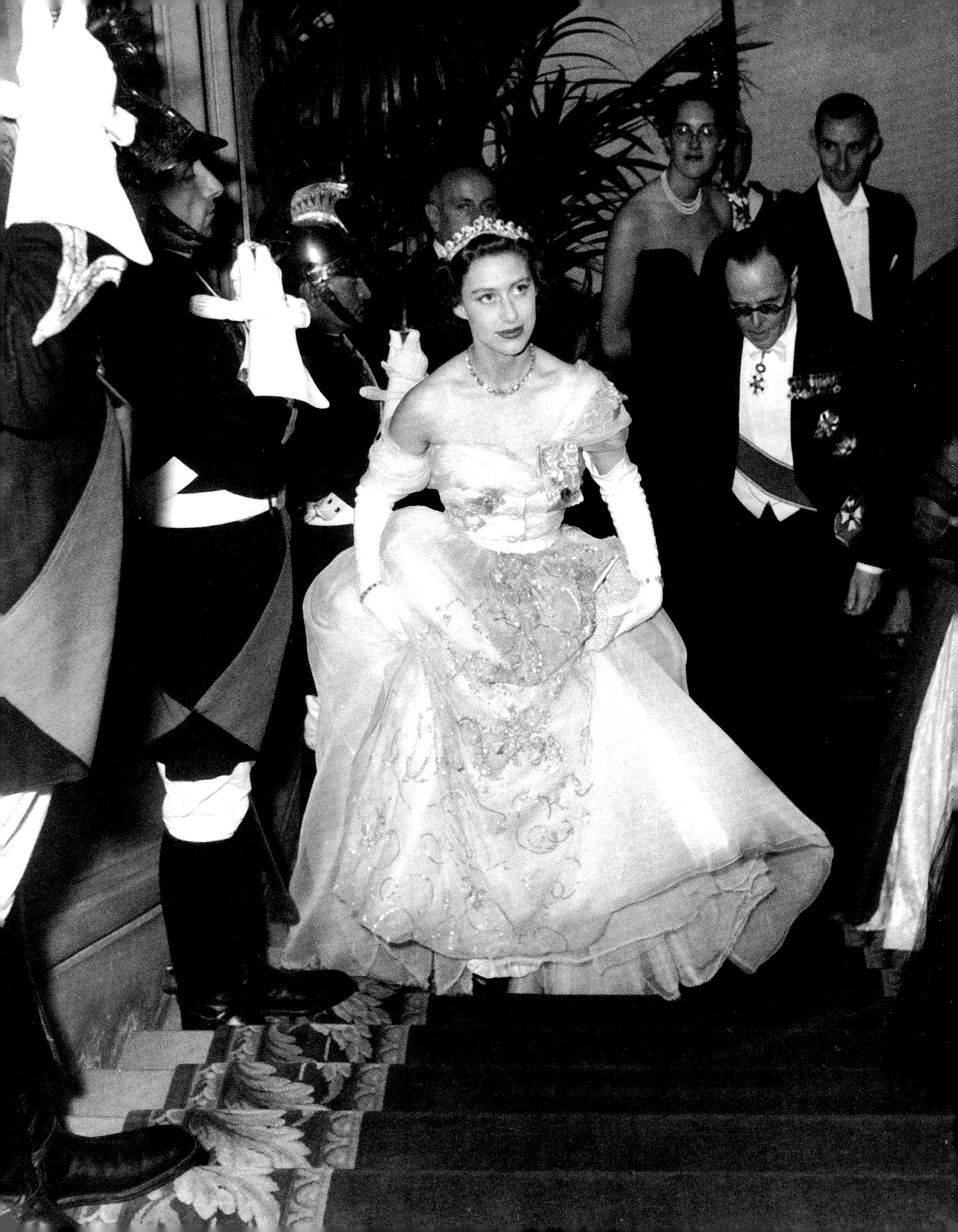

H.R.H. Princess Margaret

Princess Margaret was responsible for making the New Look popular in Great Britain despite the attacks from those who deemed the fashion scandalous during the years of rationing. On May 28, 1949, the Princess arrived in Paris. After visiting the Versailles Palace and dining at La Pérouse, two days later she went to 30 Avenue Montaigne. "Princess Fascinated by Dior's Fashions": the headlines in the British press proclaimed the Princess's interest in Dior, who had personally presented the *Trompe l'Œil* line to her. British protocol, however, required that she only be dressed by the official royal supplier, Norman Hartnell. Won over by Dior's designs, she stubbornly caused a stir some months later by being one of the first members of the royal family to order her dresses from a Parisian couturier.

Dior conceived an exceptional creation for her, inspired by two emblematic designs from the Autumn-Winter 1949 collection (*Trompe l'Œil* line): *Phalène*, a grand gala gown, and *Fidélité*, a crinoline wedding dress. This "bouffant tulle crinoline gown," which required almost twenty meters of tulle and five meters of satin, was fitted on Ghislaine de Boisson, a young model who had the same measurements as the Princess. "The dress is difficult to manage," the latter confessed. "It has so much whalebone I could hardly breathe, and it has a big hoop over the hips, so the only way the Princess can sit down in it is to slide the hoop over and squeeze on to about half a chair."[1] The Princess had a little shawl added to cover her shoulders. She wore this dress for the first time at a private dinner held by the King.

Two years later she ordered a white dress for her twenty-first birthday. In July 1951, Cecil Beaton photographed her wearing it between two pale pink hydrangea bushes. "The Princess looked like a little girl in front of my camera," said the man whom Christian Dior considered "a prince of English society." "Through the lens I could see her fabulous complexion, the fresh pink of her cheeks, the deep blue of her cat-like eyes. She was wearing a Dior dress that she was extremely proud of."[2] A dress that the young Princess wore to her birthday party at Balmoral Castle on August 21 and then one last time in Paris, on November 21, 1951, at the Franco-British ball held at the Cercle Interallié. The French press adored her appearance: Princess Margaret was definitively exquisite, "*l'exquise.*"

---

[1] *The Australian Women's Weekly*, February 4, 1950, quoted in Jérôme Gautier, *Dior New Looks* (London: Thames & Hudson, 2015).
[2] *Beaton in Vogue* (London: Thames & Hudson, 2012), 198, quoted in Jérôme Gautier, *Dior New Looks* (London: Thames & Hudson, 2015), 209.

Princess Margaret accompanied by Sir Oliver Harvey while arriving to the *Bal du Cercle Interallié* benefitting the British Hertford Hospital in Paris, November 21, 1951.

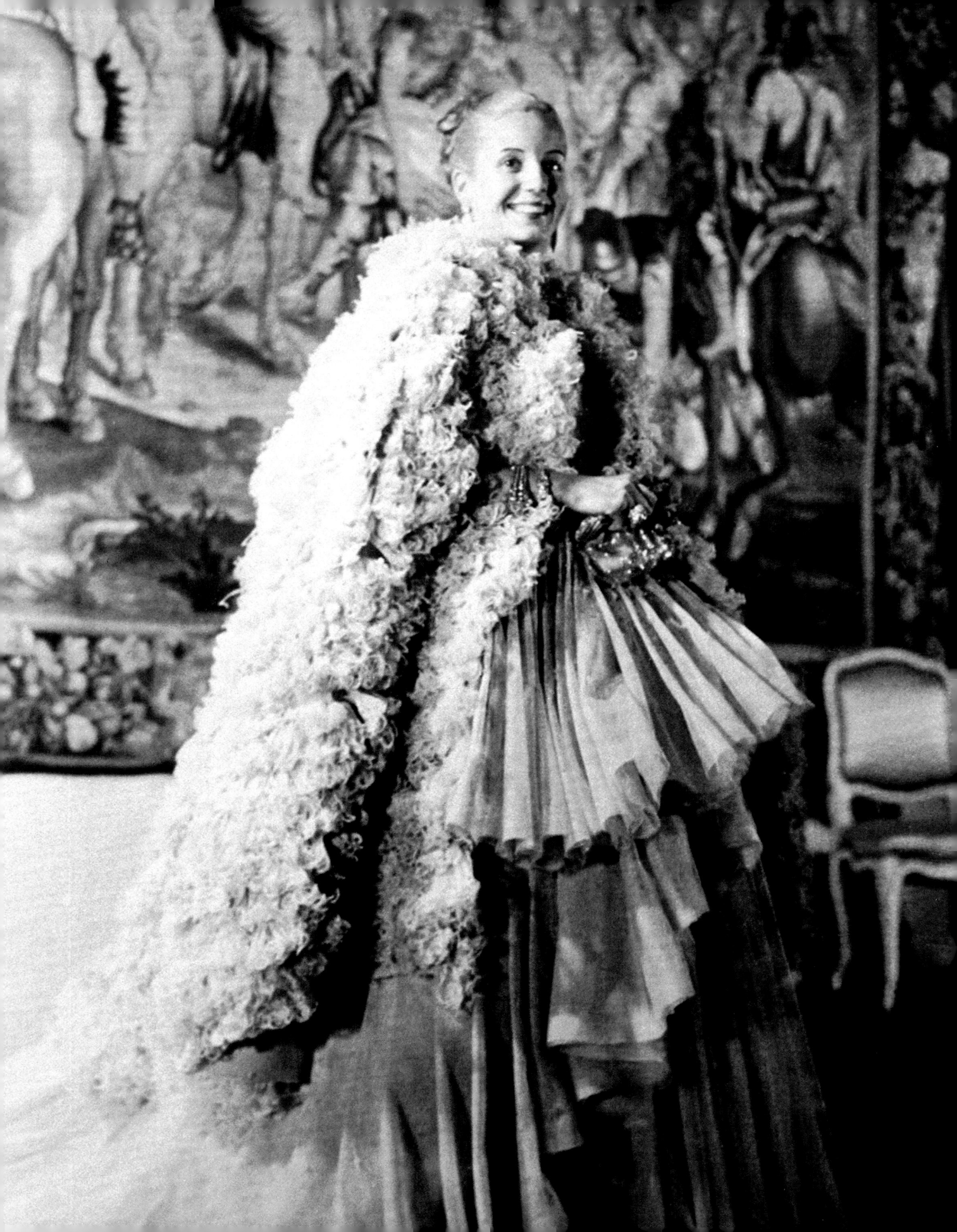

Eva Perón

In July 1947, during an official visit to Paris—where she arrived with an escort of forty cars—a mini-couture presentation was organized in Evita Perón's suite at the Ritz. It was there that she met Christian Dior. The couturier suggested she change her hairstyle and wear gold lamé for her evening events.... The new Eva adopted a chignon at the nape of the neck, "woven like two interlocking hands." From that day on she ordered several outfits from Dior, from suits to coats, gowns and dresses—all the day and evening wear required to dress a woman who had grown up marveling at Hollywood and who ruled her country like a sovereign.

For the 141st anniversary of the Independence of Argentina, she wore the *Amérique* dress, a fairy-like apparition of star-studded tulle. A client statement dated May 13, 1952, addressed to her Excellency Madam E. M. Duarte de Perón shows that the President's wife made regular purchases. Her love for fashion is part of her legend: When she died in 1952, she left no fewer than 150 evening gowns in her wardrobe. A *Caprice* early evening gown, or a *Rocaille* dancing gown, season after season saw her add new designs to her collection. The Dior ateliers at Avenue Montaigne excelled when it came to magnifying Argentina's First Lady, whose natural figure featured a relatively thick waist and small bust. The "Madonna of the shirtless ones," who was purported to savor emeralds as if they were candy, had a special fondness for the house of Dior: Beginning in 1947, she adopted the black houndstooth suit as a "little work outfit"— with two rows of buttons and a black velvet collar—in which she famously appeared at the balcony of the Casa Rosada to harangue the crowd.

Eva Perón during celebrations for Argentina's national holiday in 1950. She wears the *Bach* dress, Spring-Summer 1950 haute couture collection, *Verticale* line.

imposed by etiquette, listening to all the desires and details that will spark so many comments, pictures, and emotions—communion between the ateliers, the creative studio, and the saleswomen is the paramount rule. "One day a saleswoman came back from vacation with blond hair. Suzanne Luling immediately asked her to go back to being a brunette," recalls Sophie Gins, who was an haute couture saleswoman from 1952 to 1972. "Monsieur Dior imposed his own protocol: 'Everything had to be impeccable, and above all discreet.'" Elegance beyond the pageantry and splendor.

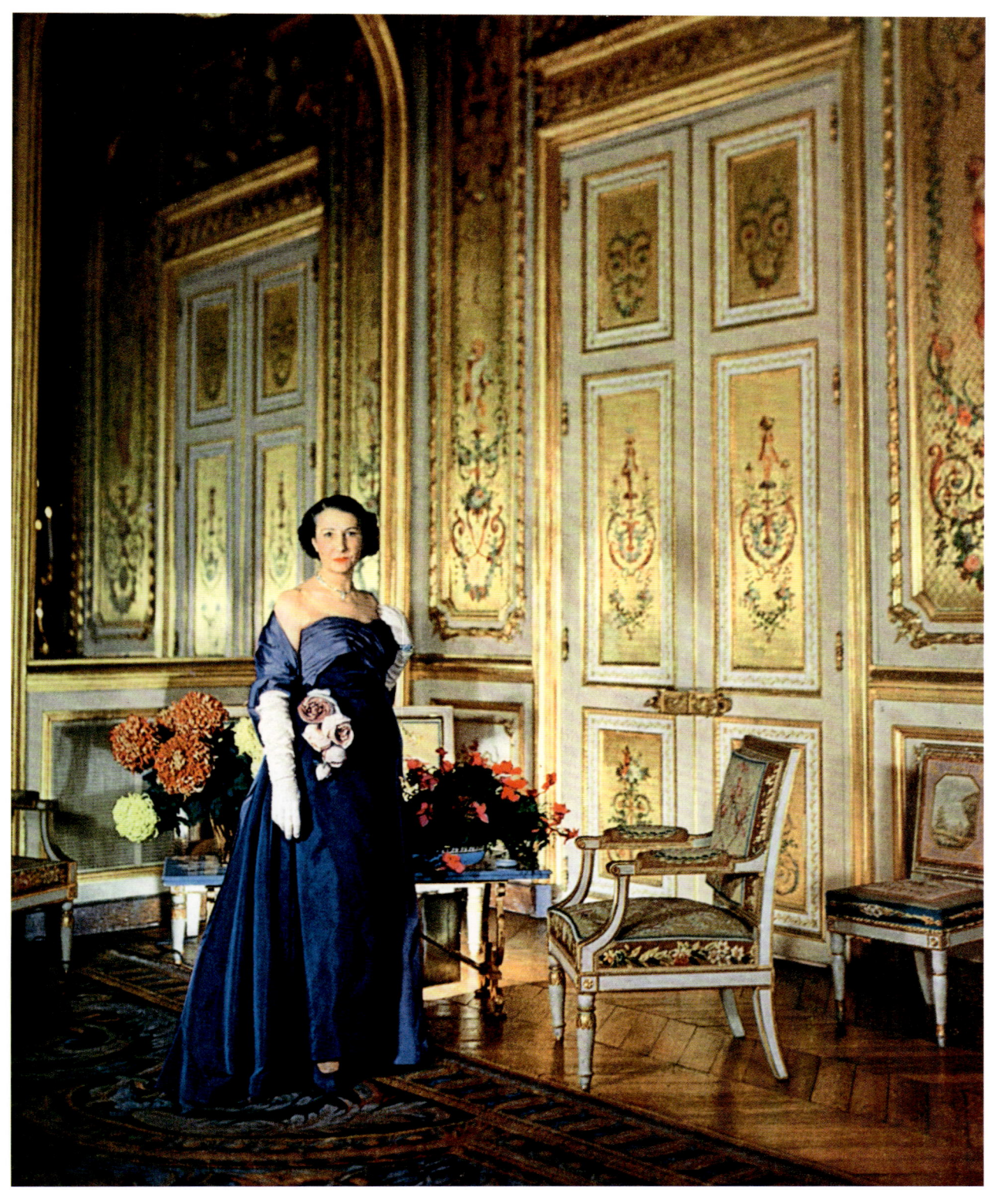

Michelle Auriol, wife of President Vincent Auriol, poses in Dior before Cecil Beaton's lens at the Élysée Palace for *Vogue* Paris, February 1951.

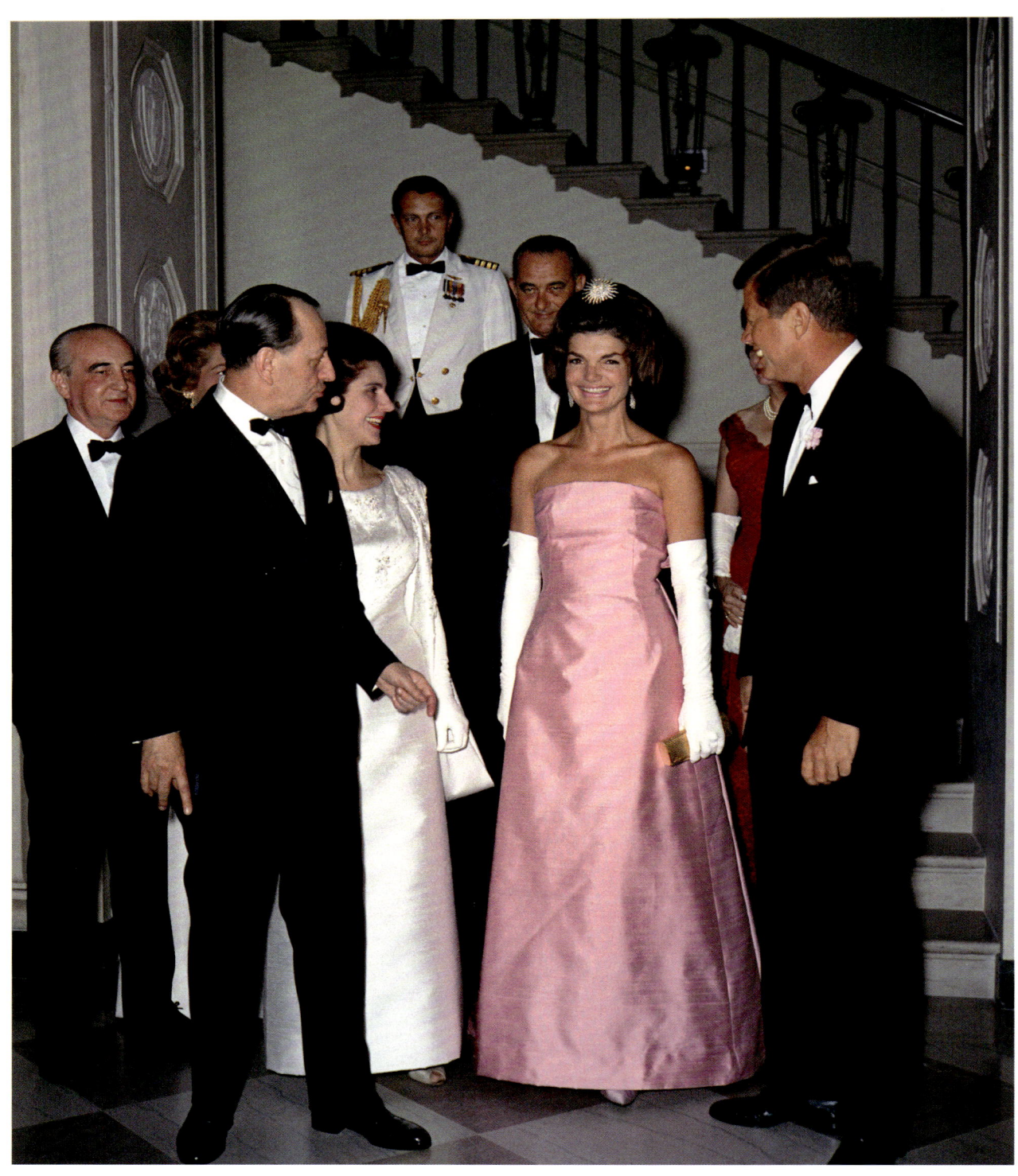

PREVIOUS PAGE
Vintage Christian Dior boxes.

ABOVE John Fitzgerald and Jackie Kennedy receive André Malraux, then France's Minister of Cultural Affairs, for a dinner given at the White House, May 11, 1962. Mrs. Kennedy wears a design by Guy Douvier for Christian Dior-New York.

Wardrobes and Protocol

For a First Lady of the United States there was a very special significance to dressing in Dior: A passionate fan of history and literature who spoke excellent French, which she perfected during a year at university in Paris in 1949, upon entering the White House Jackie Kennedy ordered dresses and suits from Dior. For Grace Kelly, dressing in Dior symbolized the end of her career as an actress and the start of a new, more official life. For her engagement party to Prince Rainier of Monaco at the Waldorf Astoria in Manhattan, the American film star wore a special creation made by Christian Dior-New York. For her life as a princess filled with society events, she wore a white guipure dress to the *Bal des petits lits blancs* in 1966; a gown in multi-colored striped silk chiffon to the Red Cross Ball in 1968; and a dress in coral jersey with a gold corsage to the *Dîner des Coiffes* in 1969. In all, over twenty haute couture designs were made for Kelly's different charity and Monaco galas. Her links with the house of Dior were so close that she became a patron of the Baby Dior boutique in 1967 when Caroline was ten, Albert nine, and Stephanie just two years old.

In haute couture, the art of official representation is a matter of protocol: When Marc Bohan created Silvia Sommerlath's dress for her wedding to King Carl XVI of Sweden in June 1976, it had to be designed to go with a fine lace veil that had once been worn by his mother, Sybilla of Saxe-Coburg and Gotha, and his sisters, Princess Margaretha, Princess Désirée, and Princess Christina. The long lace train had also belonged to the Bernadotte family for several generations.

Enough can never be said about the major role of the haute couture saleswomen at 30 Avenue Montaigne. They always wore black—and stockings, even in summer—and were trained to perfection by the aptly named Simone Noir; she was recruited by Christian Dior in 1946 and had dressed the Empress Michiko, the Shah of Iran's sisters, and all his wives. The entire art of a couture house like Dior consists in reconciling the personality of a great "lady-to-be" and her entrance into a new world. No less than forty meters of silver lamé silk re-embroidered with pearls, six thousand crystals, and twenty thousand marabou feathers were used to make Soraya's wedding dress in 1951 when she married the Shah of Iran. Yves Saint Laurent and Marc Bohan upheld the relations with the Court of Iran by dressing Farah Diba for her wedding to Mohammed Reza Pahlavi in 1959, for her coronation in 1967, and for the great Persepolis celebrations in 1971. Knowing exactly how to follow the constraints

III

OFFICIAL EVENTS

Christian Dior
30, AVENUE MONTAIGNE
PARIS

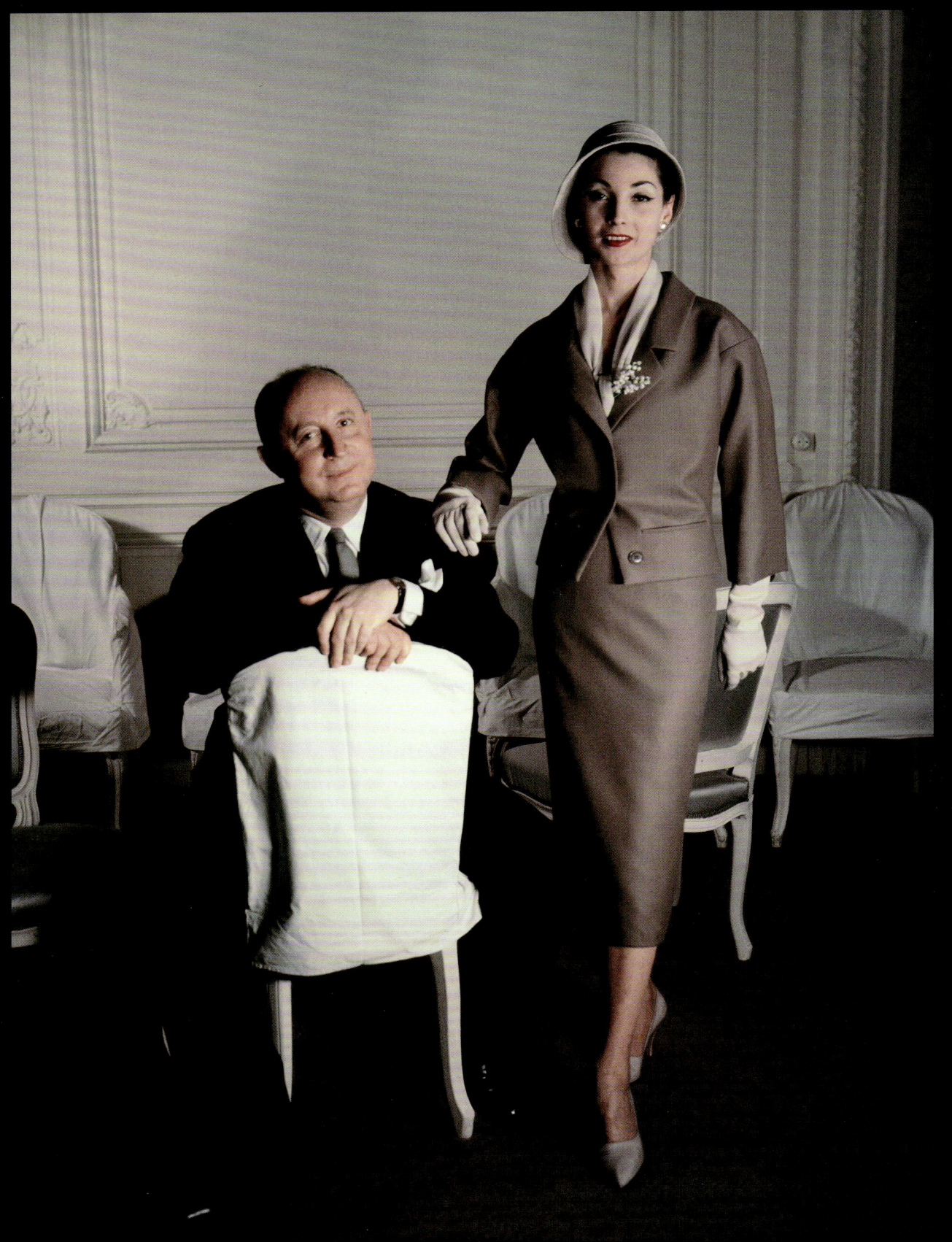

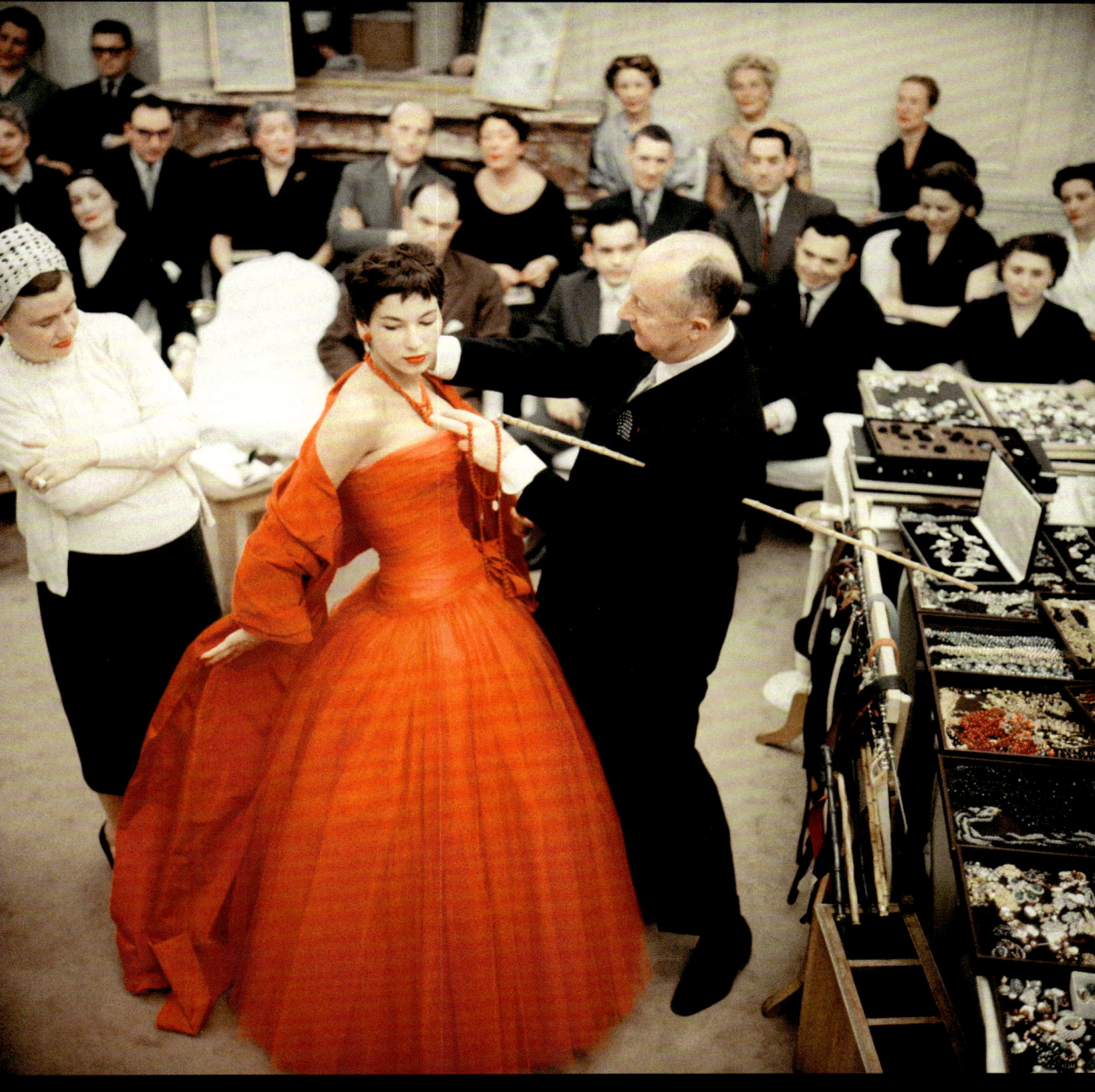

PREVIOUS PAGE Christian Bérard and model Marie-Thérèse in the Dior fitting room the day of the couture house's first fashion show, February 12, 1947.

ABOVE Christian Dior adjusts the *Zaïre*

OPPOSITE Christian Dior and the model Renée pose for Henry Clarke in the house of Dior's large salon for *Vogue* magazine, March 15, 1957. Renée wears the *Richard*

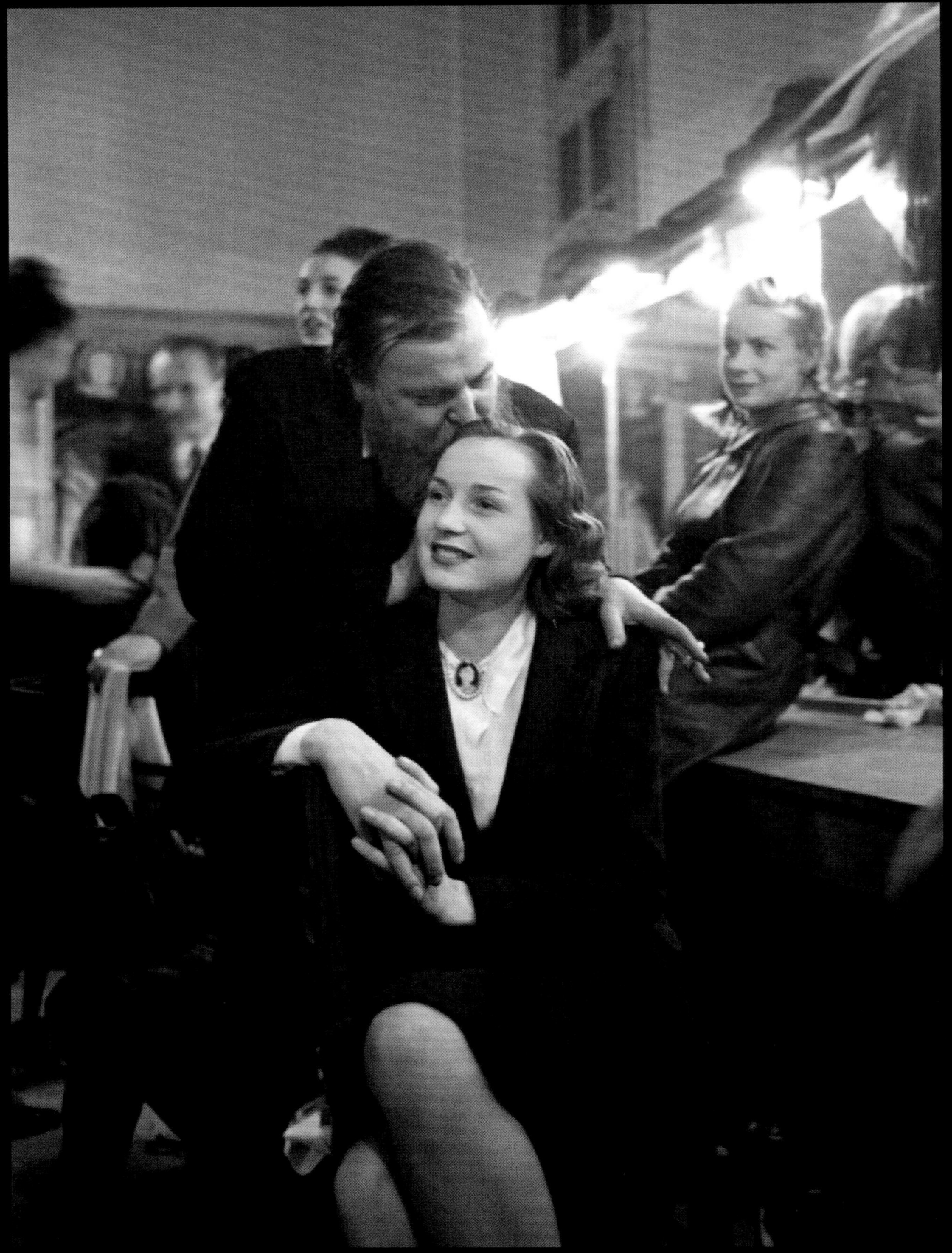

The Dior Models:
La Cabine

"My mannequins are the life of my dresses,
and I want my dresses to be happy."

Christian Dior

Marie-Thérèse, Tania, Lucky, France, Sylvie, Alla, Renée... All "*jeunes filles*" whom Dior saw "as Pygmalion saw Galatea. They alone can bring my clothes to life. In creating them even, I have had these girls in mind. It is not until they put on the design that I see the dress in its full glory."[1] From Tania, "femininity itself, with her ruses," to France, who was "so typically... Parisian French" and knew how to support "stylish dresses admirably," or the "sparkling brunette appearance" of Sylvie, the Dior mannequins always embodied a dream. "The young girls," as they were always termed, had figures the clients envied, but never "wore" the season's designs out in the city. Their role was to "grasp" the dress while knowing how to efface themselves behind it. For Dior, "Every *cabine* should employ different types of women who embody the clients' ideal image." Traveling around the world to present the collections, they became true ambassadors of the *maison*.

---

[1] Christian Dior, *Dior by Dior*, 128.

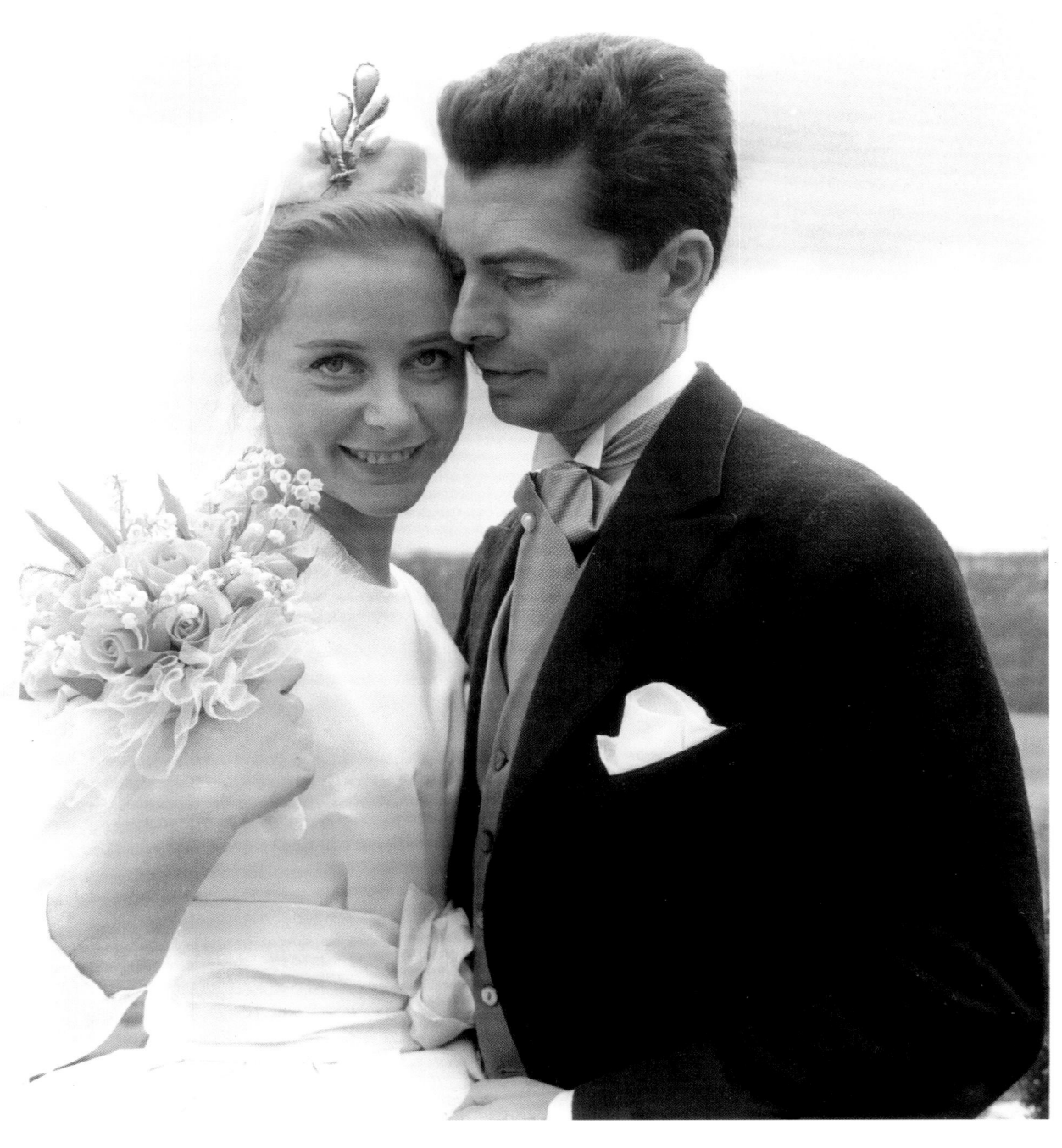

OPPOSITE Geneviève Page wears a Christian Dior dress during the French Film Festival in London in 1957.

ABOVE Geneviève Page chose a dress by her "godfather" Christian Dior for her wedding with banker Jean-Claude Bujard, April 11, 1959.

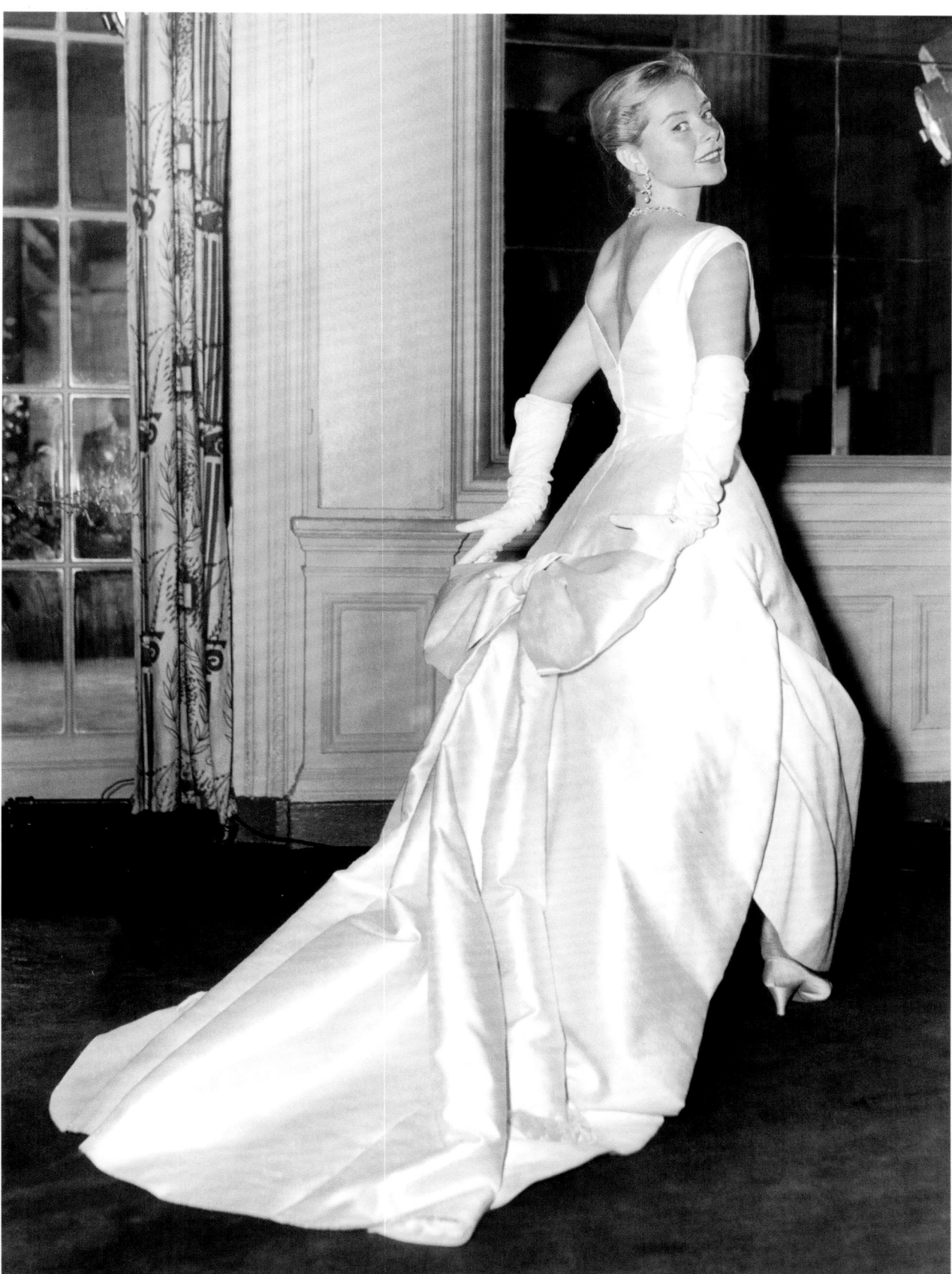

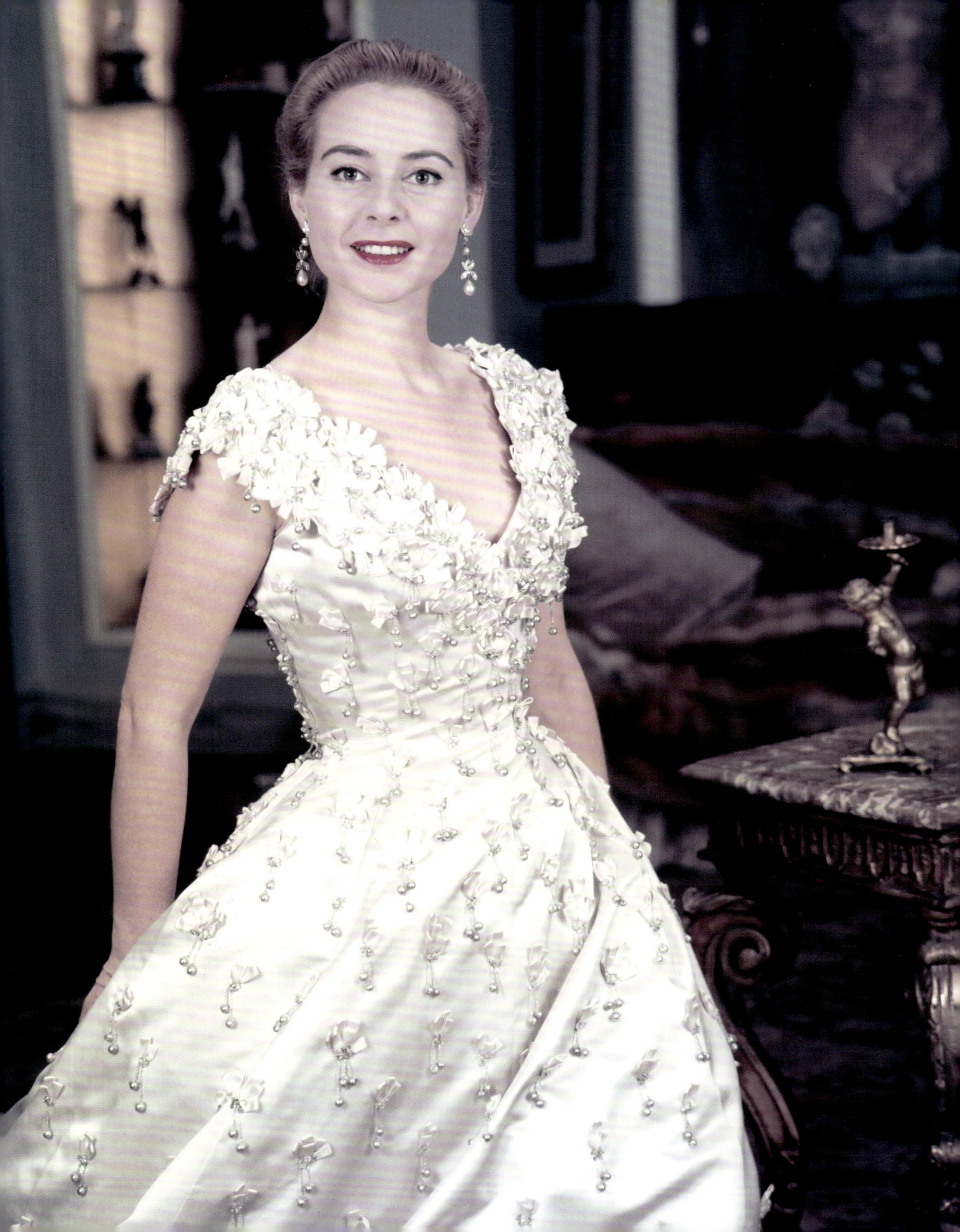

Geneviève Page

Geneviève Anne Marguerite Bonjean was the daughter of Germaine and Jacques Bonjean. Christian Dior was a close family friend; he often played *trictrac* (a form of backgammon) and piano with Geneviève's mother, and it was with her father, an antiques dealer and collector, that he opened a gallery on Rue La Boétie in 1928, representing artists such as Max Ernst, Giorgio De Chirico, and Raoul Dufy.

Geneviève Page had deep feelings for Dior, whom she saw as her adoptive godfather. Though he never dressed her for the stage or screen, from an early age he adorned her with a priceless asset: "audacity." "Godfather Christian had given me a hyacinth for my birthday and I was extraordinarily flattered that someone had given me flowers. I must have been barely six years old, and it was the first poem I wrote and which my father, who did not talk to us, liked very much."

Having brought Geneviève a "puce-red" dress back from a trip to the United States, for her eighteenth birthday Dior made her a dress that corresponded to the advent of the New Look. "For my eighteenth birthday, he had a dress made for me. I had gone to try it on and I found it a little strange: 'But how long will it be?' I said. 'That's a surprise,' he replied. Basically, it was the first dress, in black velvet, and I thought to myself: 'What will my escort say? Won't he think I look ridiculous in this dress?' But no, it was a success. Christian always flattered women. He always made them look more beautiful, more comfortable in their body."

Geneviève Page photographed by Willy Rizzo for *Paris Match* on December 29, 1956. She wears the *Première soirée* dress, Autumn-Winter 1955 haute couture collection, *Y* line.

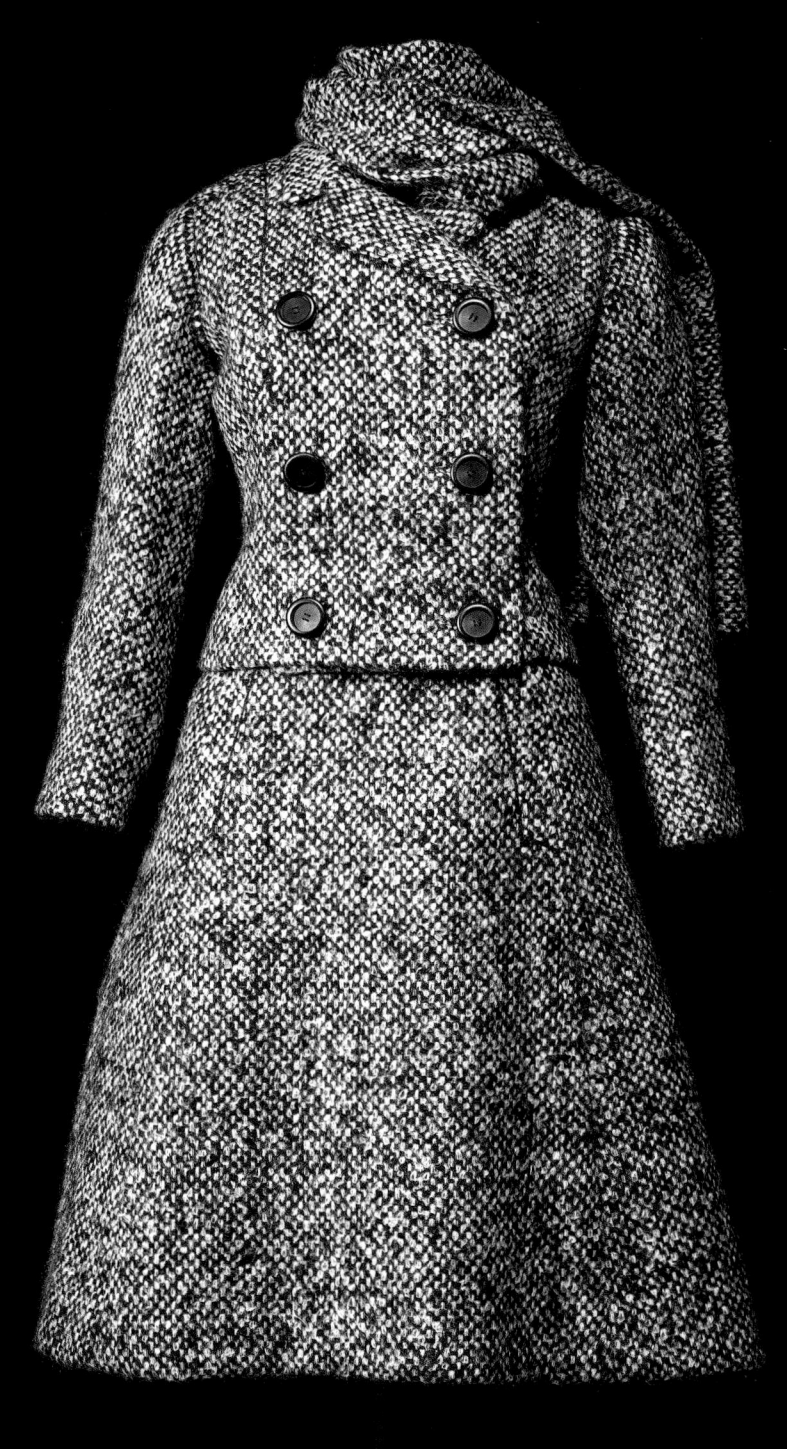

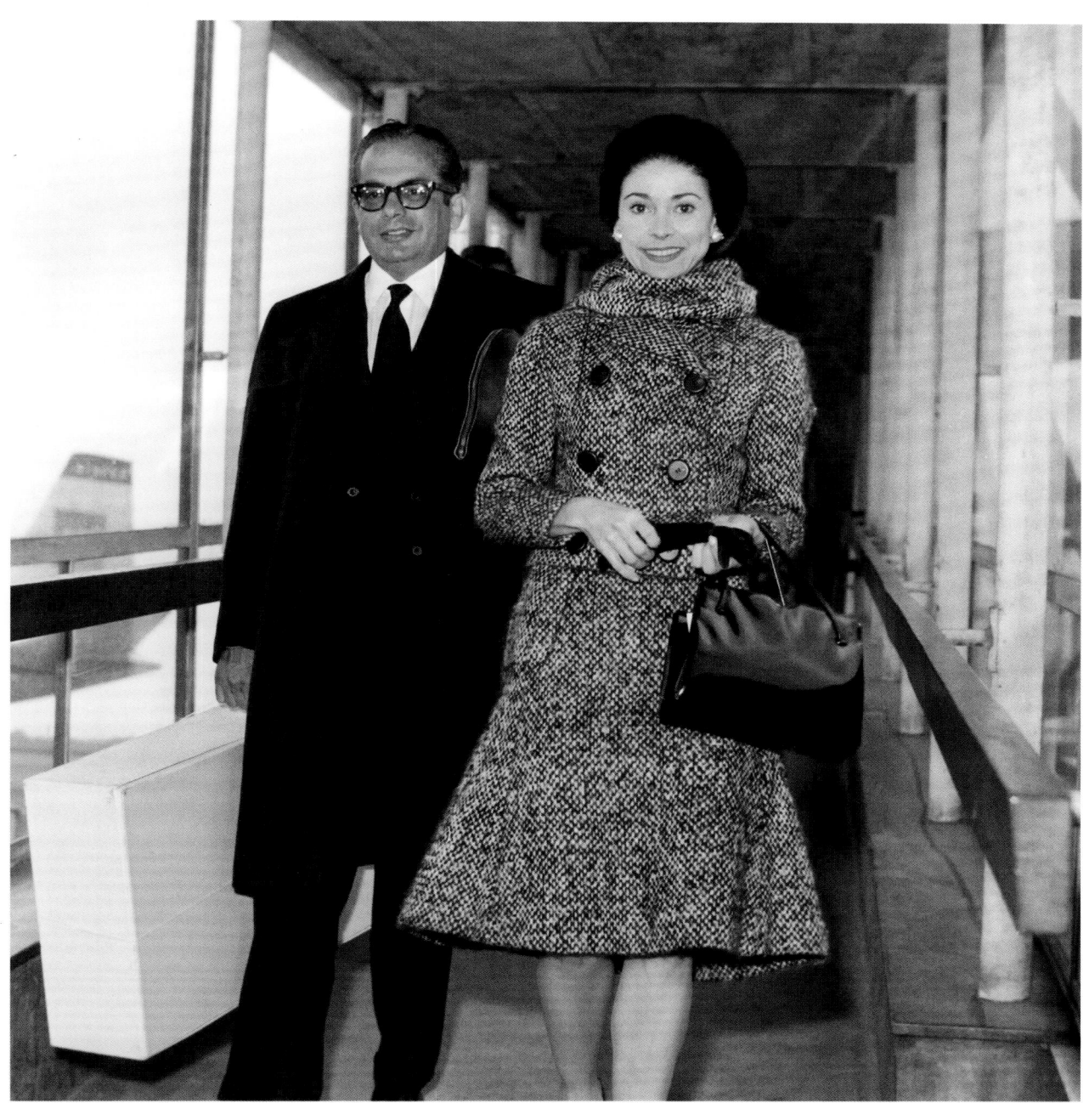

ABOVE Margot Fonteyn and her husband Roberto Arias in London in March 1962. She wears the *Gamin* suit, Autumn-Winter 1961 haute couture collection.

OPPOSITE The *Gamin* suit in black and white tweed, Autumn-Winter 1961 haute couture collection, *Charme 62* line.

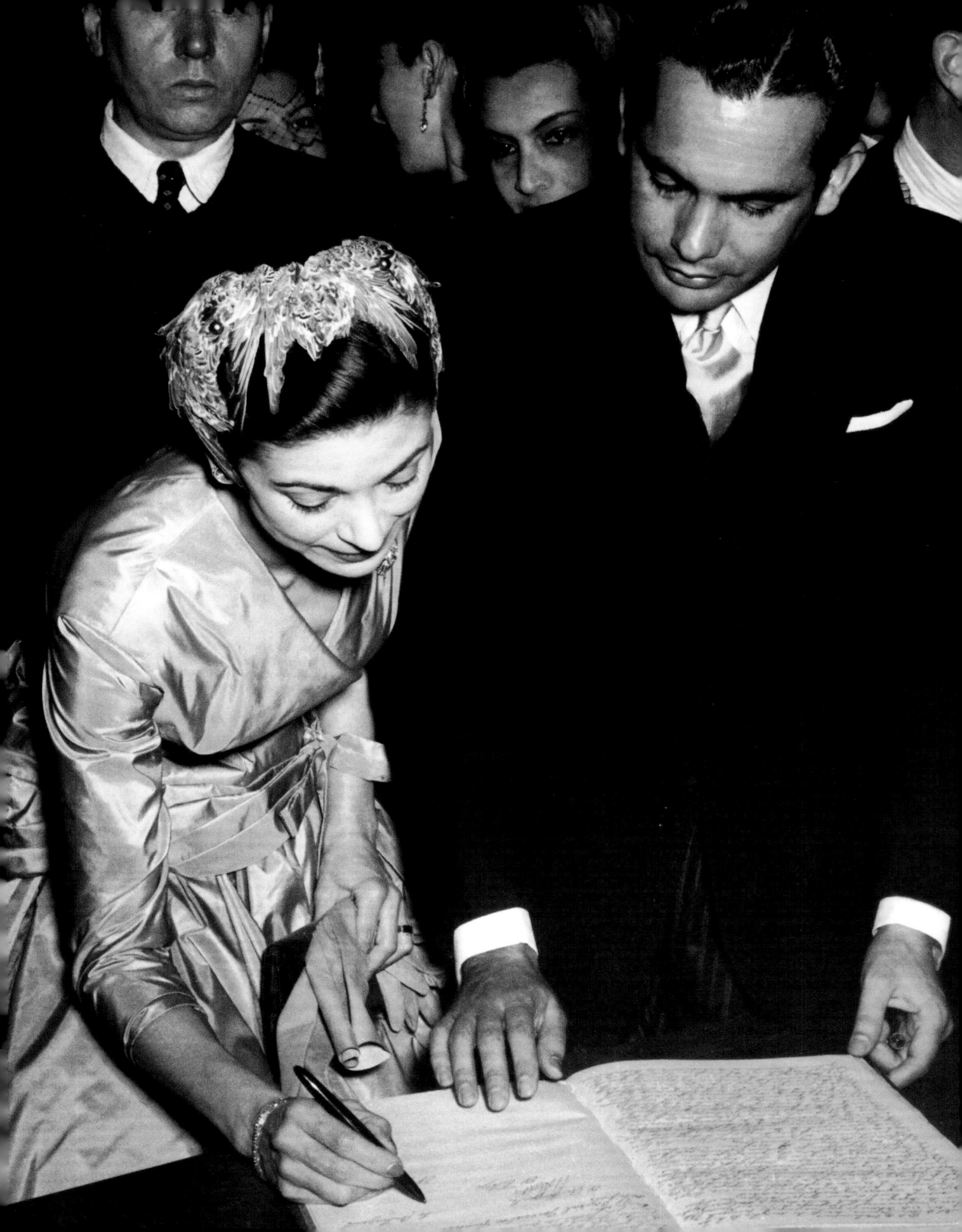

Margot Fonteyn

"The main thing I have learned over time is the difference between taking your work seriously and taking yourself seriously. The first is imperative and the second is disastrous." Née Margot Fontes in Surrey, Great Britain, the *prima ballerina assoluta* shared the same ideal of beauty as the most famous couturier in the world. Her interpretation of *Swan Lake* or *Sleeping Beauty* with Rudolf Nureyev and her *Rose Adage* performance are legendary moments in classical ballet. "Life off the stage is a world of non-choreographed surprises," she said.

Dior and Fonteyn had the same sense of discipline and career. "I was fortunate to be more or less the same size as one of Dior's favorite models, Lucky." This meant that every season Fonteyn could purchase an outfit that had been modeled on Lucky. The couturier called this "fashion itself brought to life: she can make a comedy or a tragedy out of a dress as she chooses."[1]

Fonteyn was among Dior's first clients, purchasing the *Daisy* suit in the summer of 1947: "The bust was very slim, but the hips were padded. The skirt was draped with several folds. I must admit that on the first day, I felt a bit strange, but I was quickly converted and I never looked back."[2]

In October 1949, as she prepared to perform at the Metropolitan Opera, Dior sent her flowers and a *Miss Dior* obelisk. Their destinies seem to echo one another. She was the first dancer to appear on the cover of *Time* (November 14, 1949); Christian Dior graced the cover on March 4, 1957. For Fonteyn's marriage to Roberto Arias, the son of the former Panamanian president, celebrated on February 6, 1955, at the Panamanian consulate in Paris, Dior made her a faille dress in Trianon gray cinched with a wide sash, like a queen. When she received her OBE, the unforgettable Princess Aurora wore turquoise silk court shoes adorned with blue feathers and signed "Delman, Christian Dior, Paris." From a pink moiré silk sheath dress to a champagne satin model re-embroidered with sequins and *pierrerie* for a reception at Buckingham Palace in 1956, every garment that Dior created for Dame Margot Fonteyn bears the signature of an admirer writing the choreography to his muse's every appearance. "Life creates random motifs. They hold a beauty which I try to capture as they pass, for who knows if they will be back again one day," said Fonteyn—words that could so easily have been uttered by Dior.

[1] Christian Dior, *Dior by Dior*, 105.
[2] Margot Fonteyn in the preface to *Dior in Vogue* (New York: Harmony Books, 1998).

Margot Fonteyn wears a dress specially created by Christian Dior for her marriage to Roberto Arias, February 6, 1955.

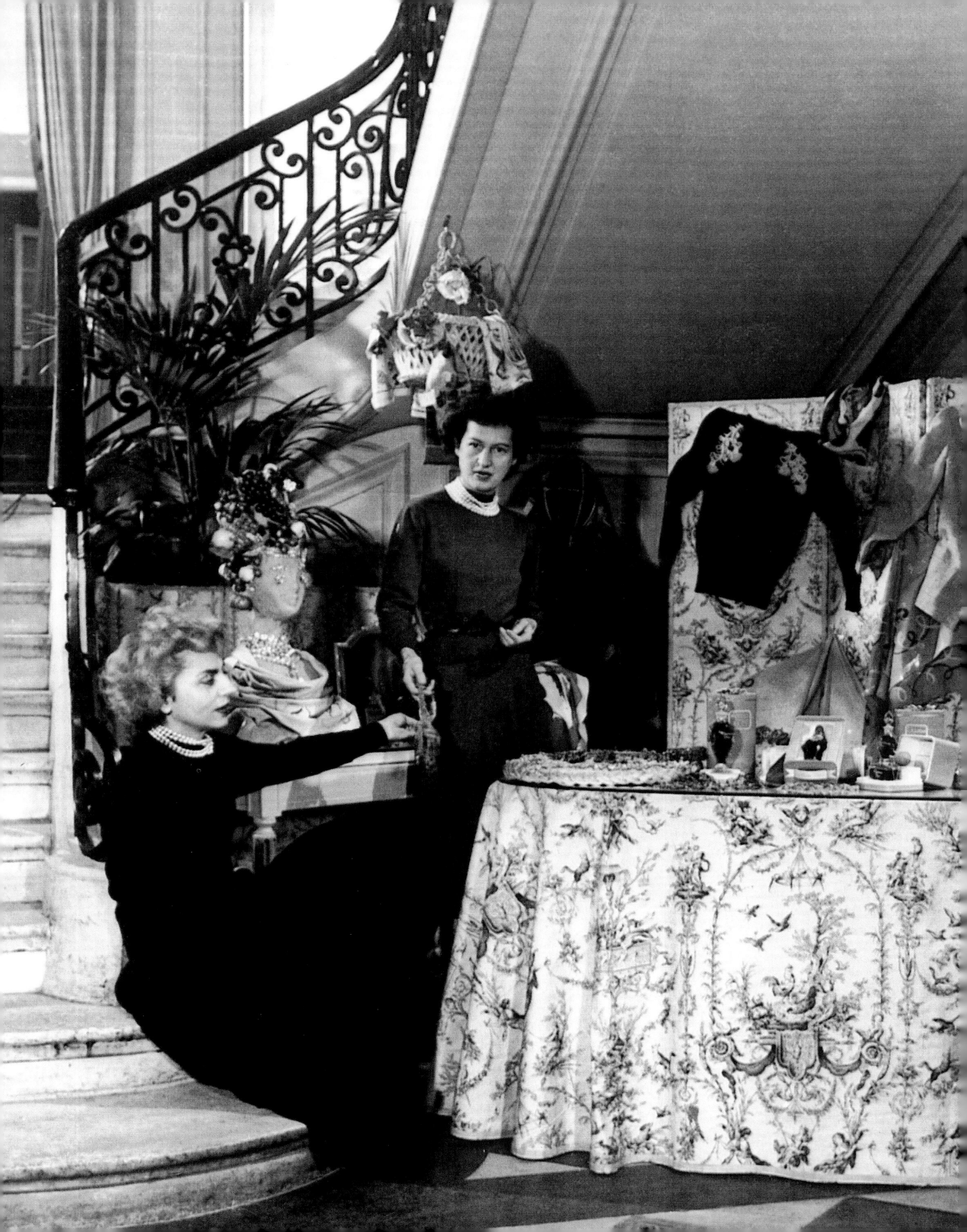

Carmen Colle

"Pierre Colle was very proud of Carmen, who was beautiful, such a chic woman with incredible human qualities, a hard worker... A fabulous girl, Carmen!" It was in these terms that Edmonde Charles-Roux described Carmen Loizaga Corcuera y de Mier, a beautiful woman of bourgeois Mexican stock, who in 1938 married Pierre Colle, an art dealer and close friend of Christian Dior's. Ten years later, following Colle's death, Carmen married her second husband, François Baron, with whom she hosted events at their apartment on Rue de Varenne, inviting Breton, Cocteau, the Noailles, the Kessels, the Préverts, the Hugos, the Poulencs, and the Aurics. Colle's family treated Dior as an adopted uncle: "Tio Christian" gave each of her three daughters, Marie-Pierre, Béatrice, and Sylvia, dolls dressed in Dior. Colle worked beside Dior beginning in 1946, but was officially appointed Boutique Director in 1948, heading the famous Colifichets boutique.

With her radiant yet sober look, a belted gray wool suit and a white blouse, she revealed another, more everyday facet of the house of Dior, which was intimately bound up in the ties she had with Dior himself, "a man with boundless heart."[1] "She wanted to keep her white hair. She was ravishingly elegant. She was what I call elegance. Never over-dressed. And a magnificent friend. She was a wonderful help to Christian," Edmonde Charles-Roux reminisced. Colle was the only person who could wear espadrilles in the boutique on Avenue Montaigne without anyone taking offence. "Come on, Carmen! Give the boutique a breath of fresh air for me," the couturier is said to have remarked, seduced by the thoroughly natural way she dressed.

"Carmen spent whole days seeing to the details and arranging the hatboxes with which 'Bébé' Berard had envisaged decorating this pocket-sized shop... In the summer of 1948, Carmen suggested that the boutique should also sell dresses, which while they adhered to the general line of the collection, would be simpler and less elaborate in execution. Her idea was received with such enthusiasm that the boutique collection was born."[2] Independent and spontaneous, she then launched the "section for young girls" in the large Dior boutique that opened in 1955 on the corner of Avenue Montaigne and Rue François 1er, drawing a large South-American clientele. She worked at Dior until 1969, nurturing passionate, lifelong memories of the couturier.

[1] Lina Lachgar, ed., *Carmen Baron, instants d'une vie*, (Paris: Du Saule, 1995).
[2] Christian Dior, *Dior by Dior*, 149.

Carmen Colle supervising the Dior perfume counter in the Colifichets boutique, 30 Avenue Montaigne, in 1948.

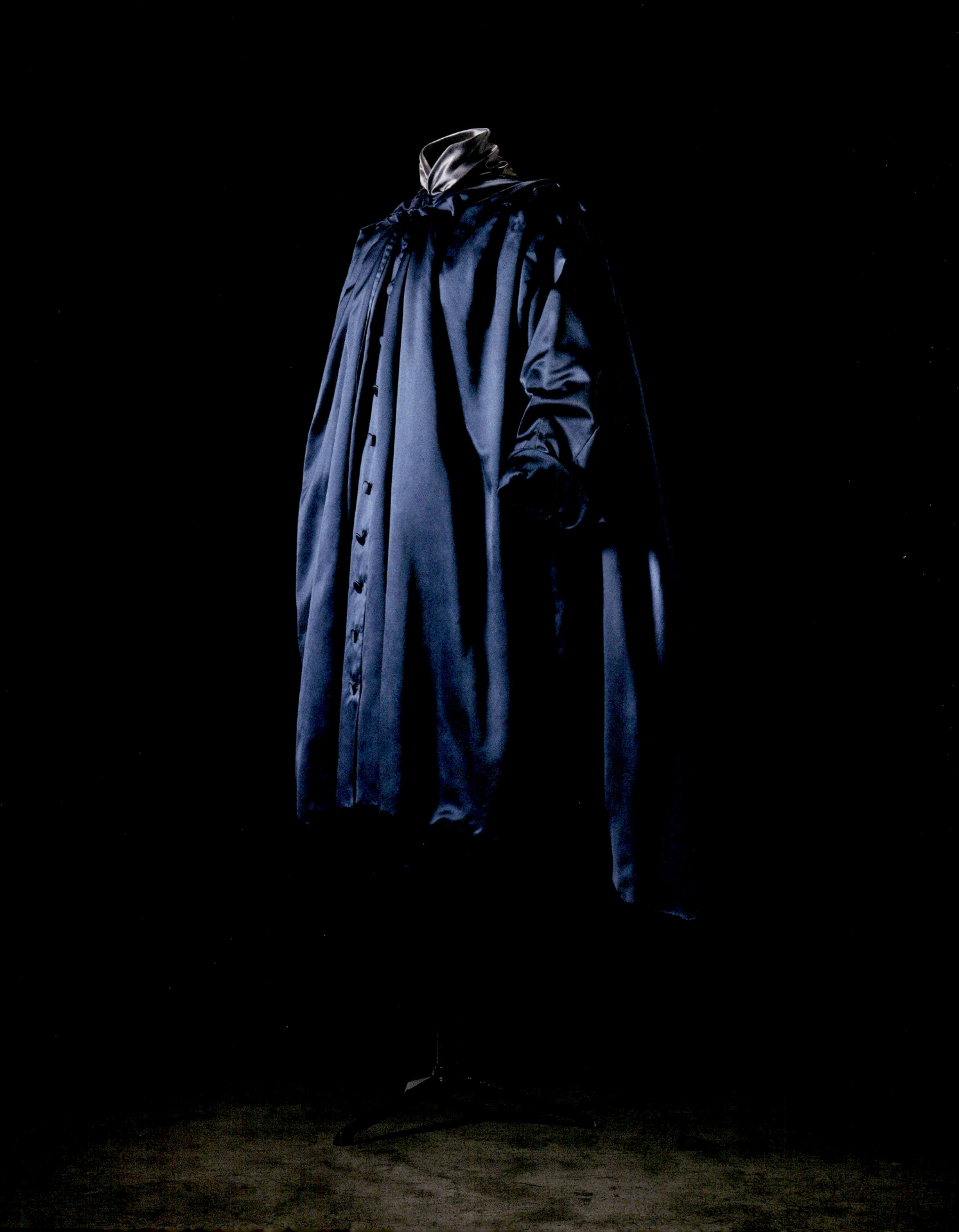

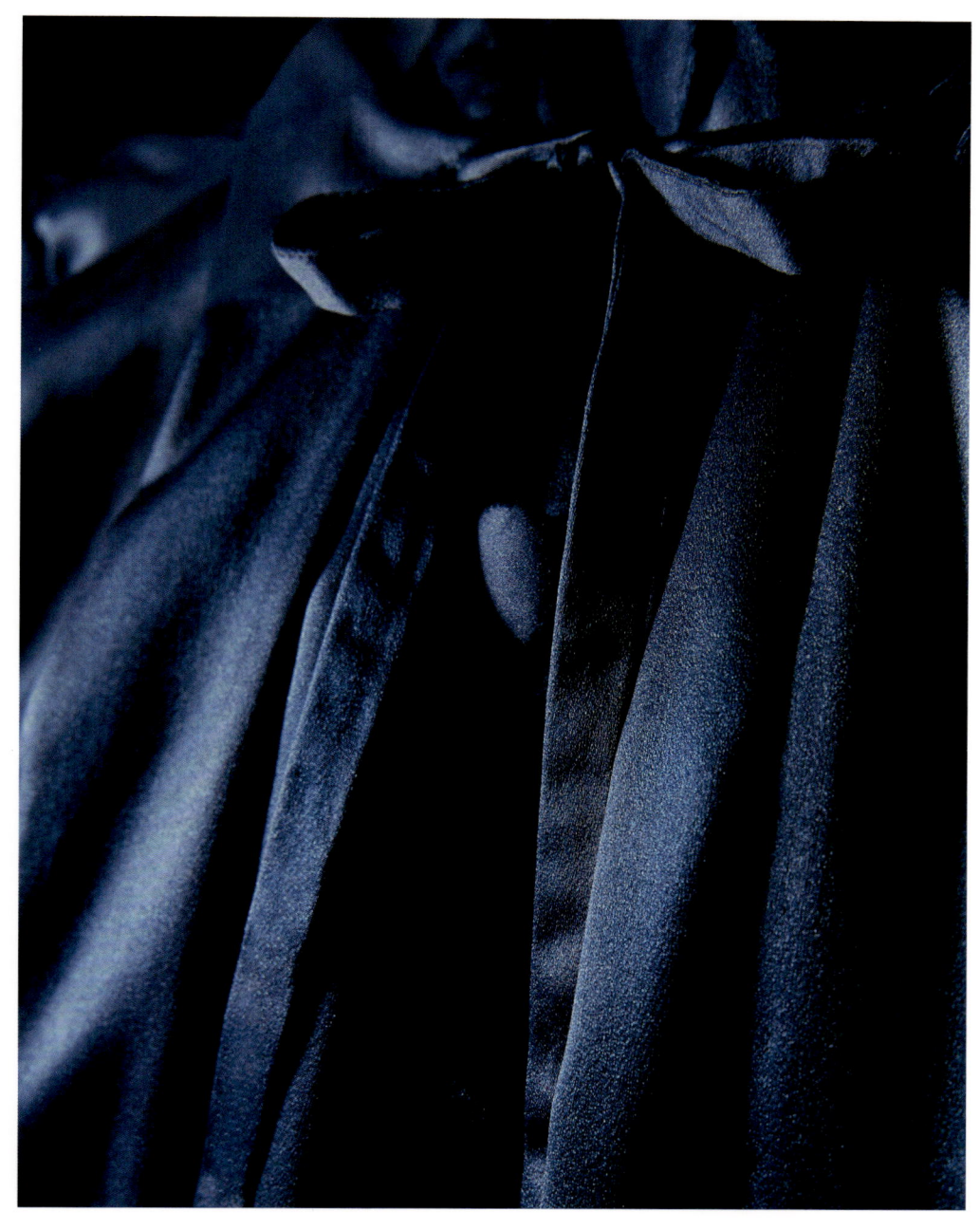

ABOVE AND OPPOSITE The *Viet-Nam* large evening coat in midnight blue silk satin belonging to Suzanne Luling, Fall-Winter 1951 haute couture collection, *Longue* line.

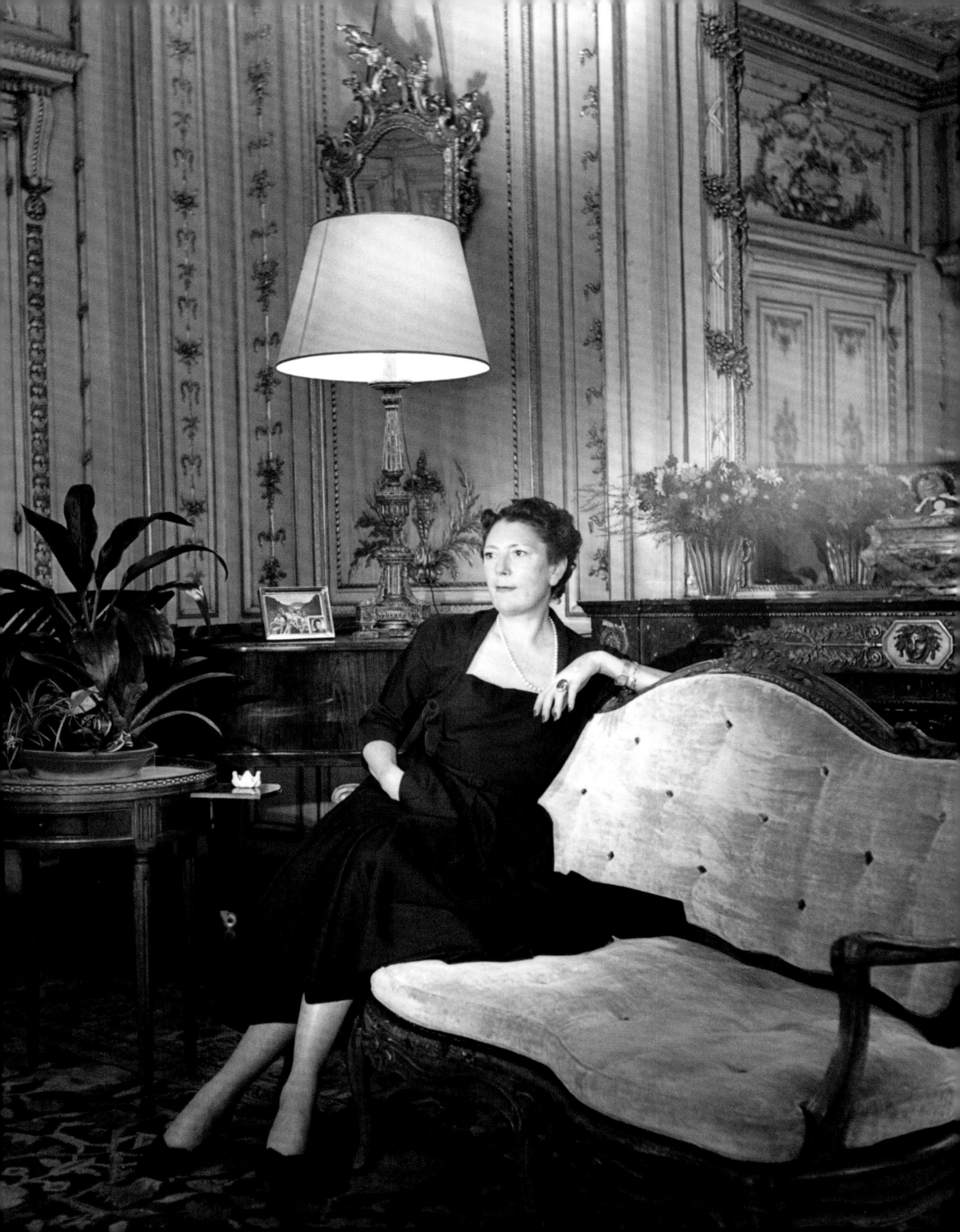

Suzanne Luling

It requires "the vocabulary of the atomic age to describe her,"[1] wrote Christian Dior about this Granville girl born and bred, for whom he designed one of his very first creations: an "island woman" dress for a costume ball in Granville. In 1946, he appointed her as Sales Director at Dior: "It is not enough simply to say that she is dynamic, and explosive scarcely conveys her quality. She is never out of sorts, never flags, never lets us down: She rallies the saleswomen's spirits when they are sinking, soothes the clients when they are fractious, and infects us all with her buoyant enthusiasm."[2] By day, Suzanne Luling was the woman who waited steadfastly for the clients, calling them "with a mixture of sarcasm and affection, her 'darlings.'" She had an open table at the Relais Plaza and held a cocktail party twice a year in her apartment on Quai Malaquais, where she greeted buyers "always with a pleasant smile on her lips." She knew better than anyone how to make friends with the goddesses of the silver screen, how to be invited by Marlene Dietrich for a "nice little French dinner" at the actress's flat on Avenue Montaigne, how to seduce "unfaithful" clients, eke out the undesirable or "fake" ones, or spot the woman in the third row who had the cheek to come with her "little seamstress." In her private diary, Luling noted: "What a curious thing couture is! Getting dressed up is a touching gesture—for there is something moving about wanting to be beautiful—and something a little annoying sometimes, of course, but nearly always enlightening."[3]

[1] Christian Dior, *Dior by Dior*, 18.
[2] Ibid.
[3] Suzanne Luling, *Mes années Dior, l'esprit d'une époque* (Paris: Le Cherche Midi Éditeur, 2016).

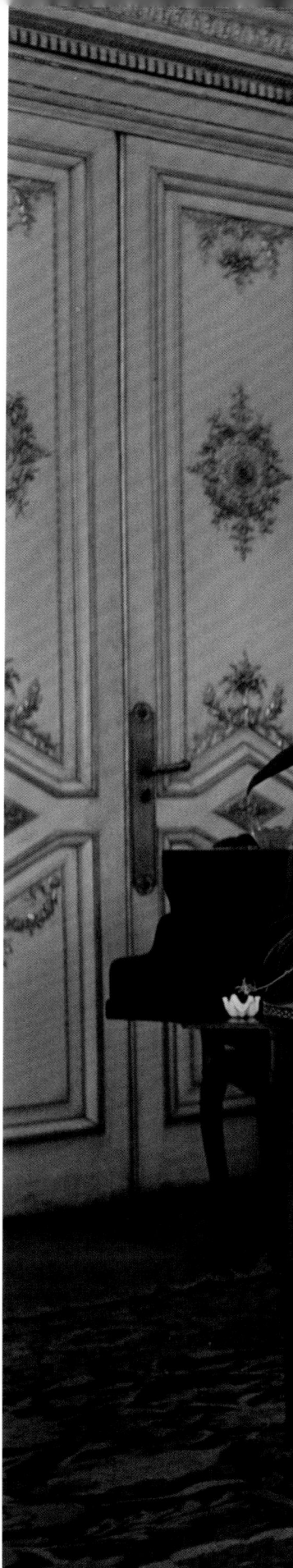

Suzanne Luling poses in her apartment on the Quai Malaquais in Paris.

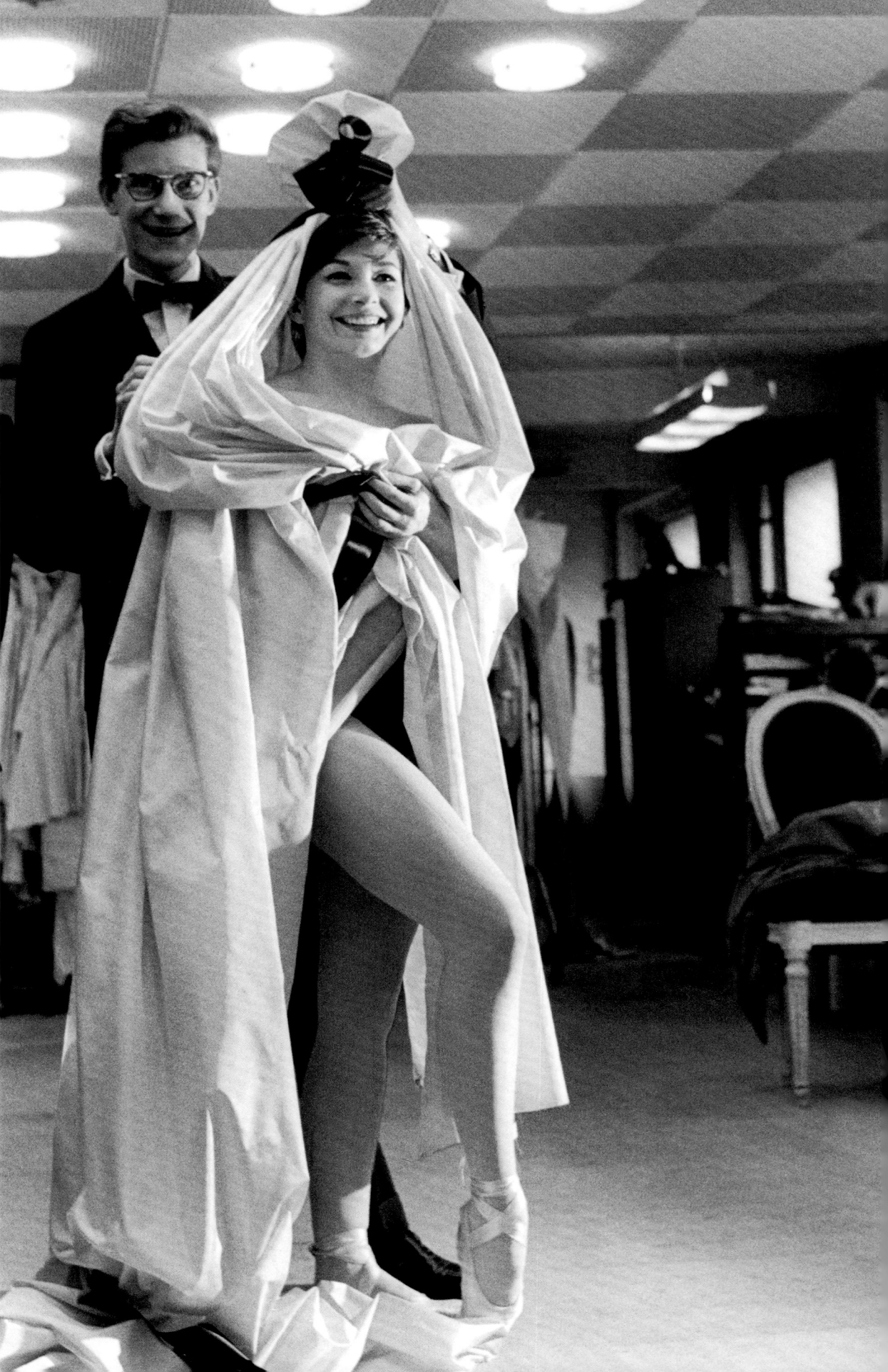

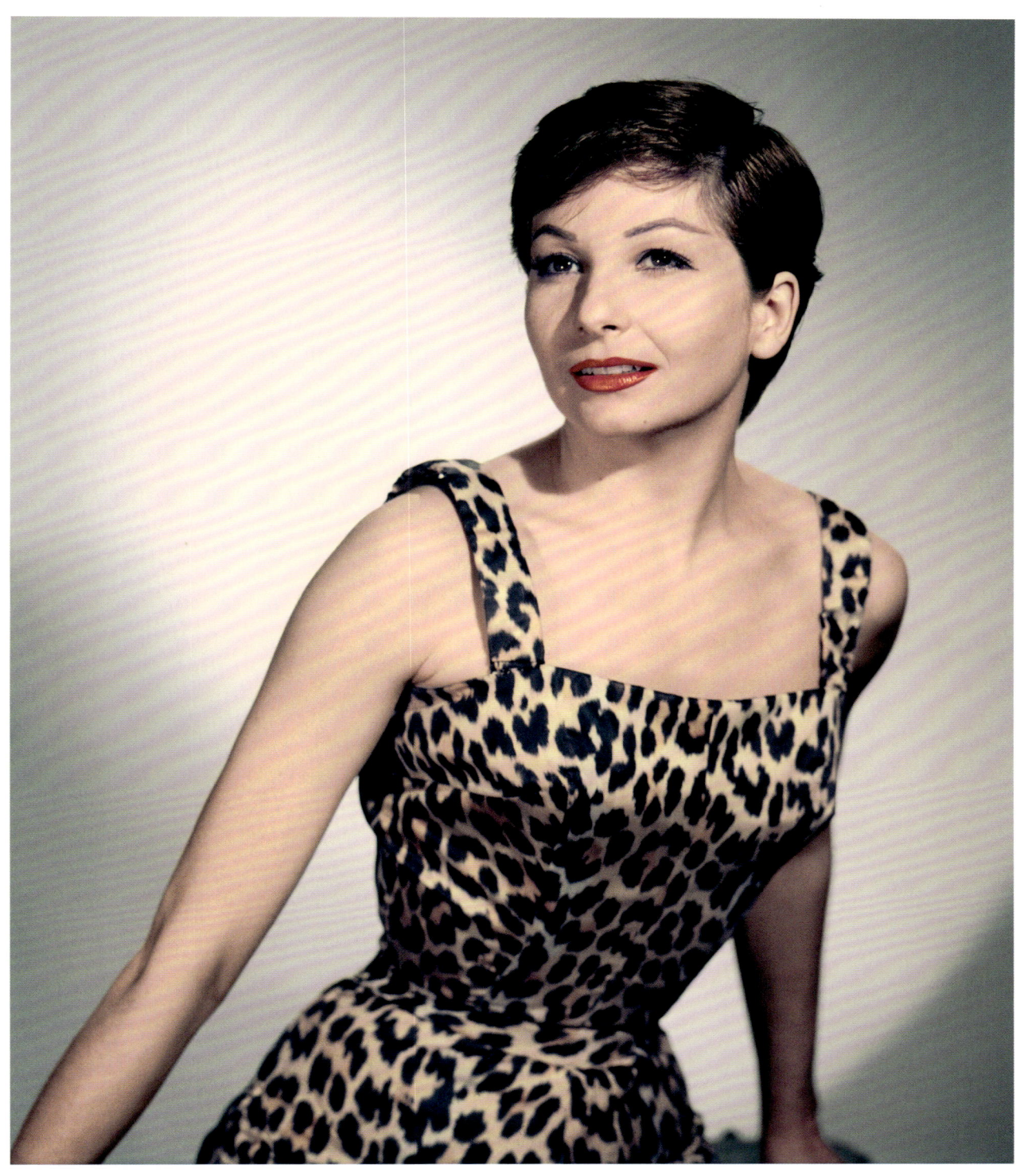

ABOVE Zizi Jeanmaire in a panther suit specially created by Christian Dior for the film *Charmants garçons* directed by Henri Decoin (1957).

OPPOSITE Zizi Jeanmaire with her friend Yves Saint Laurent, then creative director of the house of Dior, who designed her costumes for the film *Les Collants noirs (Black Tights)* directed by Terence Young (1961).

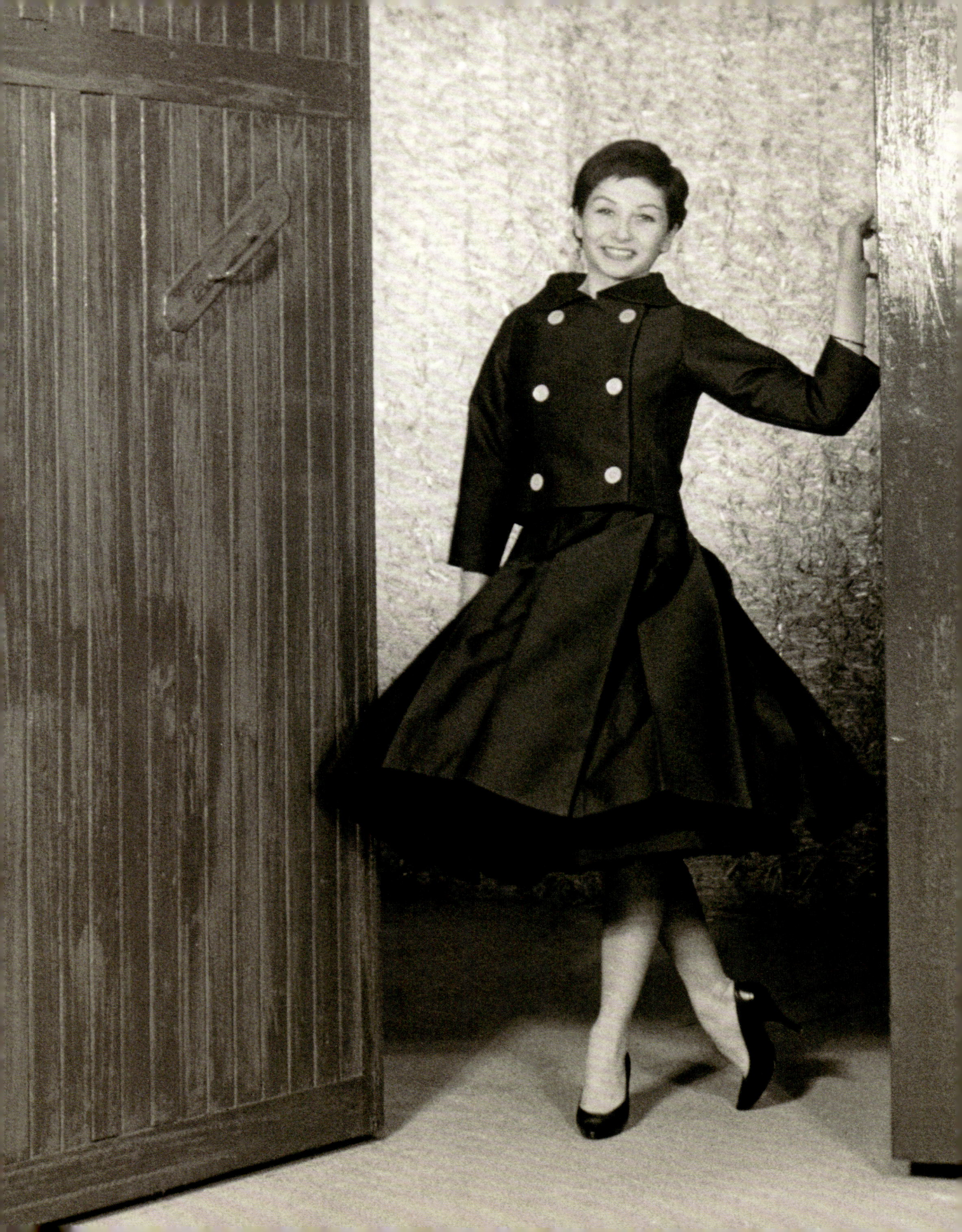

Zizi Jeanmaire

Zizi Jeanmaire, famed for having "the most fabulous legs" in Paris, was dressed by Christian Dior. They met long before he founded his couture house. He designed huge coats, strict shirts, high collars, and tall, stiff lapels for her. "Zizi does not like blousy backs, voluminous pockets, or combinations of fabrics," was already the word in the press in 1949. Even when she sang "*Mon truc en plumes*" ("My Feathery Thing"), she wore black court shoes designed by Roger Vivier for Christian Dior that were as black as her eyeliner.

For her wedding to Roland Petit in December 1955, she wore a Dior dress and mink jacket to keep the winter chill at bay. *Paris Match* covered the event with a three-page spread: "Their honeymoon starts with the Dior 'torture.'" We see Jeanmaire "submitting" to the trial of the toile that would enable Dior to create all the dresses she wore in *Anything Goes* with Bing Crosby in 1956, even from a distance.... When she flew off to the U.S. she wore a navy blue alpaca outfit by Dior: "You too can look like a star," wrote *Vogue* in May 1958.

Then came new dresses and coats, like the *Dame Blanche* design in gabardine satin with a mink collar. The friendship between Dior and Jeanmaire was maintained by Yves Saint Laurent after he took over from the couturier and at his own couture house later. He marveled at the style and audacity of this star who could seamlessly switch from ballet to music hall with such panache. "Mademoiselle Jeanmaire shines. She only needs to enter the stage for it to blaze with life."

Zizi Jeanmaire, photographed by Guy Arsac for *Vogue* Paris. She wears the *Miss Dior* outfit, Spring-Summer 1958 haute couture collection, *Trapèze* line.

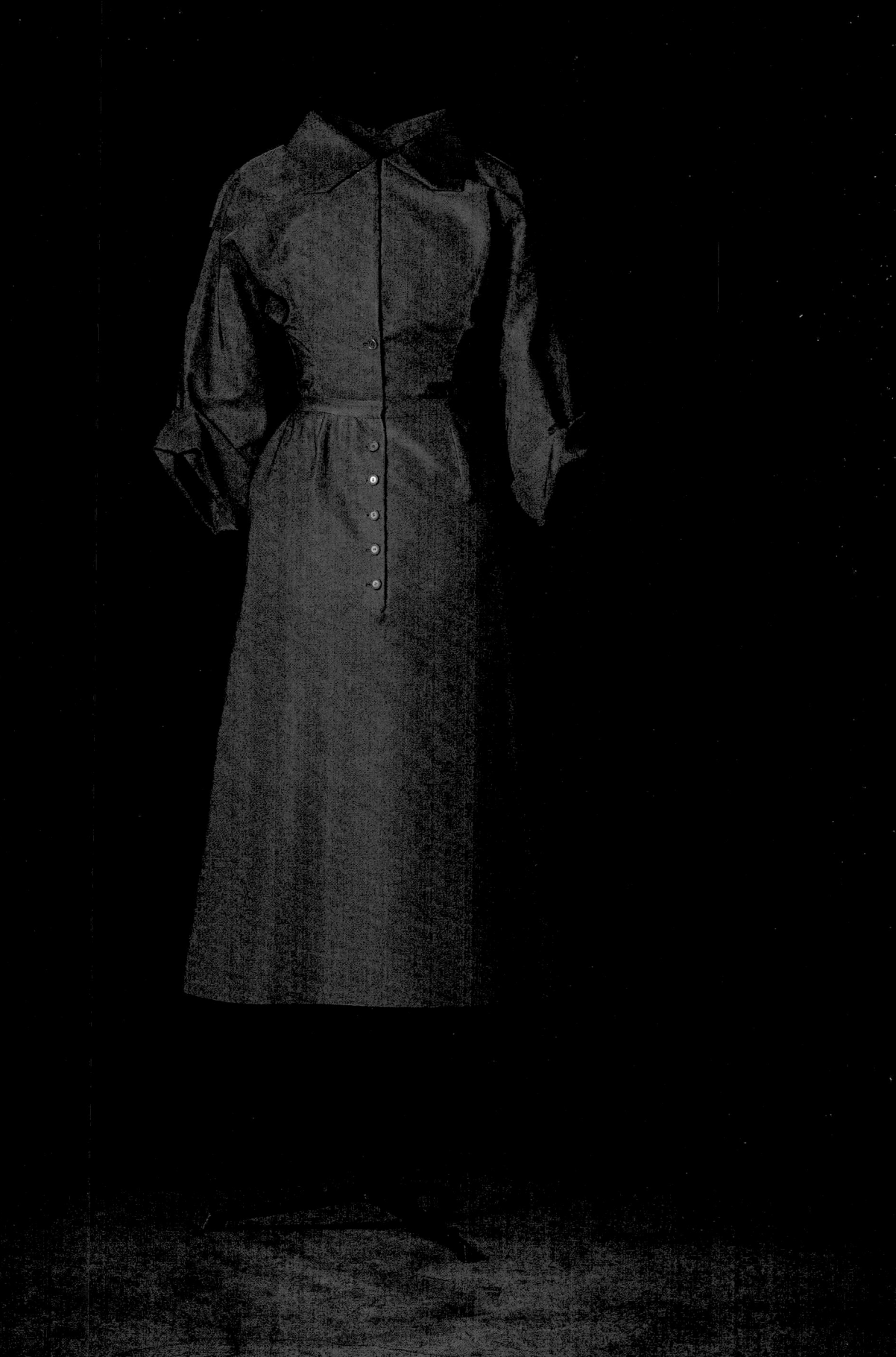

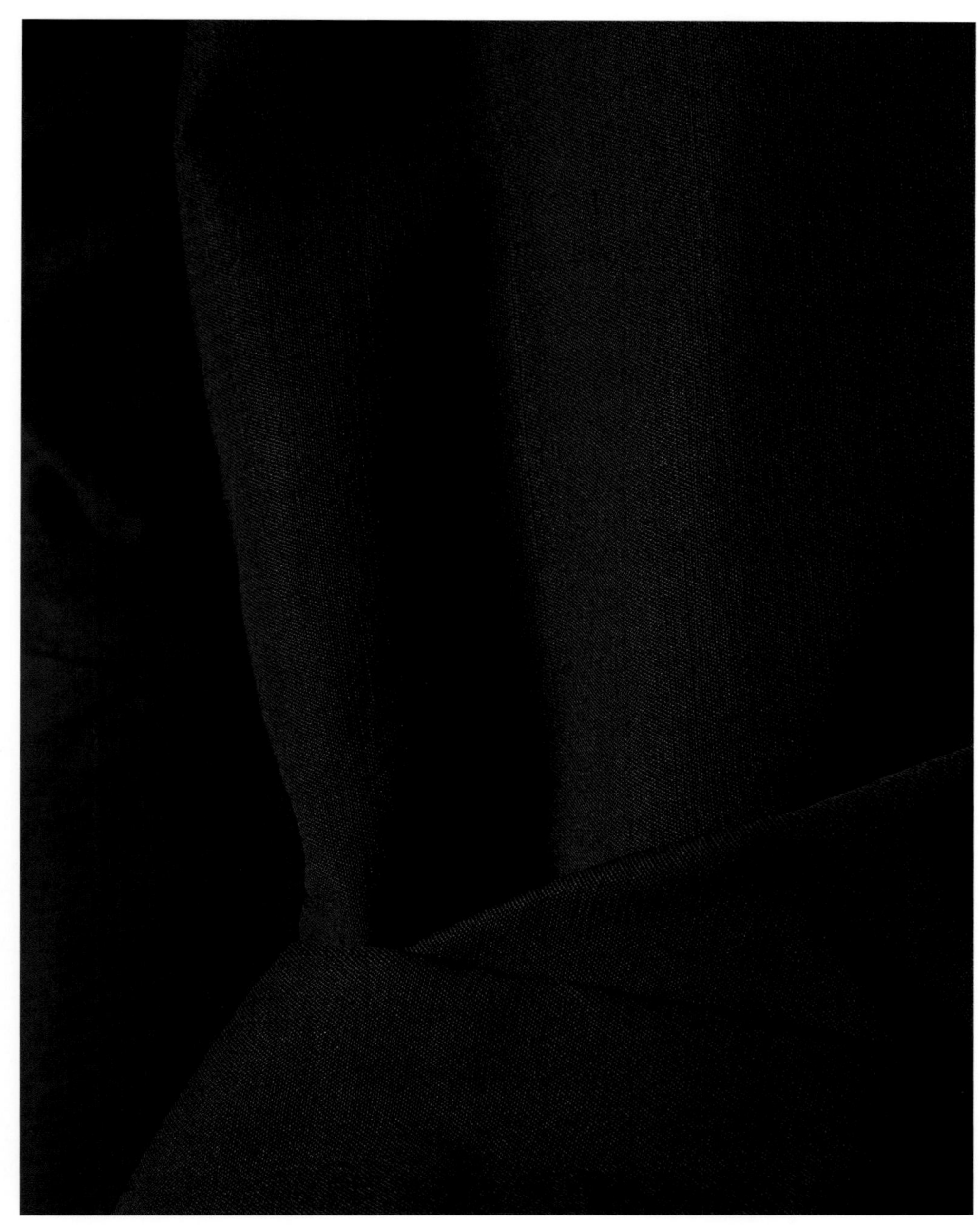

ABOVE AND OPPOSITE Blue marine silk taffeta outfit belonging to Mitzah Bricard, circa 1947.

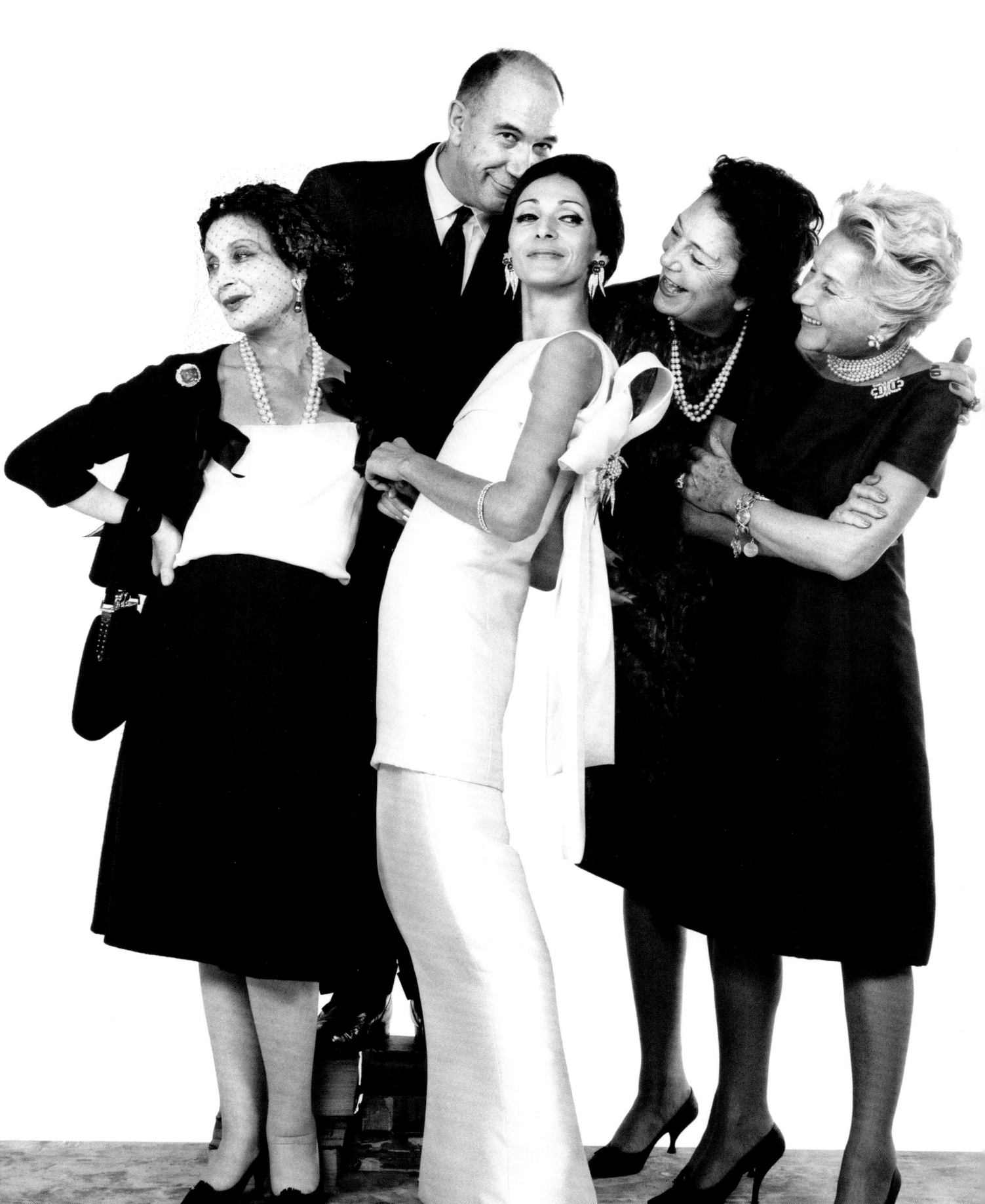

Mitzah Bricard

It was for her experience as much as her international network that Christian Dior chose to work with Mitzah Bricard, née Louise Neustadtl. Having worked as a stylist for Doucet and Molyneux and created the "fashions" department at Balenciaga, she had a unique way of condemning an unfortunate fabric "with a look," or suddenly plumping "for a daring color."[1] She proclaimed to abhor anything "half good."

Her life was a mystery, rich with numerous lovers and marriages doubled by her enigmatic presence. In 1947, it was she who inspired Dior to use the "jungle" print and adopt the color lilac, which was her favorite shade. She embodied a "sense of elegance taken to its paroxysm. One of a kind, she cannot be classified. She belongs to nothing, she dares."[2] In contrast to the rigorist presence of Madame Marguerite, Bricard sported hat veils and Cartier diamonds night and day, as well as a knotted leopard-print scarf around her right wrist to hide a scar that was the source of endless rumors. She brought the house of Dior the "spot of excess," "the hint of scandal" that made each of her appearances infallible signs of style, her naked frame corseted in black lace under a white blouse and pearls.

Time has passed, her aura remains. In 2010 a fragrance named *Mitzah* was dedicated to Madame Bricard in the Christian Dior Collection Privée. "Madame Bricard is one of those people, increasingly rare, who make elegance their sole *raison d'être* . . . gazing at life out of the windows of the Ritz."[3]

---

[1] Christian Dior, *Dior by Dior*, 73.
[2] Suzanne Luling, *Mes années Dior. L'esprit d'une époque* (Paris: Le Cherche-Midi Éditeur, 2016).
[3] Christian Dior, *Dior by Dior*, 12.

Mitzah Bricard, Jacques Rouët, Kouka, Suzanne Luling, and Yvonne Minassian, Paris, August 1961. Photograph by Richard Avedon.

living room—her Dior outfits are invariably protected by a canvas cover tied with black satin ribbons. It's all about maintaining an allure. "Haute couture is seen and experienced from the inside, it's a question of proportions and centimeters," they say at Dior. Altering a line and adjusting a toile so that the seams are in the right place, lowering a shoulder a few millimeters, lifting a hip—the myriad details that are invisible to the naked eye are part of the daily work of these ateliers, which knew how to decipher Christian Dior's "hieroglyphical figures." "They keep their heads among a forest of pins, apparently stuck in completely haphazardly, and a spider's web of threads. I have never been able to understand how they manage it," Dior himself avowed.[1] The magic results from metamorphosis, from a sketched dress that the couturier referred to as a "perpetually erased manuscript," to a finished garment so perfect it looks entirely untouched. The absolute privilege of a mystery proudly proclaimed by his *couturières*: "Haute couture is the opposite of effect, it does not tolerate the slightest imperfection."

---

[1] Christian Dior, *Dior by Dior*, 79.

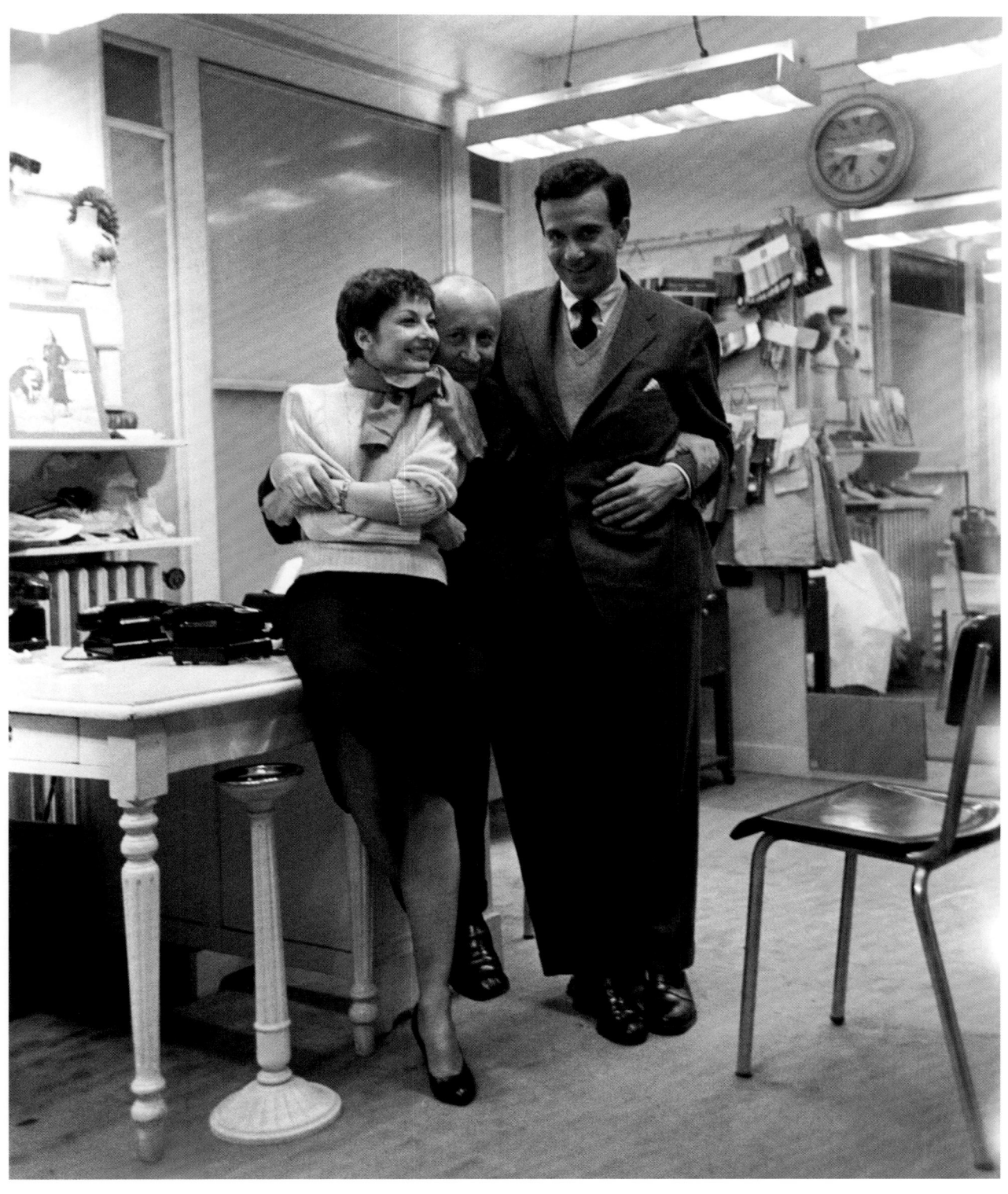

Following their marriage and just before leaving for a trip to New York, Zizi Jeanmaire and Roland Petit meet up with their friend Christian Dior in his studio, January 1955.

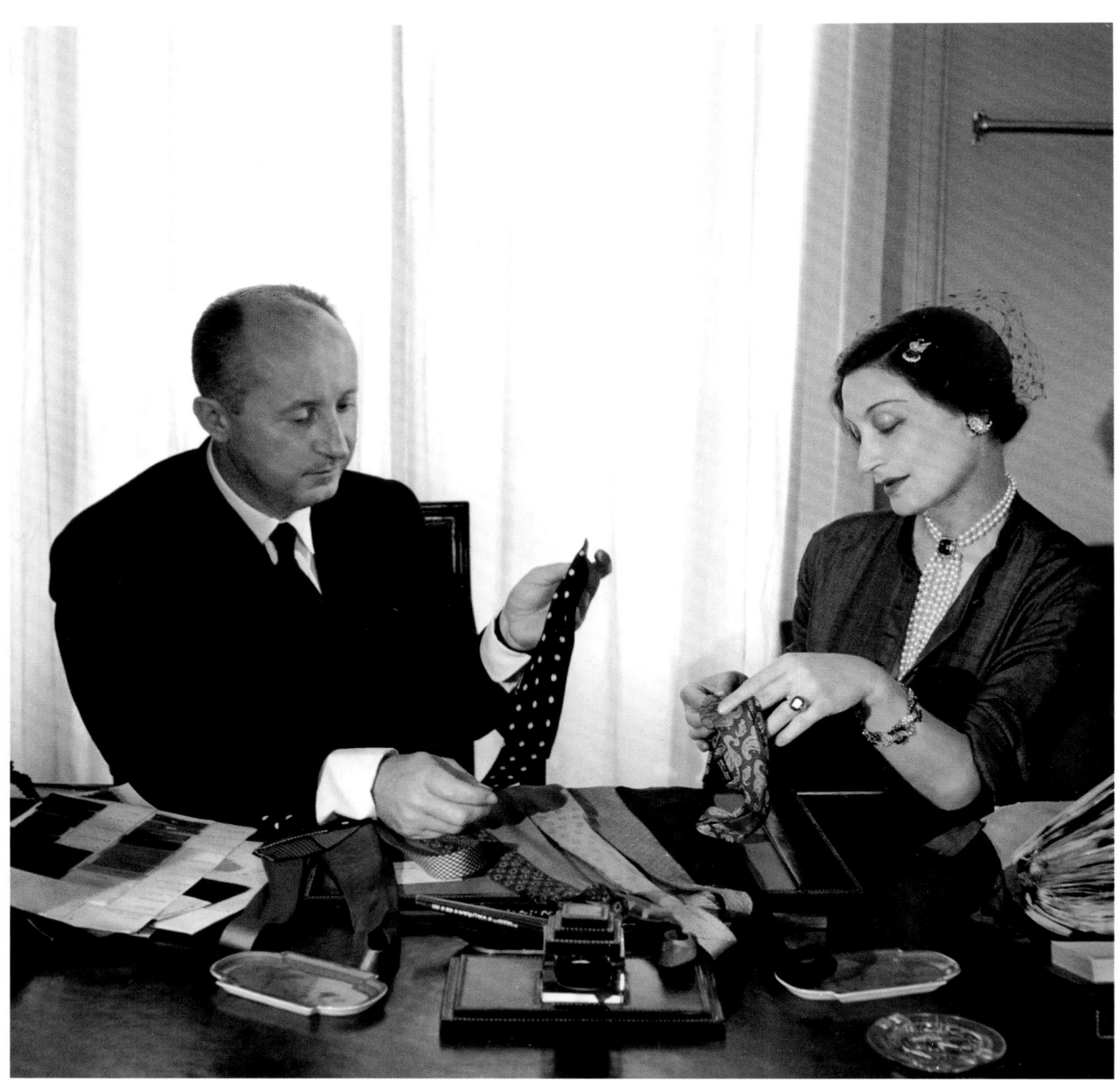

PREVIOUS PAGE Stockman mannequins adapted for different clients.

ABOVE Christian Dior and Mitzah Bricard choosing ties.

53

Queens of
30 Avenue Montaigne

"Yes, a fairy tale has to be deserved, prepared, adapted.
For me, couture is not a lie, it is more a kindly
conspiracy, an understanding."

Suzanne Luling, private diary

"We were a group of people who shared the same way of living, working, and creating," Edmonde Charles-Roux used to say. Given the close circle that helped the house of Dior to thrive, from Carmen Colle to Margot Fonteyn or Leonor Fini, the couture house has often been compared to the *École des Femmes*: a place whose eminently Parisian décor was painted in watercolors by Dior's trusted friend Christian Bérard. *Premières*, ateliers, saleswomen, clients, entourage—the order was subjected to a strict protocol whose rituals were codified by the "discipline" crossed with "freedom" that meant so much to Dior. Christian Dior's entourage had been primarily female from the start, for the couturier's close circle was comprised of Marguerite Carré, Raymonde Zehnacker, Suzanne Luling, Mitzah Bricard, and Carmen Colle. A person would fit into the Maison Dior in the same way they would fit into a Dior suit or dress, supported by the "hand" that literally structured the fabric and determined the perfect fold. "*Je maintiendrai*," or "I will maintain": Christian Dior's favorite motto defied time and fashion to make its mark on the veritable essence of couture and his solid belief in values. Each seamstress would have a pattern and follow it to the letter.

Today, fittings mostly take place outside the salons of 30 Avenue Montaigne, but the highest standards remain de rigueur; two months of work are needed to make a suit and up to twice as much time to create a gala gown requiring four hundred hours of couture. From the preparation of the toiles—the sample muslins which can "sculpt" the body from the very first fitting—to the basting and then the "finish" of final execution, the time it takes to make haute couture is replete with secrets brimming with reinvented handiwork: "When I enter my board meeting dressed in a Dior suit, I know something happens," says a certain loyal New York client who only ever orders daywear. In her dressing room—which is as spacious as a large Parisian

II

THE CLOSE CIRCLE

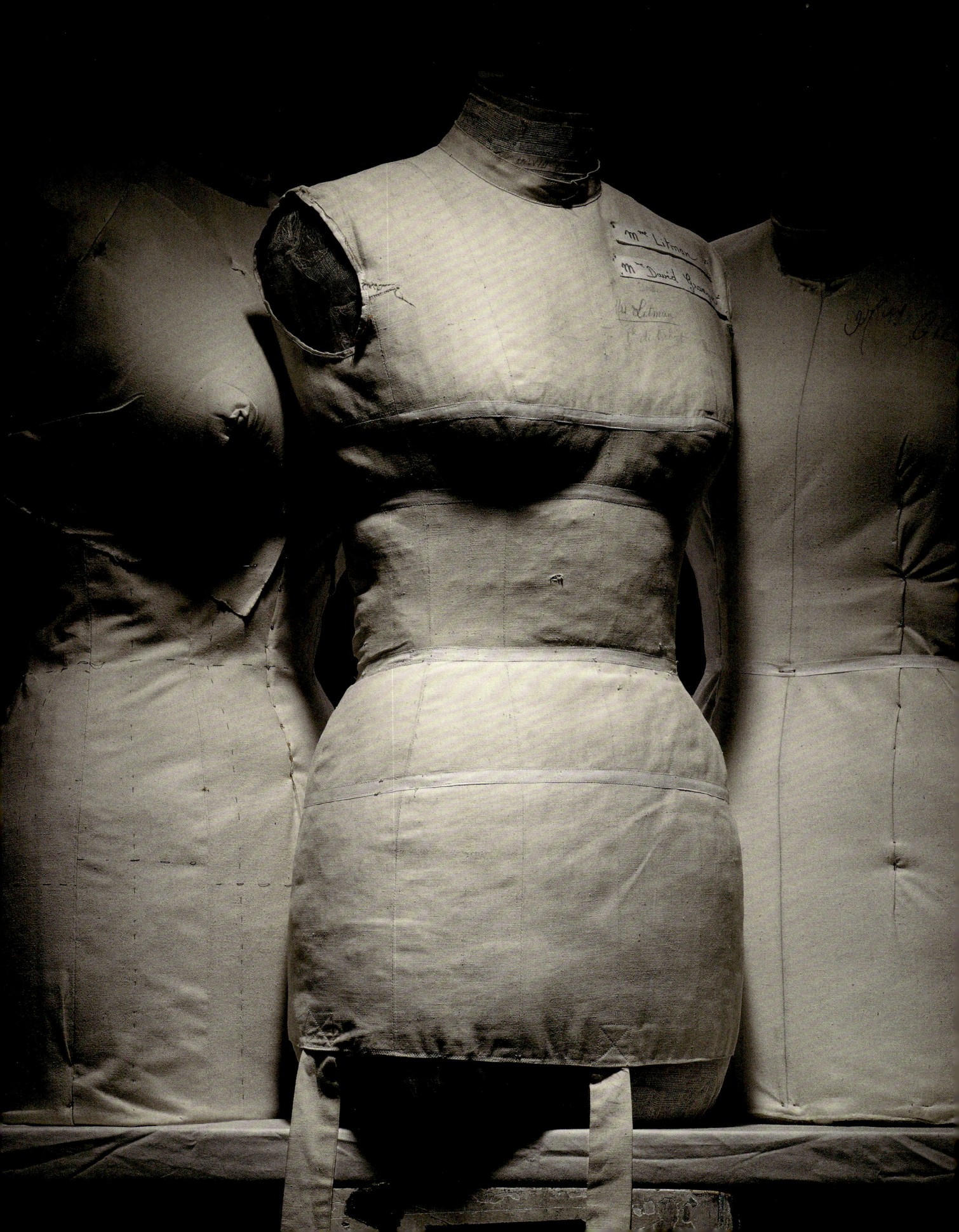

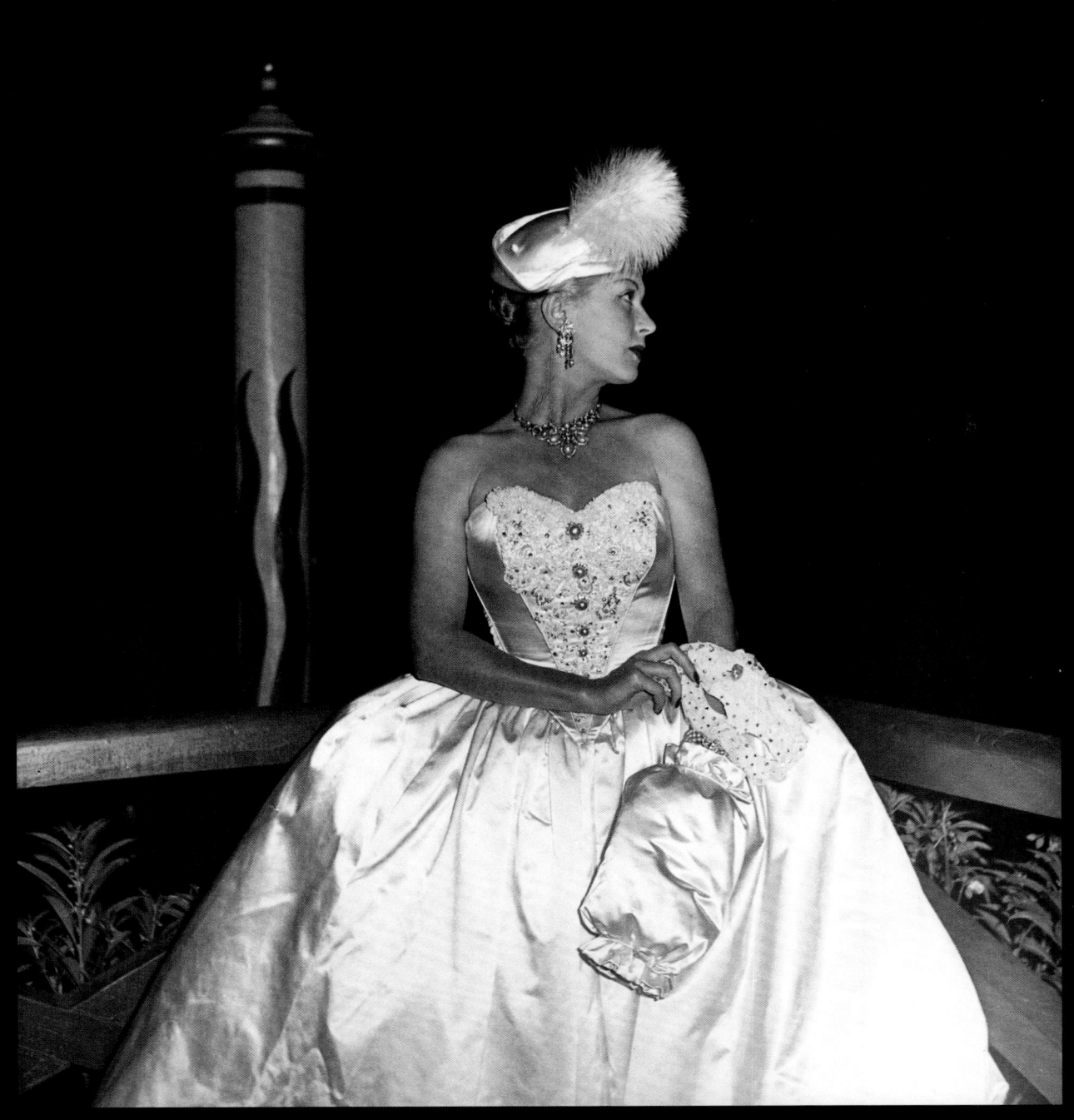

The actress Josette Day in a Christian Dior dress at the *Bal des Masques et Dominos* given by Charles de Beistegui on September 3, 1951, at the Palazzo Labia in Venice.

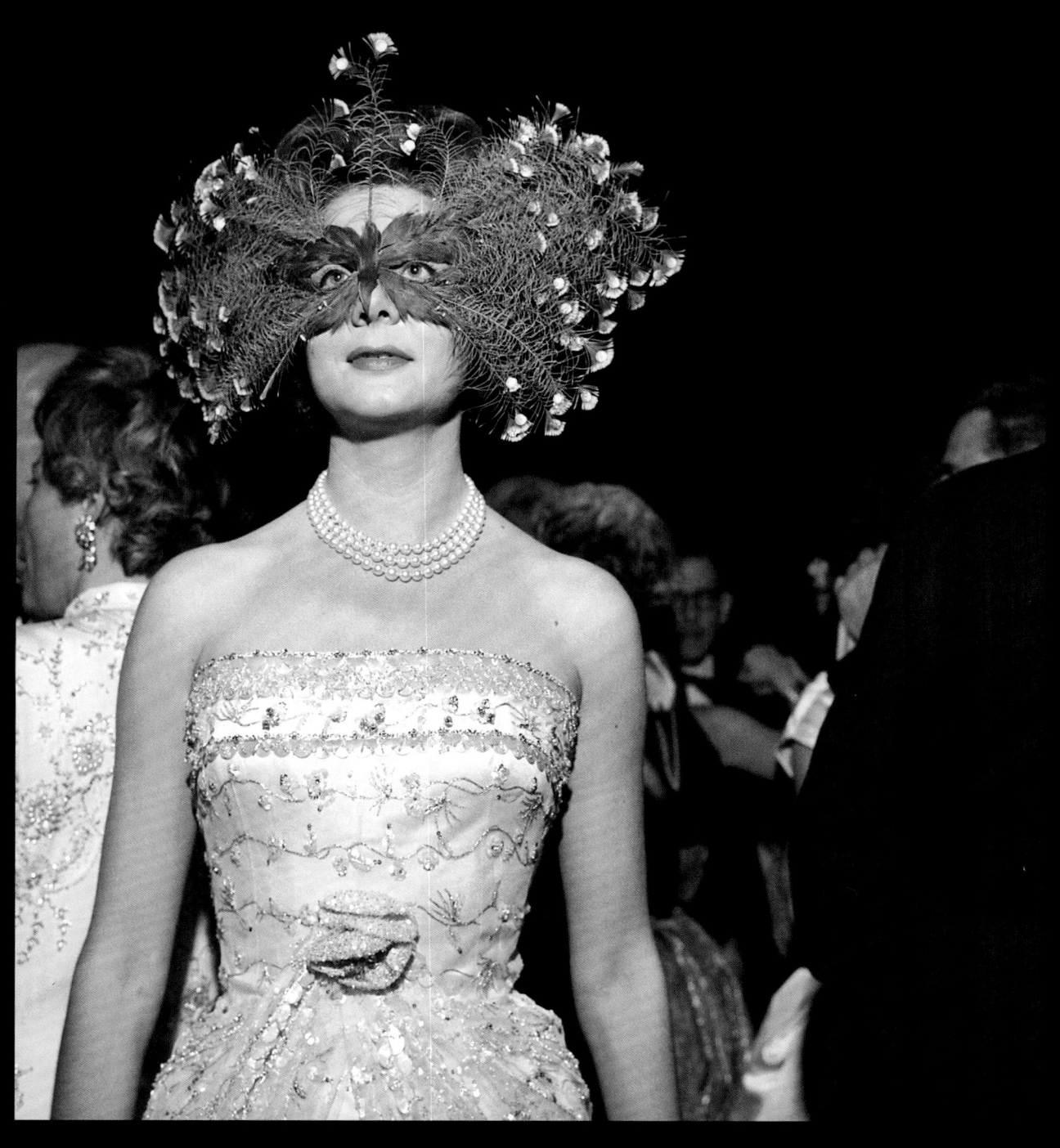

Madame Malard wears the *Musique* dress, Autumn-Winter 1956 haute couture collection, *Aimant* line, at a ball held at the Hôtel de Coulanges, December 3, 1958.

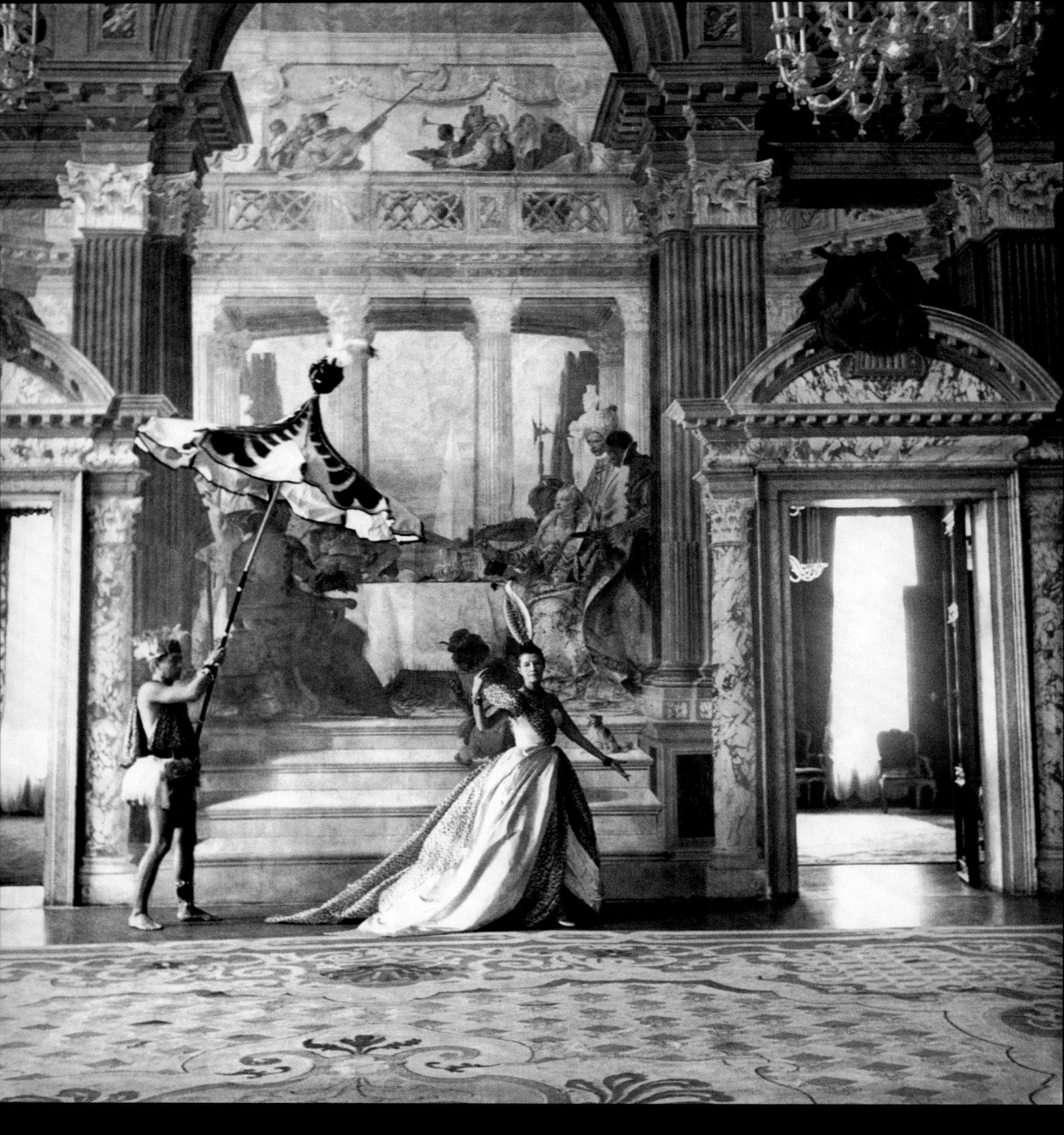

Mrs. Reginald Fellowes and James Caffery photographed by Cecil Beaton at the *Bal des Masques et Dominos* given by Charles de Beistegui on September 3, 1951, at the Palazzo Labia in Venice. Daisy Fellowes wears a special creation by Christian Dior.

Society Balls

For the ball that Charles de Beistegui held at the Palazzo Labia in Venice in September 1951, he drew strongly on the eighteenth century: Alongside six costumes designed with Salvador Dalí for their "Entrance of the Giants," Dior created the dress worn by Daisy Fellowes, "an aristocrat through her father and a millionaire through her mother."[1] It was a ball gown offset with large panels of leopard-printed silk chiffon, the famous "jungle" motif. Cecil Beaton photographed this apparition in front of a vast fresco painted by Tiepolo. "This was the most marvelous spectacle which I have ever seen, or ever shall see," wrote Christian Dior about what would be dubbed the *Bal du Siècle*. "The splendor of the costumes rivaled the splendid attire of the figures in the Tiepolo frescoes on the walls."[2] The Dior ateliers also created the grand white satin bustier dress worn by the actress Josette Day, inspired by the eighteenth-century pannier dresses, as well as a shantung shepherdess dress that came in two versions: one worn by Marie de Rothschild, the other by Nicole Champin. A loyal client, the latter was also dressed by Christian Dior for the *Bal des Artistes*, held by the de Noailles in Paris in 1956. Dior had his ateliers make the velvet doublet and the jabot worn by Suzon in the famous *Bar des Folies Bergères* painting by Edouard Manet. A year later, Christian Dior offered Fleur Champin, Nicole's daughter, her first porcelain-pink ball gown. Dior favored natural looks, recommending: "You can choose almost any material. . . silks and organdy and cotton for the young set."[3] In 1957, it was a white organdy two-piece ensemble decorated with rows of lily of the valley, his favorite flower, that he created for Marie-Christine zu Sayn-Wittgenstein, the daughter of Serge Hefter-Louiche, one of Dior's best friends and the founder of Dior perfumes. This was quite a symbol when you know about Christian Dior's love of flowers: "After woman, the most lovely thing God has given the world."[4]

[1] Jérôme Gautier, *Dior New Looks* (London: Thames & Hudson, 2015).
[2] Christian Dior, *Dior by Dior*, 35.
[3] Christian Dior, *The Little Dictionary of Fashion* (London: V&A Publishing, 2007), 13.
[4] Ibid.

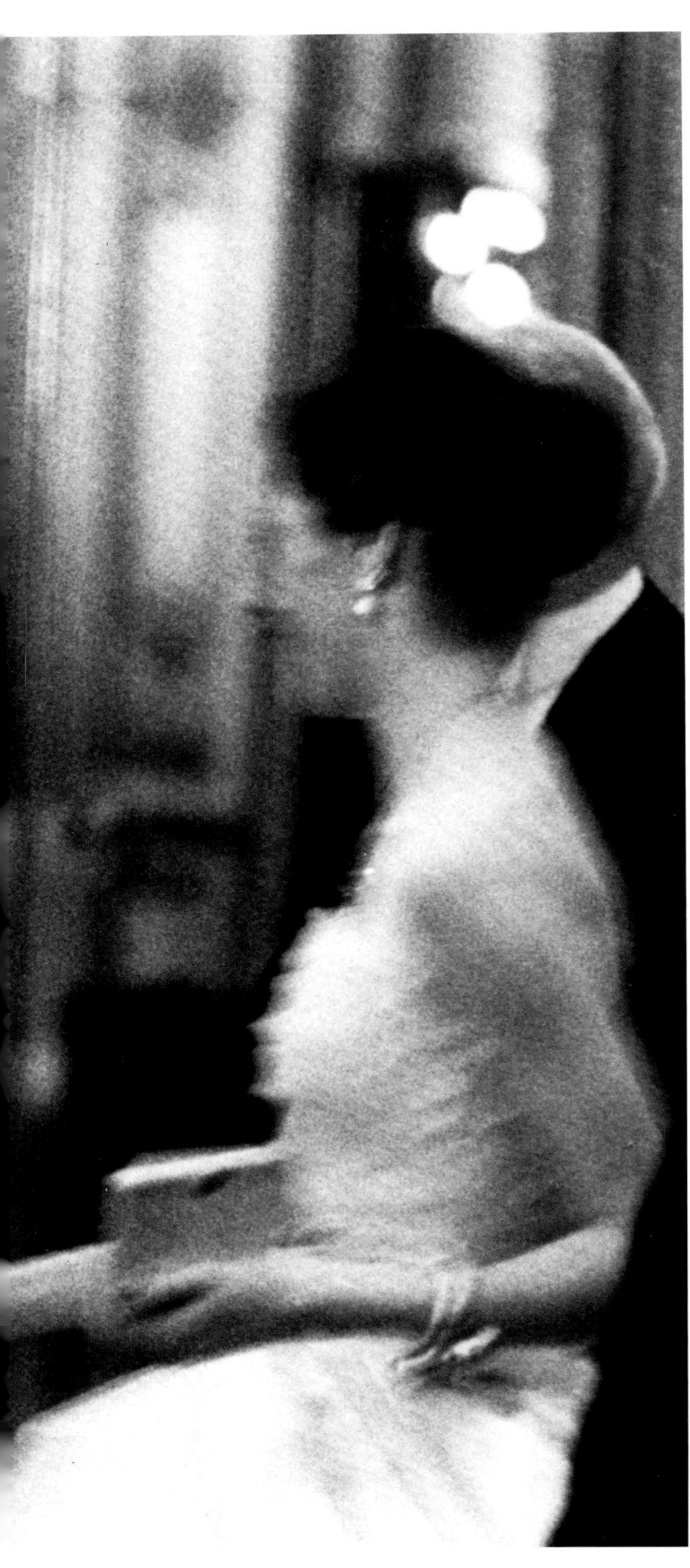

Patricia López-Willshaw receiving her guests during a ball organized in Neuilly in 1952. She wears the *Miguel Zamacoïs* dress, Spring-Summer 1952 haute couture collection, *Sinueuse* line.

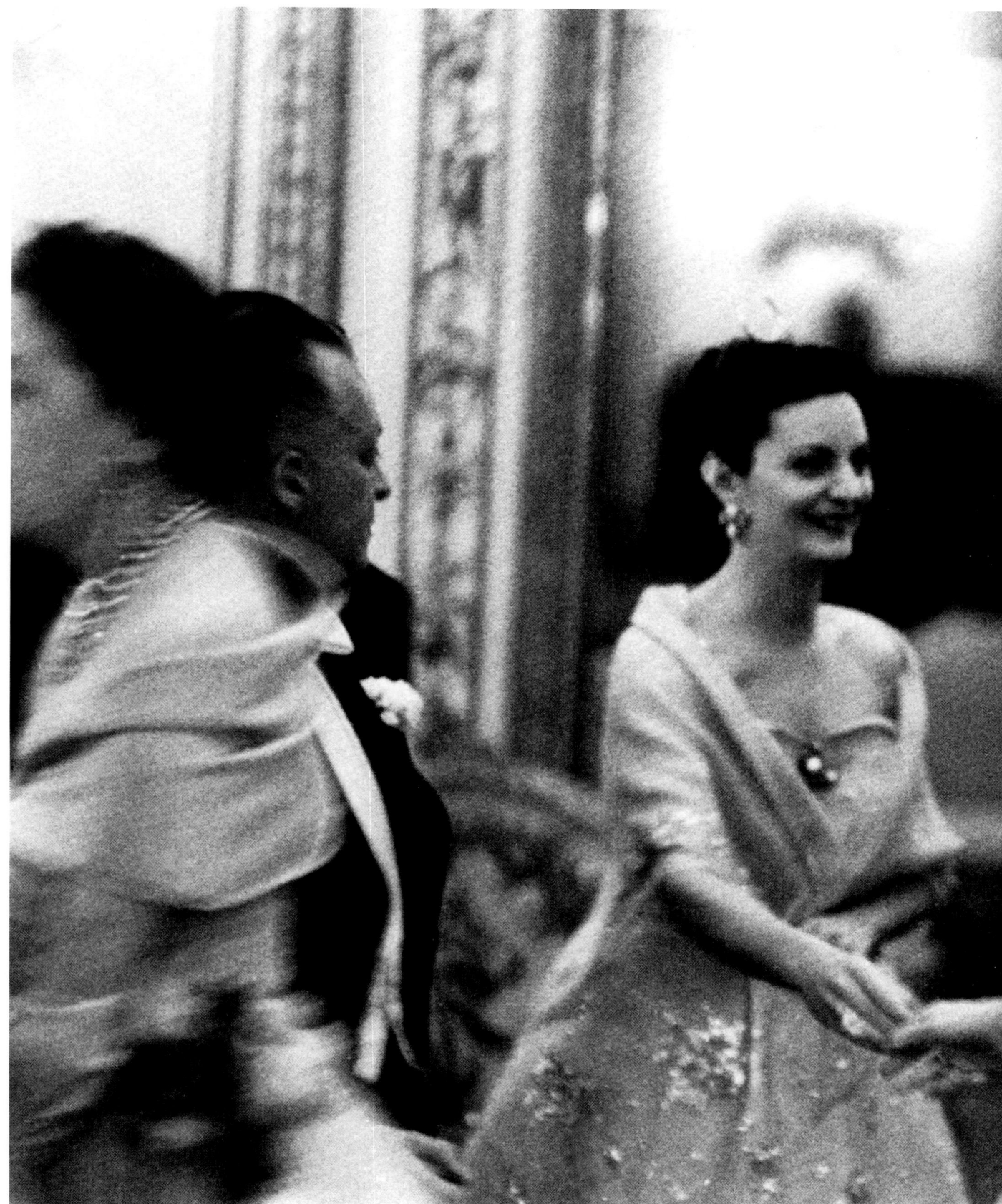

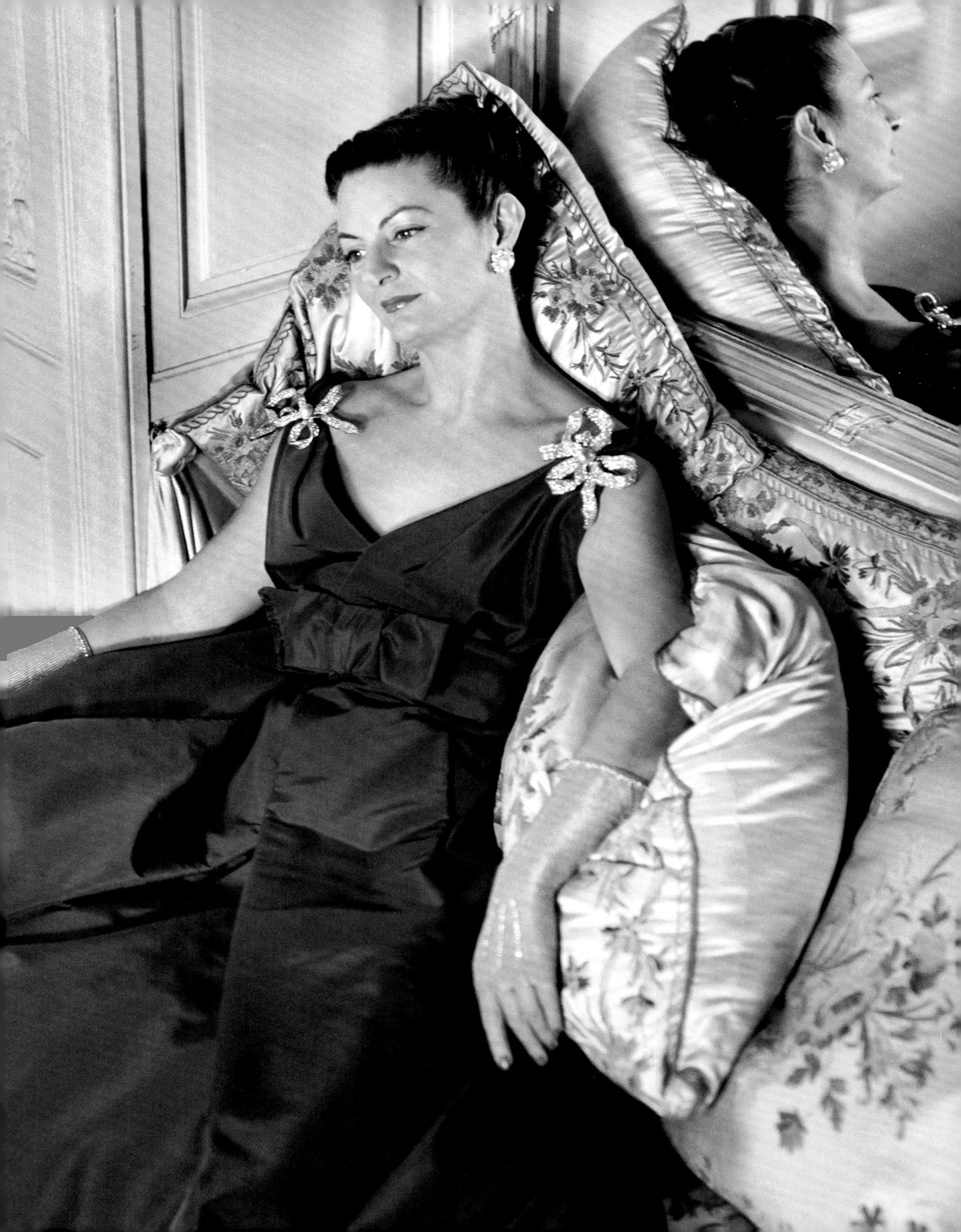

Patricia López-Willshaw

"Her long eyes and high cheekbones suggest the feline beauty of a regal panther," wrote *Vogue* in December 1956. Sublime in a preciously luminous taffeta Dior dress, Patricia López-Willshaw, who had "all the fragility of a Tanagra figurine, but not discounting a sculptural reality," embodied Café Society with brio. "When I left New York after the war, I was regularly dressed by Dior. Most of my friends were clients as well, it was the most fabulous thing to do," López-Willshaw confided.

The South-American socialite lived between Paris and St. Moritz and shared a love of partying with her husband, Arturo, the heir to a Chilean fortune built on tin mining and guano trading. This extremely wealthy couple attended parties thrown by Étienne de Beaumont, Marie-Laure de Noailles, and Charles de Beistegui and sailed the Mediterranean in a yacht adorned with gilt and Chinese furnishings, the famous *Gaviota*. "While his taste does not open up any new perspectives, the grandeur of the style and the perfection of the theatrical effects do at least have the merit of keeping up a life and an activity along a path drawn by Largillère," wrote Cecil Beaton about Arturo López-Willshaw, whose private mansion in Neuilly was like visiting a museum.[1]

When it came to Dior, Patricia López-Willshaw was a staunch lover of faille, chiffon, and the embroideries that would magnify her every appearance. On September 3, 1951, she arrived at the ball given by Charles de Beistegui at the Palazzo Labia in a large Chinese junk, like an empress let out of the Forbidden City. The costume was not designed by Dior, who reserved the luxury of dressing her like a fairy from the city: black organza sheath dresses bathed in tulle; pink organdy dresses with silver flower blades; pink organza dresses sewn with pink and white daisies... At 30 Avenue Montaigne, López-Willshaw's dresses frothed gracefully on the dressmaking tables of the Flou atelier. She was considered one of the best-dressed ladies in Paris.

After Dior died, she remained a loyal client, ordering designs created by Yves Saint Laurent: When Dior's heir apparent opened his own haute couture house in January 1962, she was his first client with a cult black dress signed 00001.

[1] Cecil Beaton, *50 ans d'élégance et d'art de vivre* (Paris: Amiot-Dumont, 1954).

Patricia López-Willshaw photographed by Henry Clarke for *Vogue* Paris, December 1956–January 1957. She wears the *Circé* dress, Spring-Summer 1956 haute couture collection, *Flèche* line.

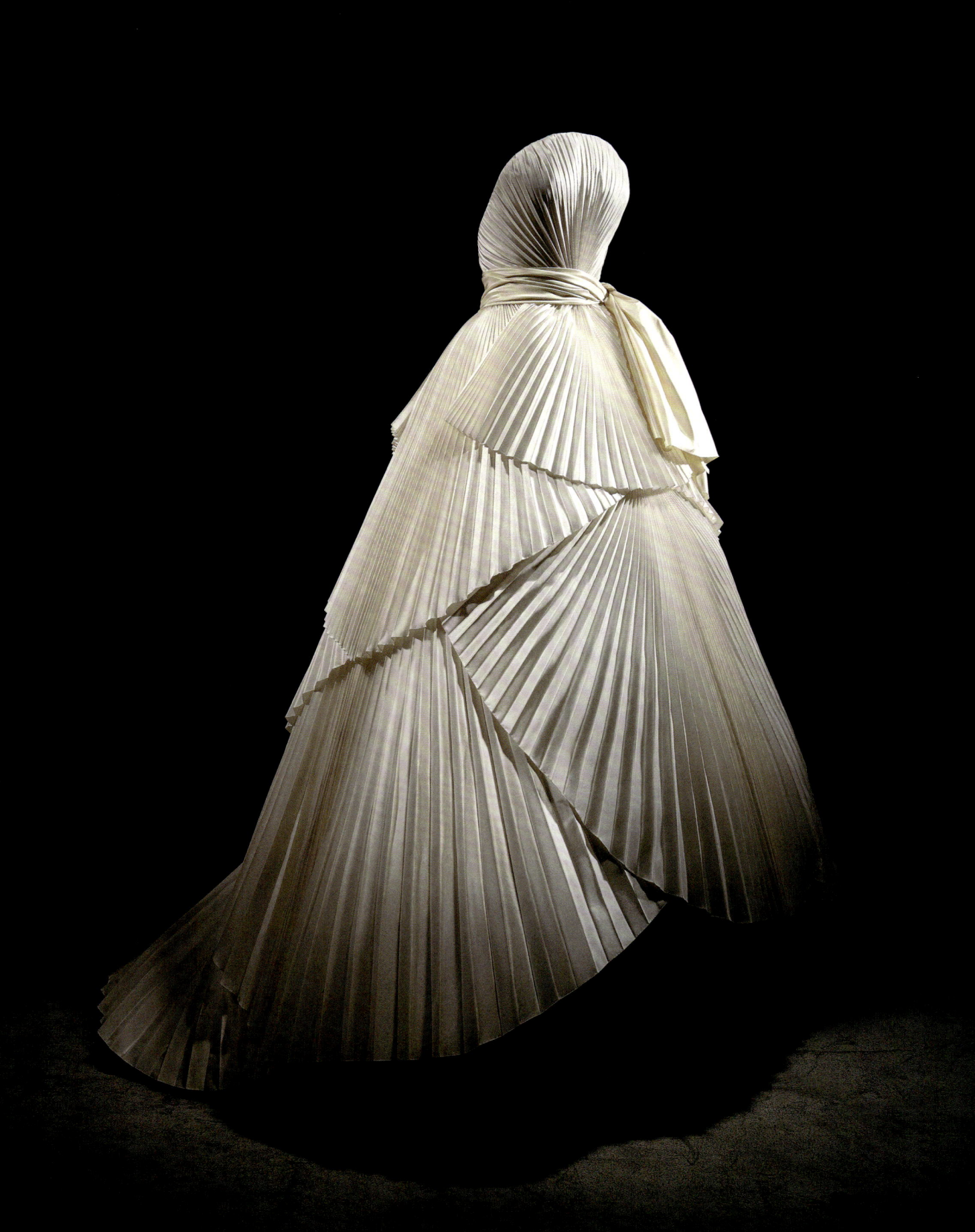

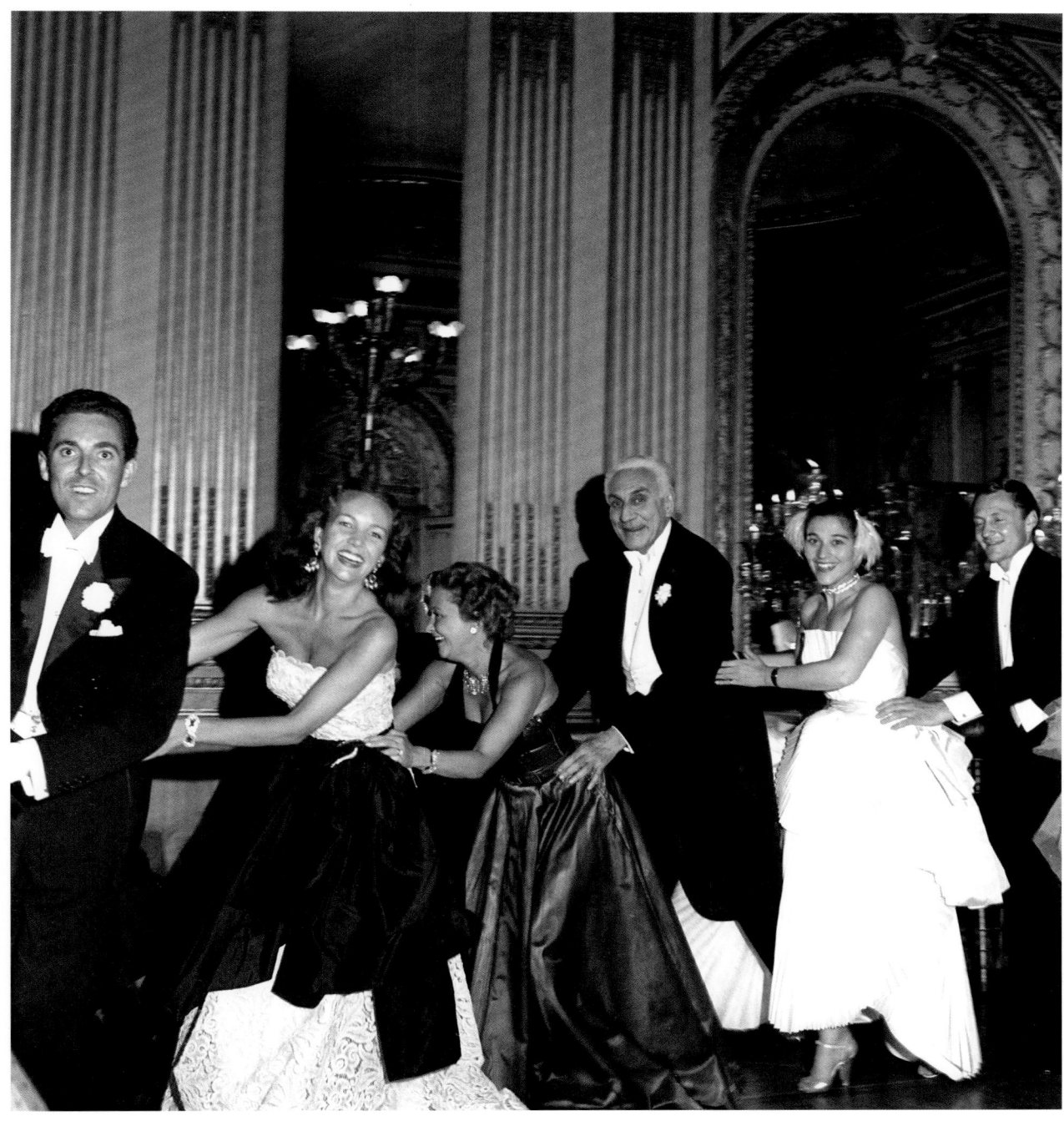

ABOVE Count Henri de Beaumont, Mrs. William Woodward, Madame Vlasto, Count Étienne de Beaumont, Edmonde Charles-Roux, and Count James de Pourtalès photographed by Robert Doisneau at a ball organized at the home of Étienne de Beaumont, June 19, 1950. Edmonde Charles-Roux wears the *Francis Poulenc* dress, Spring–Summer 1950 haute couture collection, *Verticale* line.

OPPOSITE The *Francis Poulenc* dress, Spring–Summer 1950 haute couture collection, *Verticale* line.

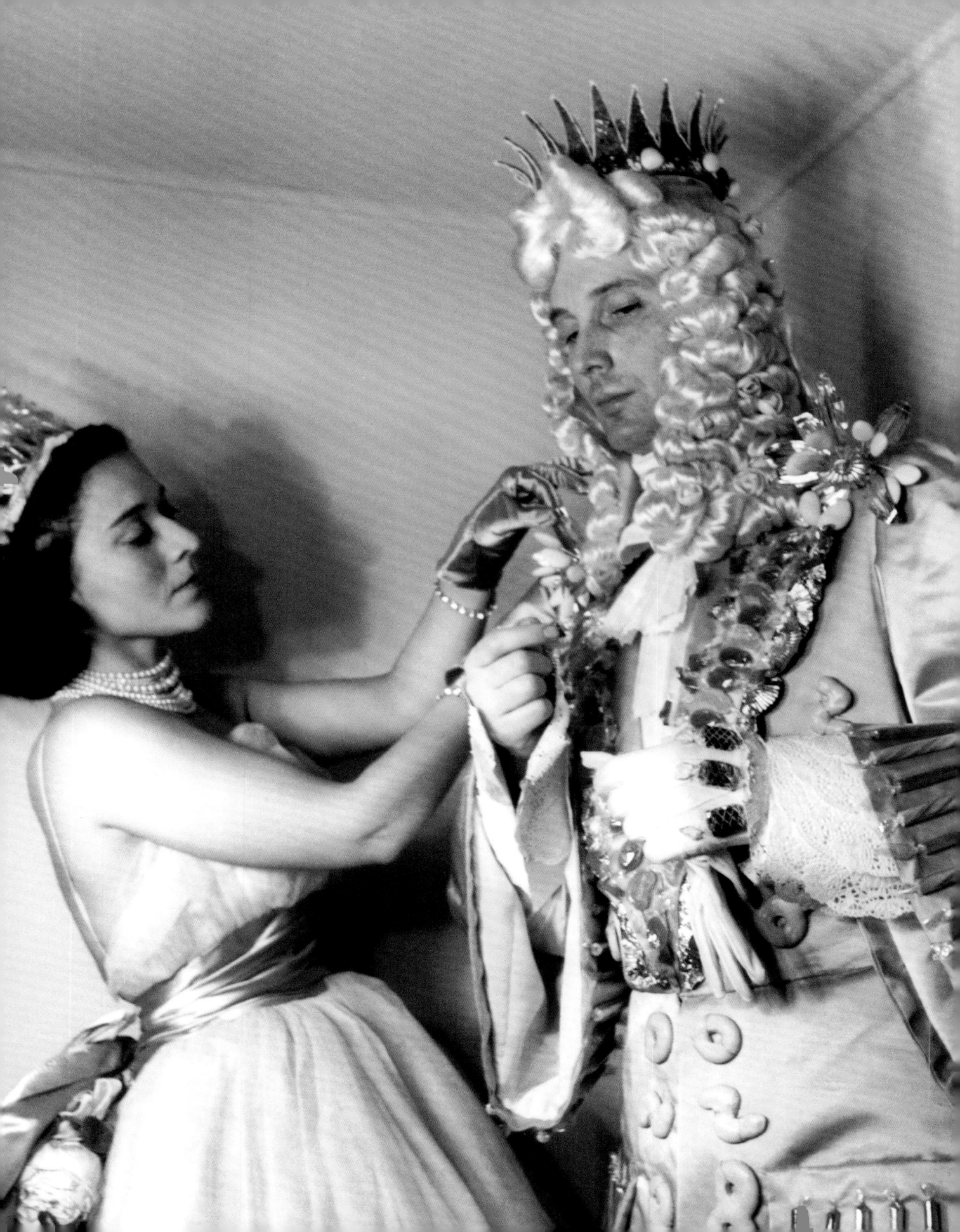

Edmonde Charles-Roux

It was in 1946 that Edmonde Charles-Roux met Dior. An ambassador's daughter decorated with the Military Cross and several medals—notably Knight of the Legion of Honor in 1945 with the distinction "*vivandière d'honneur*"—she was inquisitive about everything. It was she who transmitted a love of painting to Christian Bérard.

The flower market beside Notre Dame Cathedral was the setting for an impromptu meeting between Dior, who was on the cusp of leaving his job as a designer for Lucien Lelong, and the young journalist who was starting out on a new magazine, *Elle*. Edmonde Charles-Roux was a witness to the anger sparked by the New Look. She was just twenty-seven years old when the couturier made her a design that she remembered her entire life: "I put on this unforgettable coat-dress, which fastened with a zipper, and I was staggered when a respectable gentleman wearing an Eden hat and spats called out to me as I walked down Rue des Saints-Pères: 'It doesn't bother you in the slightest, does it?'" To which she replied: "I don't know what you're talking about." "Look how much you've cost in fabric! When there's no fabric, you don't make that kind of fashion!" It did not stop her from being loyal to her couturier friend, even when she went on vacation: "With a light-colored dress in clean lines, whose supple flow will have a slimming effect, she will be perfect at any hour of the day."[1]

Later the columnist who became editor in chief of French *Vogue* in 1954 was a frequent guest at Dior's home ("The food there was a masterpiece!"). Through his creations, Dior symbolized a break from the past that she was among the first to observe: She never forgot the extent to which fashion is a unique expression of its time. She hailed Yves Saint Laurent's early work at 30 Avenue Montaigne and consistently defended everything that brought back elegance and tradition while denouncing the taboos of the bourgeoisie that she, like Christian Dior, had inherited.

[1] *Elle*, April 11, 1949.

Edmonde Charles-Roux in the *Libellule* dress (Autumn-Winter 1947 haute couture collection, *Corolle* line) and Count Sforza photographed by André Ostier during the *Bal des Rois et Reines* at the home of Count Etienne de Beaumont in Paris in January 1949.

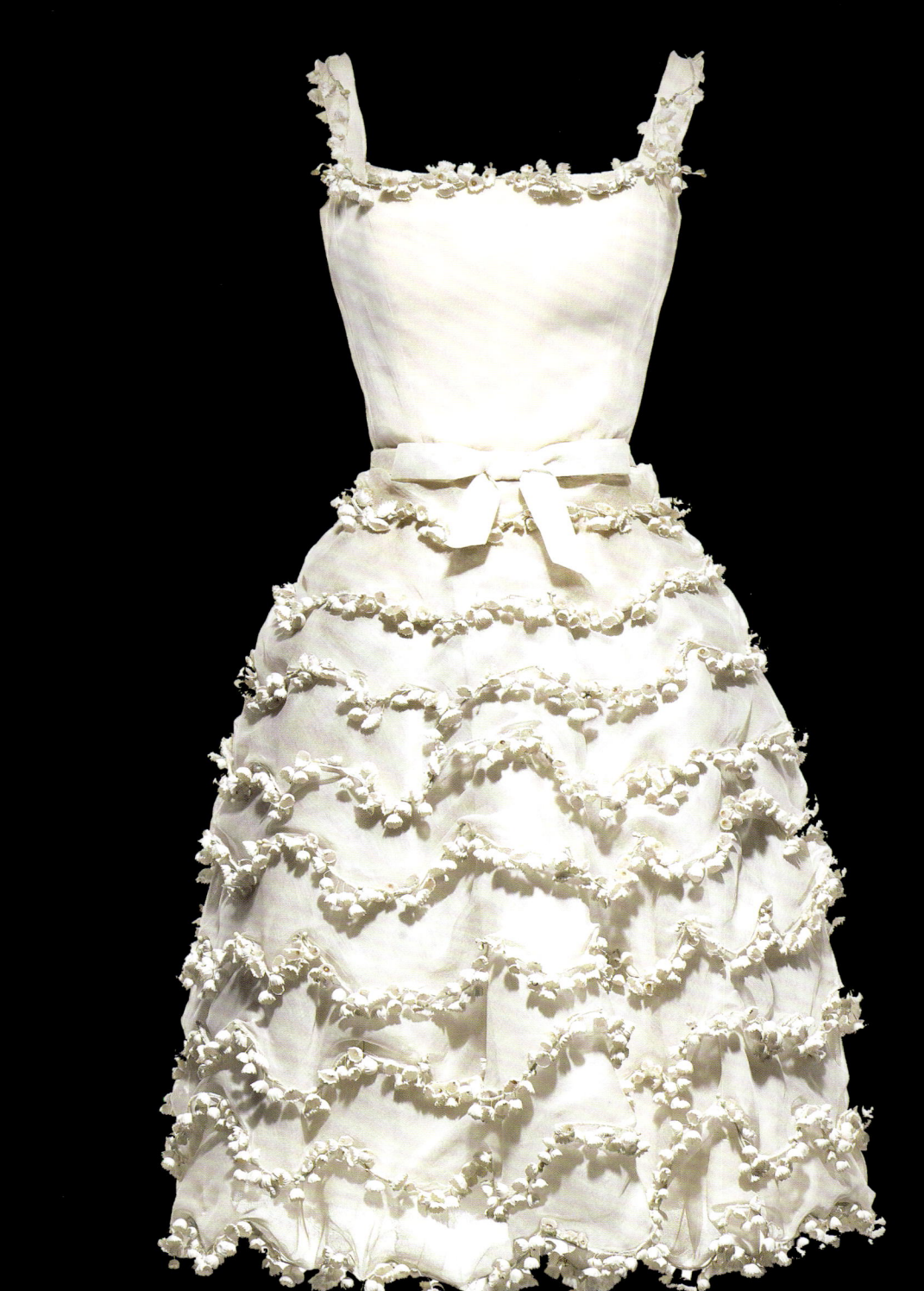

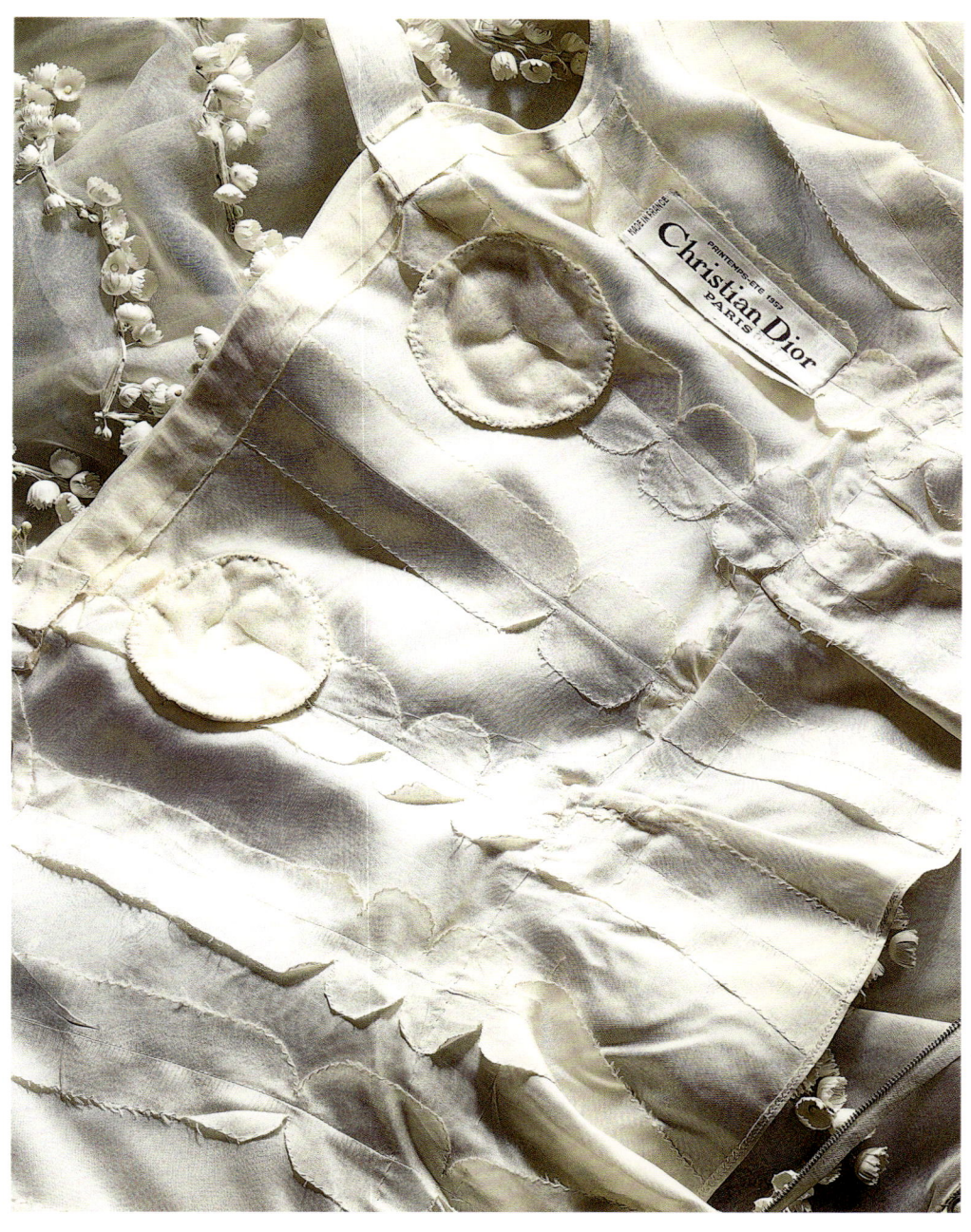

ABOVE AND OPPOSITE Commissioned by Francine Weisweiller, the *Muguet* dress in white organdy embroidered with lily of the valley, Spring-Summer 1957 haute couture collection, *Libre* line.

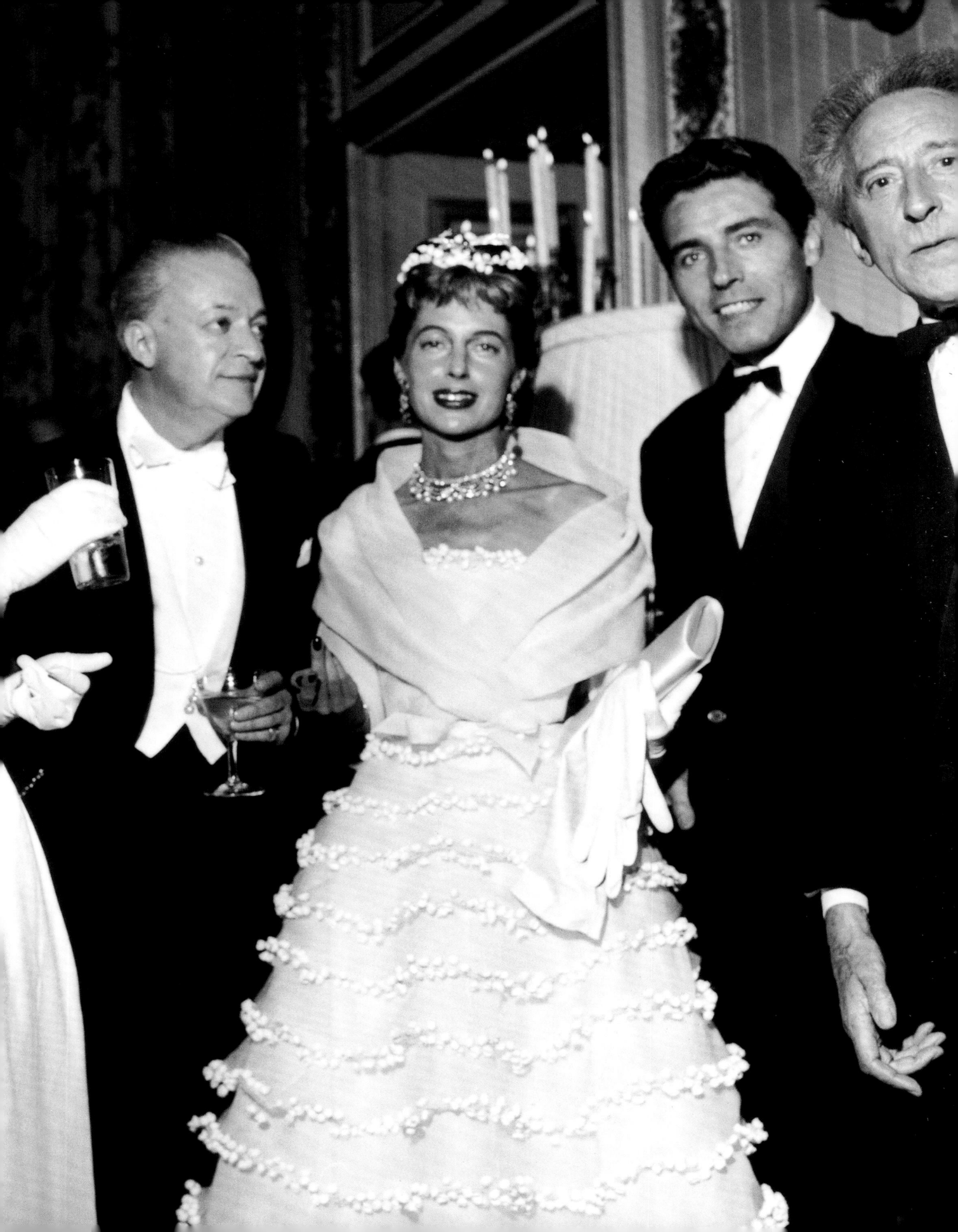

Francine Weisweiller

"The black with shining teeth is black on the outside and pink inside; I am black inside and pink on the outside." So the granddaughter of Alexandre Deutsch de La Meurte, the inventor of the first gasoline pumps, supposedly said, citing Jean Cocteau. During the occupation, Francine née Worms had to change her surname. Her brother had enlisted in the army and was killed while driving his Jeep. Her mother-in-law was arrested and deported to Auschwitz. Francine was married to Alec Weisweiller, the heir to Shell oil, and stood out in 1950s Paris as a patron of the arts, welcoming countless guests to her private mansion at 4 Place des États-Unis, from Georges Auric to Marlene Dietrich and Picasso.

Whenever she visited Dior she was accompanied by Cocteau, whom she had met in 1949. Cocteau painted murals all over the Villa Santo Sospir, her magnificent house in Saint-Jean-Cap-Ferrat. The dresses she ordered from Dior are testaments to the feast of parties and joy for which Paris was the enchanted stage at the time: The blue organdy *Musique en Fête* dress (Spring-Summer 1955), the black velvet and grosgrain *Soir à Tolède* dress (Autumn-Winter 1955), the white organdy *Muguet* dress (Spring-Sumer 1955), the early evening *Velours Rouge* dress (Autumn-Winter 1957), and *Marivaudage* were just some of the designs that Weisweiller ordered—souvenirs of a Café Society heroine who passed away in 2003. The house of Dior acquired these pieces in 1993. "This evening Francine was wearing a very beautiful Dior dress and all her pearls. A woman's eye is never mistaken. We were immediately plunged into a pool of vinegar," wrote Cocteau in passing in his journal in 1955.[1]

[1] Jean Cocteau, "Journal, February 27, 1955," *Le Passé Défini* (Paris: Gallimard: 1951–1963).

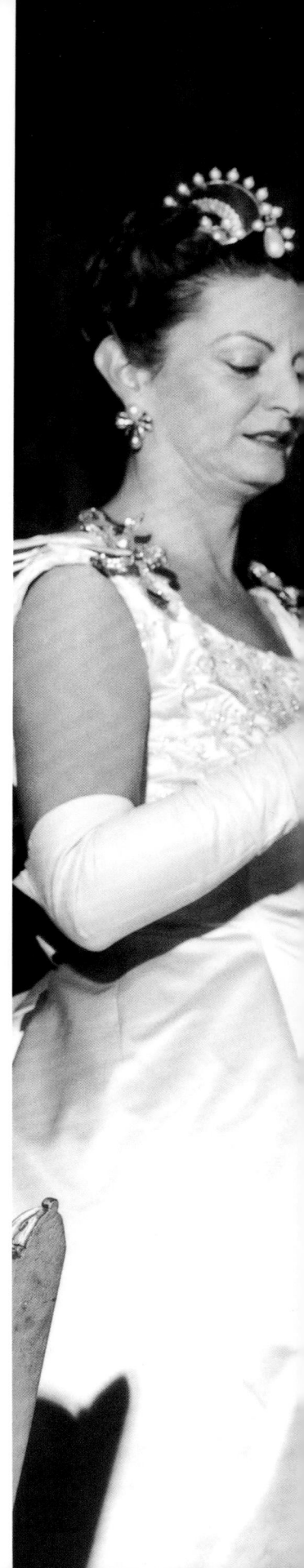

Francine Weisweiller (center) poses next to Patricia and Arturo López-Willshaw, Édouard Dermit, and Jean Cocteau before André Ostier's camera during a ball at Charles de Beistegui's home, the Château de Groussay, March 18, 1957. Patricia López-Willshaw wears the *Festival* dress, Autumn-Winter 1956 haute couture collection, *Aimant* line, and Francine Weisweiller dons the *Muguet* dress, Spring-Summer 1957 haute couture collection, *Libre* line.

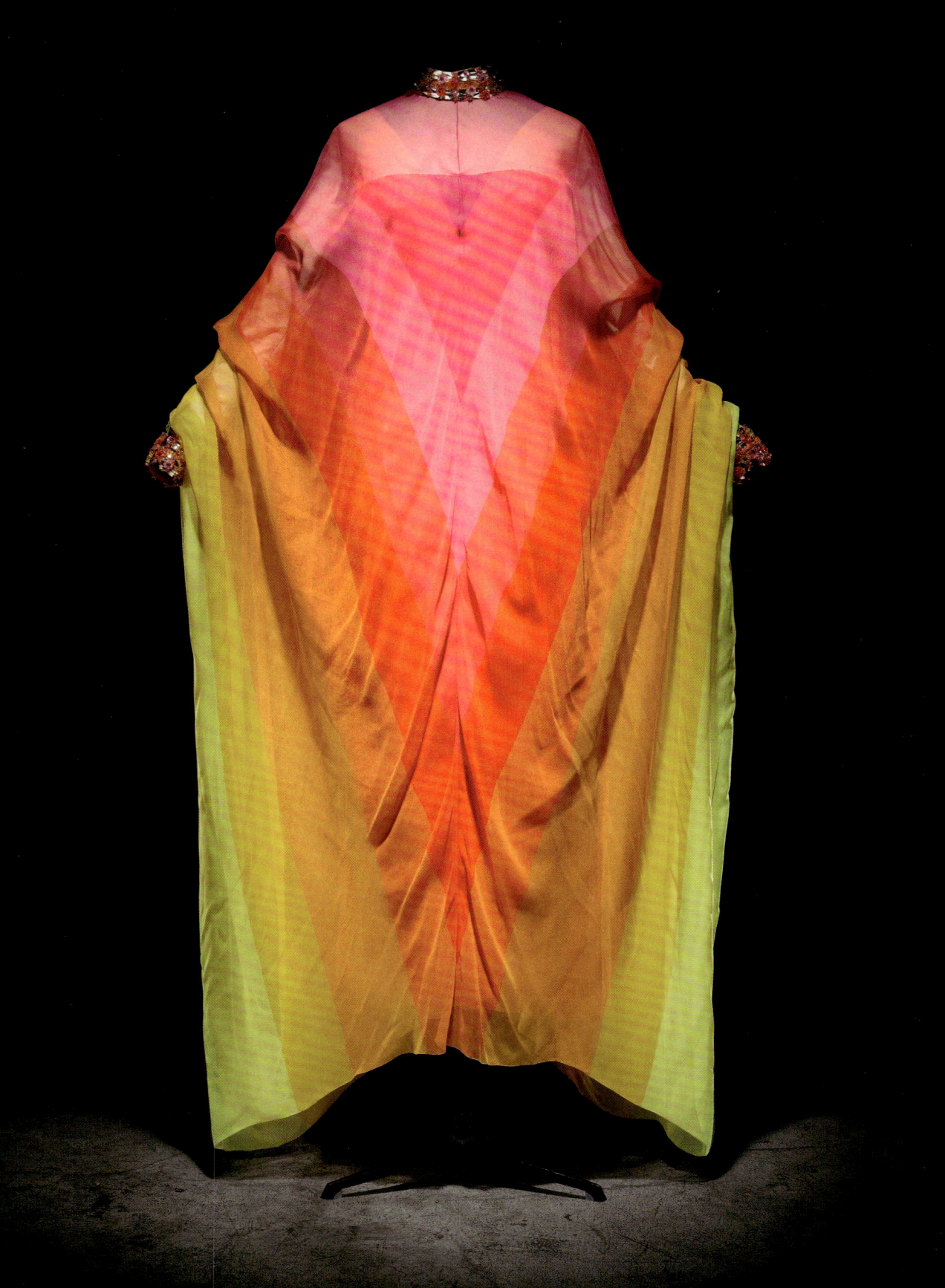

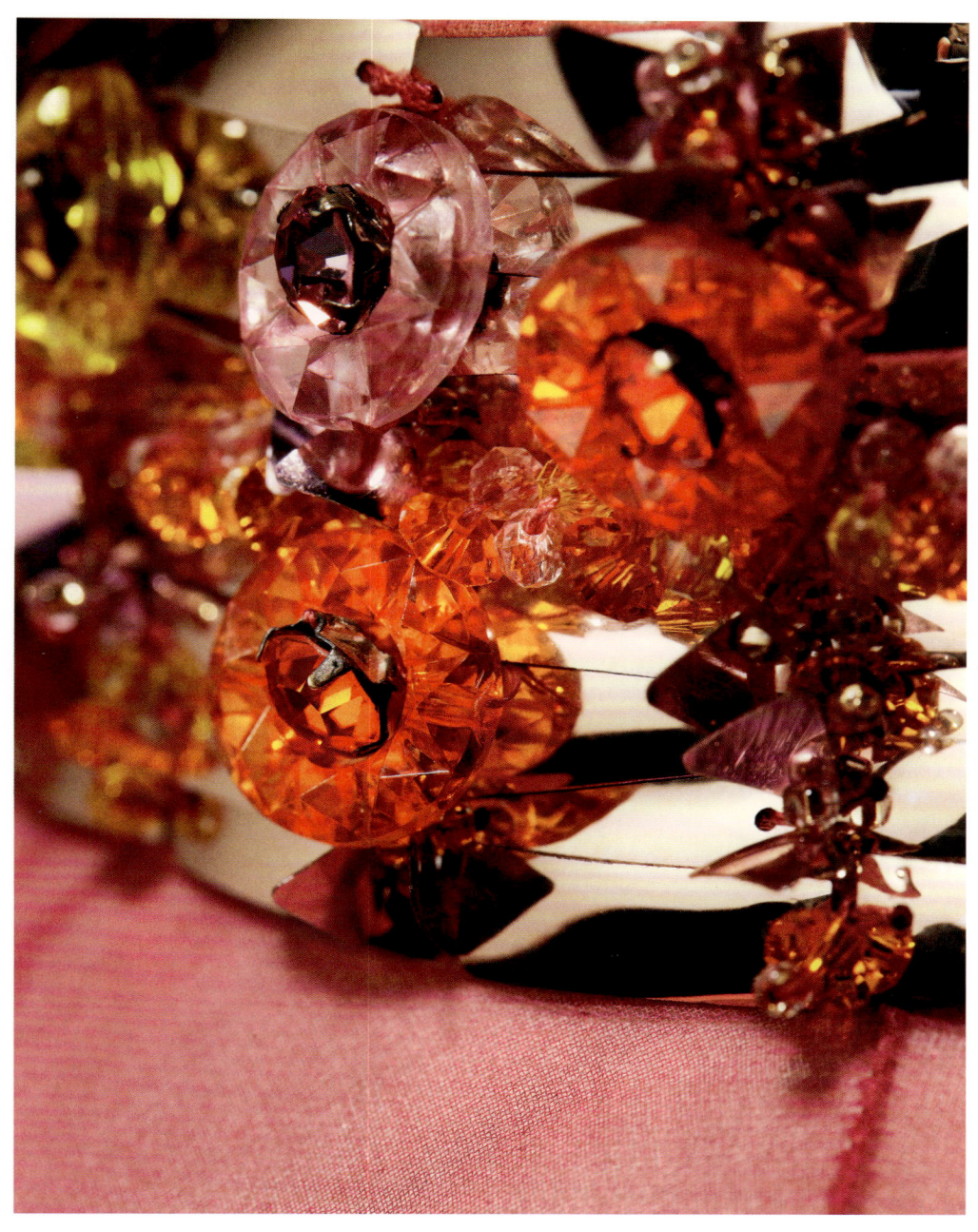

ABOVE AND OPPOSITE An evening dress in striped and embroidered silk chiffon, Spring–Summer 1967 haute couture collection.

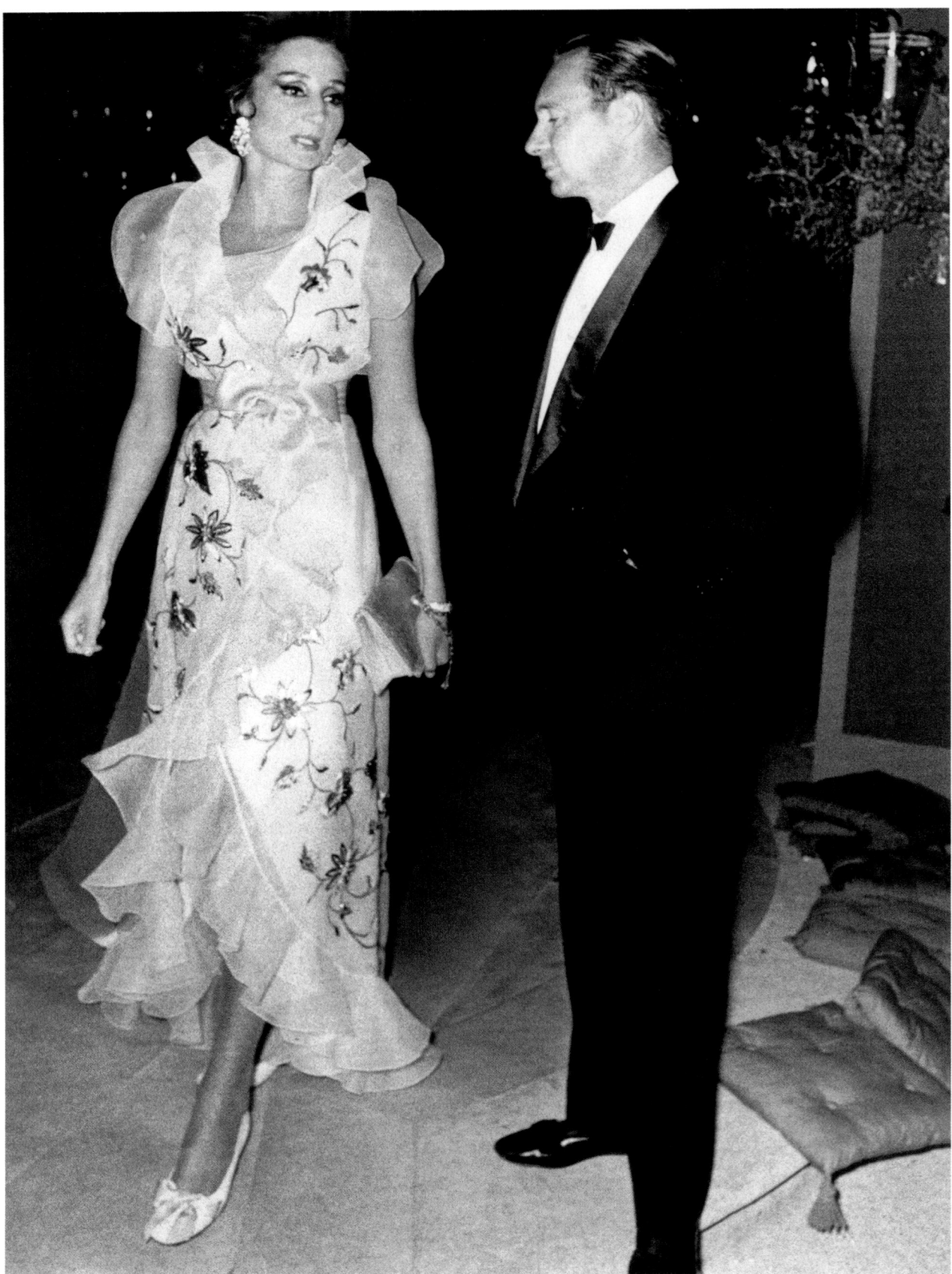

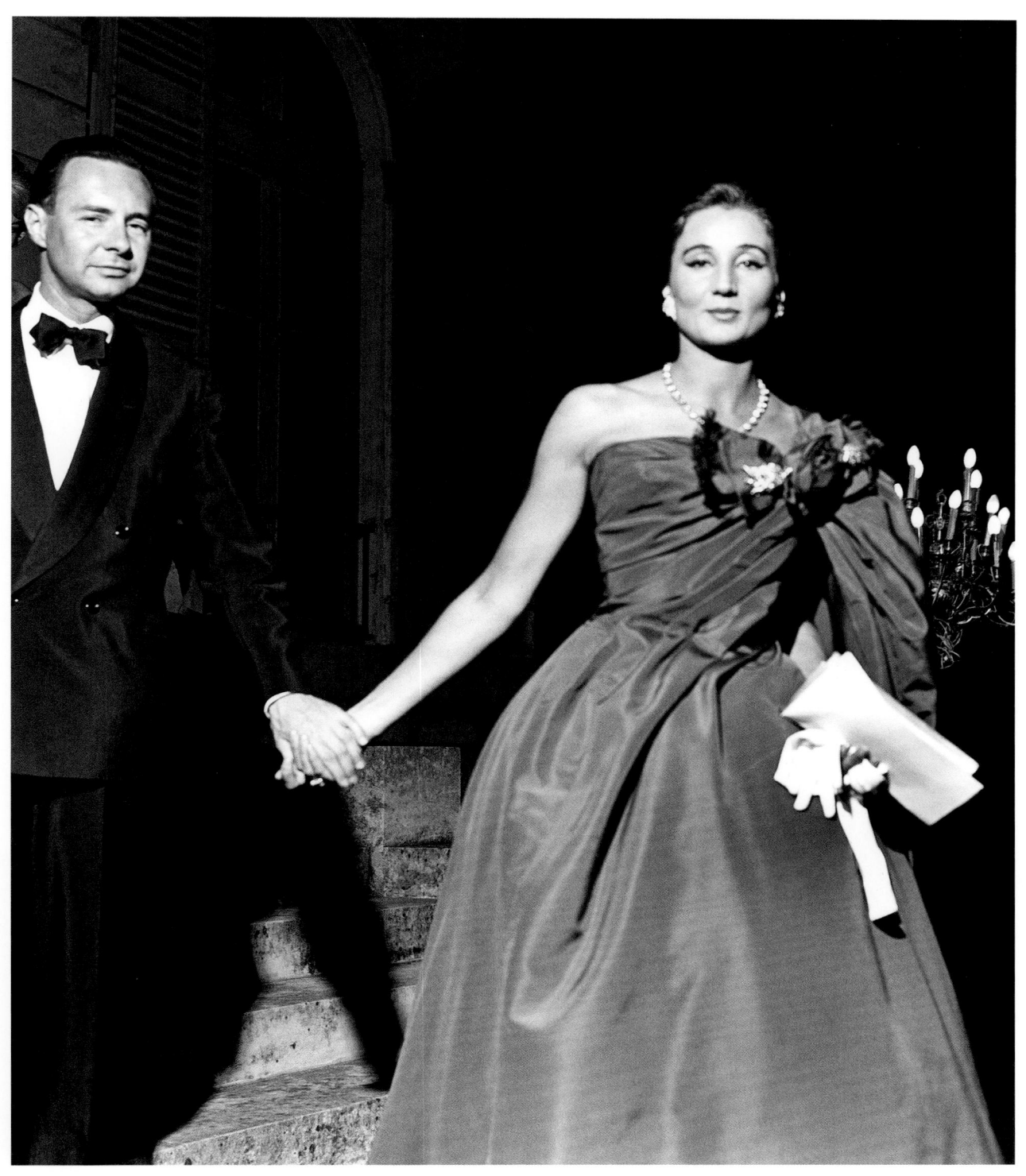

ABOVE The Viscount and Viscountess de Ribes photographed during a ball at Charles de Beistegui's home, the Château de Groussay, on June 26, 1959. She wears the *Rose rouge* dress, Spring–Summer 1958 haute couture collection, *Trapèze* line.

OPPOSITE The Viscount and Viscountess de Ribes photographed during a ball given by Anténor and Beatriz Patiño at the Quinta Patiño, Cascais, Portugal, September 6, 1968.

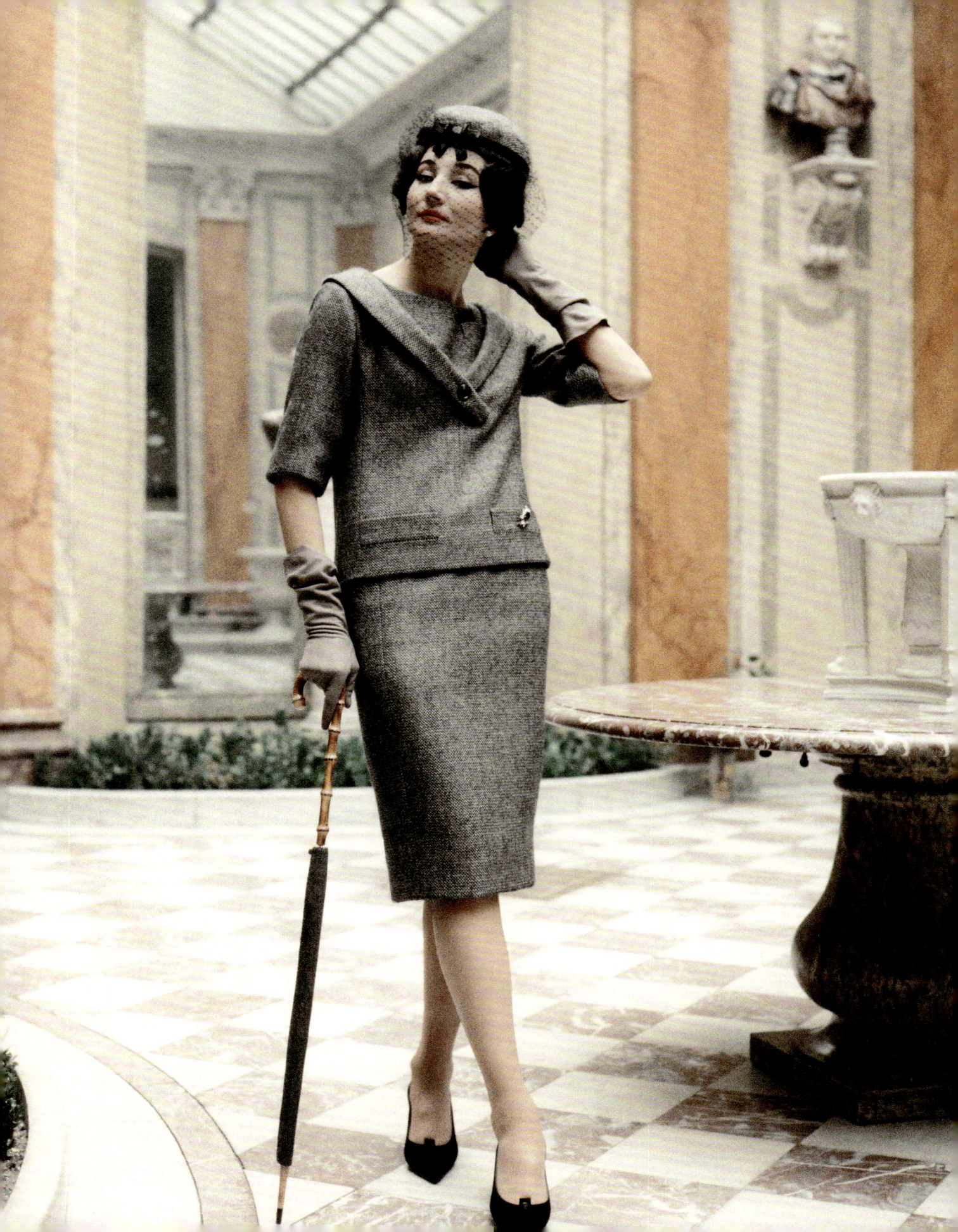

The Countess de Ribes

She talked about Dior, even when she was at convent school... Her introduction to the world of haute couture came from her uncle, Étienne de Beaumont. The pupil from the convent boarding school Les Oiseaux was hoping to find sequins, embroideries, and dresses "of all colors": Her first visit to the house of Dior rhymed with sample toiles—"a rather rough material"—pins and wooden dummies... On meeting with Dior that day, Jacqueline de Beaumont felt that she had met "a doctor": "My God, in a white coat, it was not at all how I imagined a couturier to be."

Having become the Viscountess de Ribes (and then Countess de Ribes in 1980), she was a fervid lover of haute couture. She dressed in Dior for both daywear and gala evening wear. She was never afraid of literally cutting up her haute couture dresses to reconstruct them as the whimsy took her. She did this with a satin and tulle dress "embroidered with thousands of little diamond stars," for which she kept only the base, and with a red faille dress (1959) that the Flou atelier entirely recreated for the exhibition at the Costume Institute, a mighty whirl of folds and bias cuts. "When you're twenty or twenty-five and you wear a Dior evening gown, you feel like you've been turned into a fairy..." From lowering or raising a décolleté to widening sleeves or shifting a length, there was no match for her tailor-made perfectionism. After thirty years of fittings and techniques, de Ribes was an expert of her own body. "Although I feel that elegance starts with a certain elimination, in the evenings I'm never afraid of a certain extravagance."

In 1983, when she presented her first collection bearing her name, she chose to wrap around a model's neck her famous black jade necklace, a cult piece that Dior had given her when she visited him that day. Dior was always a "magical" name for her, as was Avedon as well. "Climbing the staircase of 30 Avenue Montaigne time after time, either for the first presentation of the collection to the press, an atmosphere buzzing with intensity, or for the joy of attending the fitting sessions that I always found so fascinating, allowed me to perceive the world of haute couture—a world apart, surrounded by mystery and dreams."[1]

---

[1] Preface to *Dior by Avedon* (New York: Rizzoli, 2015).

The Viscountess Jacqueline de Ribes photographed by Mark Shaw in the Hôtel de Ribes, Rue de la Bienfaisance, in Paris. She wears the *Macadam* dress, Spring-Summer 1959 haute couture collection, *Longue* line.

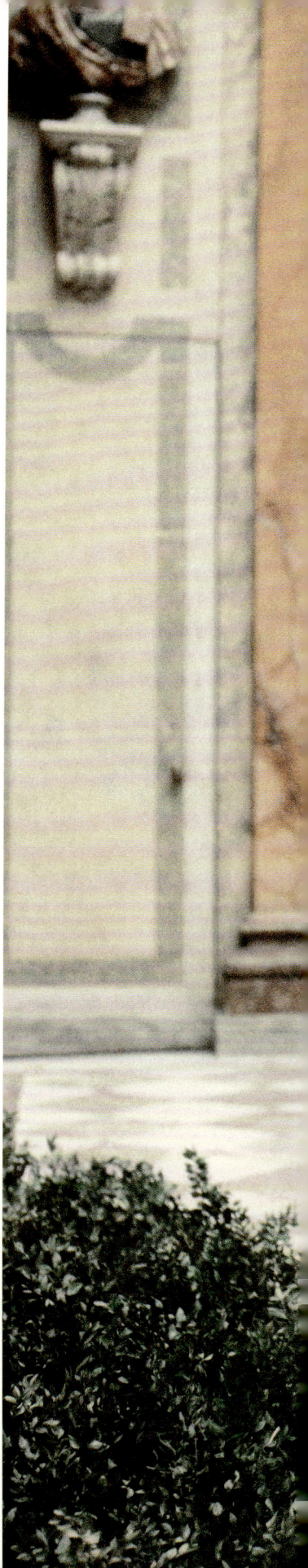

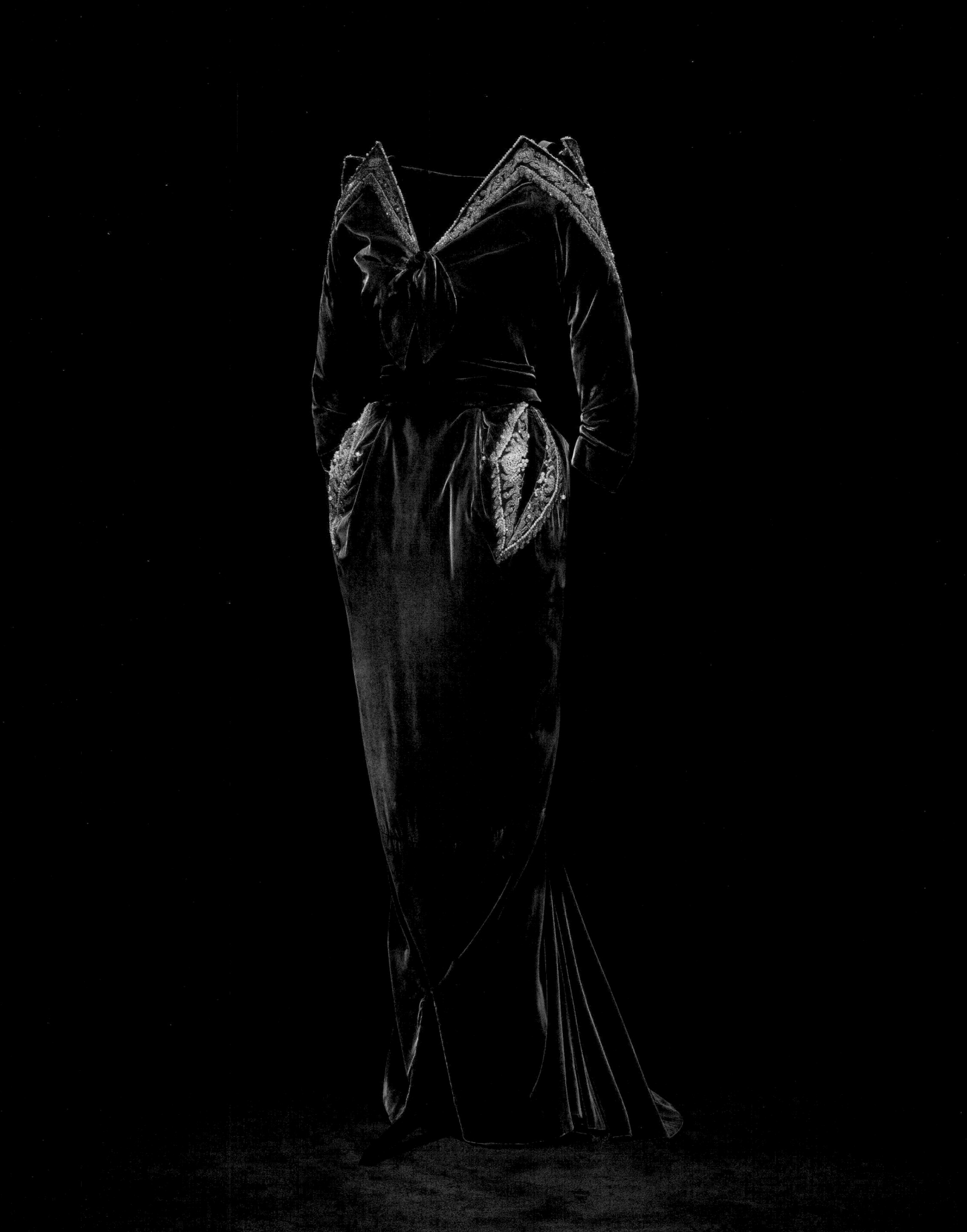

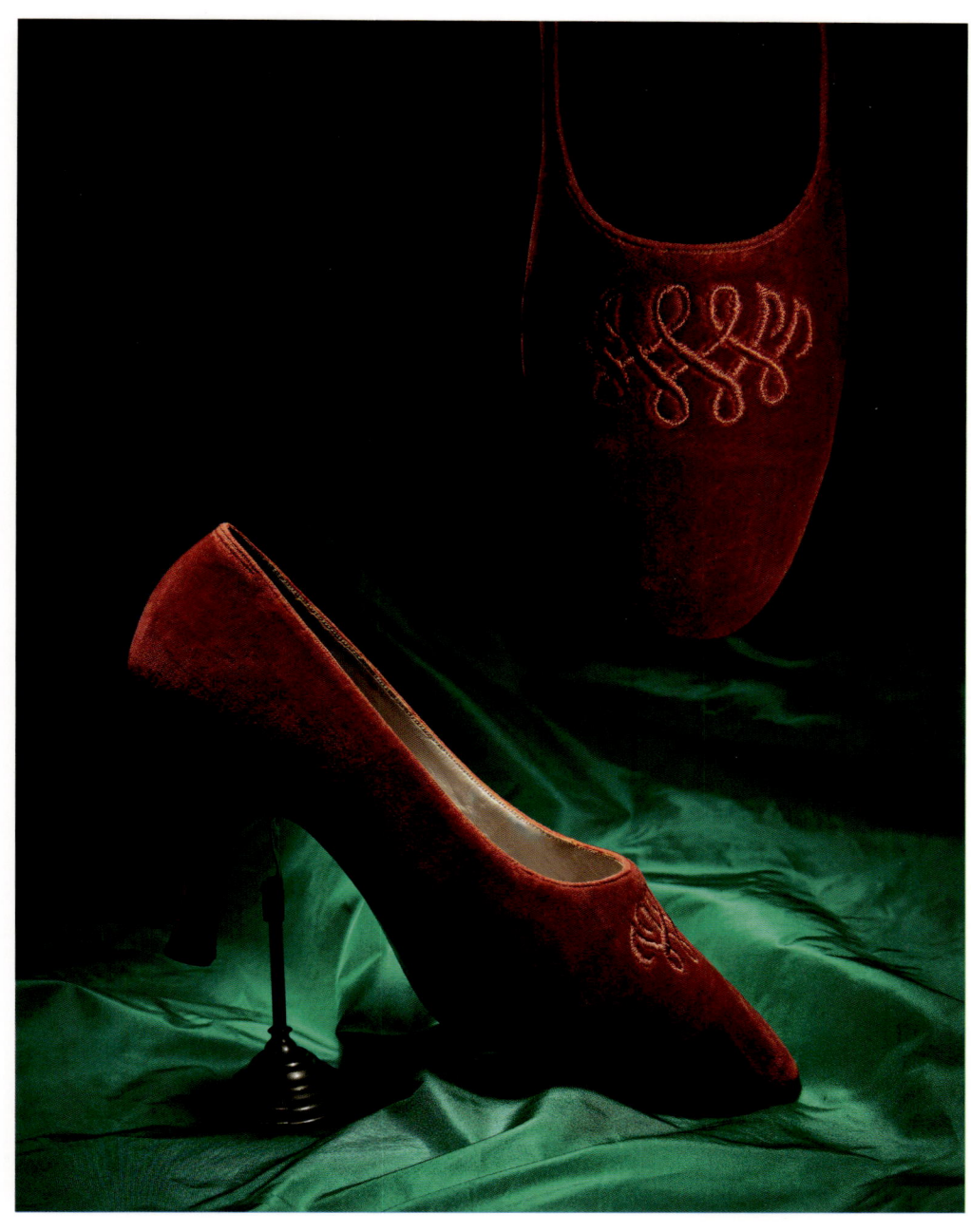

ABOVE Christian Dior-Delman cherry velvet court shoes monogrammed with two intertwined "Ws" for Wallis and Windsor, circa 1955.

OPPOSITE The velvet *Lahore* dress in midnight blue silk embroidered with silver thread and fine pearls, Autumn-Winter 1948 haute couture collection, *Ailée* line.

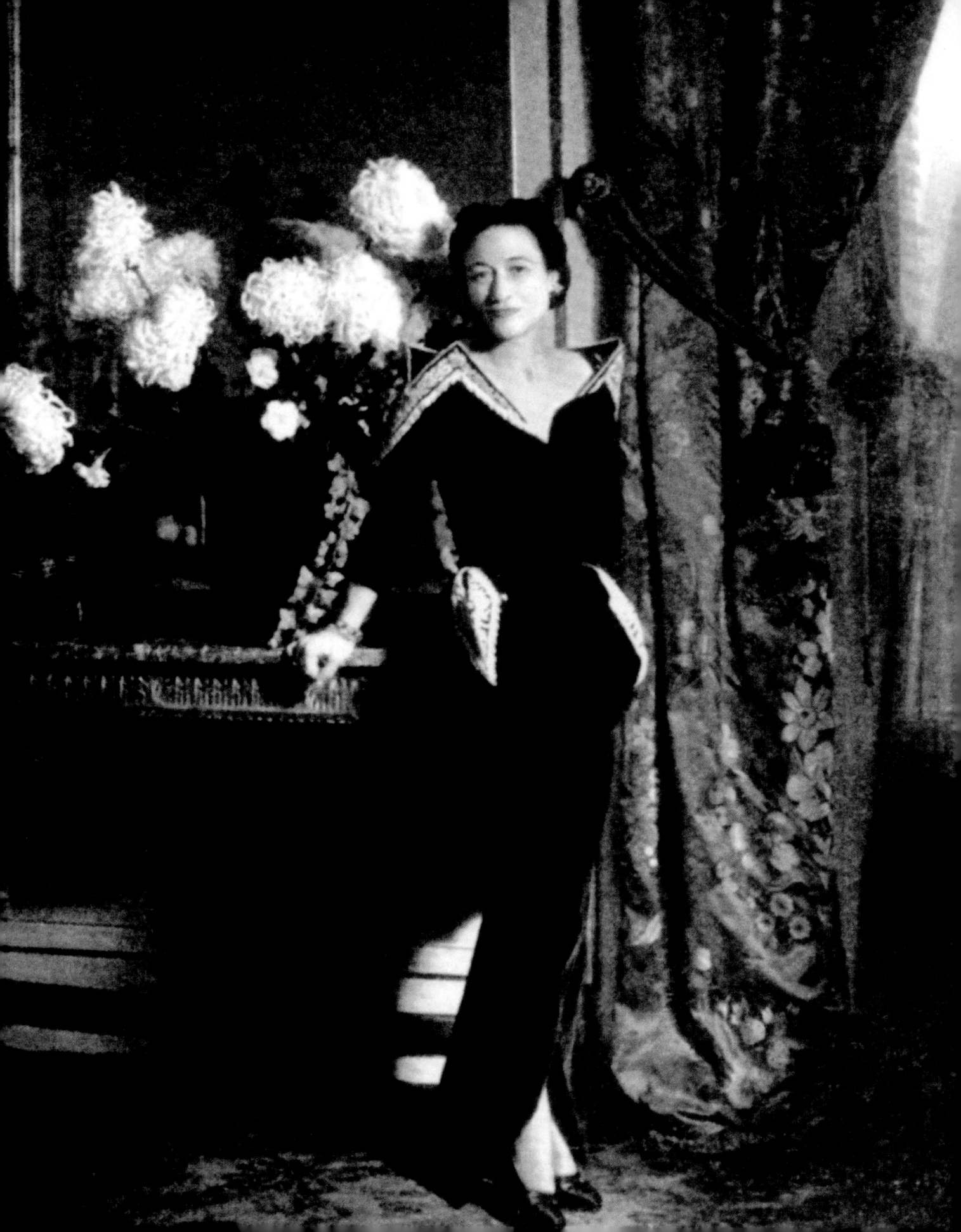

The Duchess of Windsor

In July 1948 the launch of the *Ailée* line (Autumn-Winter 1948 haute couture collection) coincided with the Duchess of Windsor's first orders at Dior. "This season interest is not focused on skirt length, but on cut and ampleness that is tautly designed, not swaying and hazy," read the program. Her perfect measurements (30-21-30) were ideal for these pieces with well-styled busts, low necklines, and very graphic pockets fitted against the hips. Cut in midnight blue silk velvet, the siren sheath dress re-embroidered with beads and silver thread revealed an emblematic look that Arik Nepo immortalized in *Vogue* in 1948. These orientalized graphics are found in the satin brocade design from Autumn 1955 (*Y* line), with a camisole top that has a simple neckline and buttons down the back, reflecting the Duchess of Windsor's mantra: "never too thin, never too rich."

The Duchess of Windsor followed a strict diet that scarcely altered her measurements over the years (33-23-33), and later ordered designs that Marc Bohan created. "She knew exactly what she wanted," Bohan recalled, "and I more or less knew that she would choose the strongest pieces in each collection... She liked blue and all the beige tones, but not apricot or gray. For daytime she preferred suits composed of a matching jacket and lightly flared skirt, dresses and coats, but they could never be in wool, which she found too warm."[1] One of the last garments he designed for her was an ivory crepe hostess dress. The cherry silk velvet shoes (circa 1960) that the house of Dior acquired in 1998 were a sign of utmost refinement: They are embroidered with the famous "W" monogram that the Duchess liked to have on her bed linen, handbags, writing paper, china, and interior items. Embroidered boleros, shantung blouses, and dinner dresses made of brocade, cyclamen gazar, or black crepe chiffon featured among the fifteen or so pieces auctioned by Sotheby's in February 1998, at which Dior acquired the famous *Lahore* dress whose price doubled the estimations.

[1] Laurence Catinot-Crost, *Wallis la Magnifique* (Biarritz: Atlantica, 2005).

The Duchess of Windsor photographed by Arik Nepo, 1948. She wears the *Lahore* dress, Autumn-Winter 1948 haute couture collection, *Ailée* line.

his film *Les Enfants Terribles*, which she funded. It was all a giddy whirl of swirling silk. "It all seemed so anachronistic and unreal to me, I felt like an eighteen year old in the last century," wrote her daughter, Carole Weisweiller.[4]

The visitor's book was like a dance card etched with the heart and soul of its silhouettes. "Everything about Dior was charm, refinement, courtesy, discreet murmurs, and rustling fabrics," recalled Jacqueline de Ribes.[5] Christian Dior's strength was that he did more than dress a period of optimism, he adorned it with everything that seemed to have been buried—the splendor of the Belle Époque, the subtle pastel colors of Molyneux, the lessons he learned at Piguet and Lelong—as though to promote the revival of "the art of pleasing." It was copied across America—in the streets, at the theater, in restaurants—but its three-tiered plunging neckline was less of a success with the ladies of Paris.

For John Galliano, Dior was a "storyteller" as much as a couturier. Like Georges Geoffroy, who designed many interiors for his clients and friends, such as Arturo and Patricia López-Willshaw and Baron de Rédé, Dior turned each dress into a benchmark for the art of living and seduction. In Autumn 1948, *Elle* magazine remarked that the *Eugénie*, an evening gown comprising sixty-five meters of tulle, was "the most expensive dress in Paris." One year later, the twelve widths of a gray shantung skirt evoked a "swirling folly from our childhood."[6] Dior was a genius magician who was just as passionate about the return of unpredictability. "The ball gown is a dream and must make you look like a dream. I consider it is as much an essential in a woman's wardrobe as a suit. And so wonderful for morale."[7]

In 2002, Victoire de Castellane organized the *Bal de la Fiancée du Vampire*, echoing the theme of her Dior High Jewelry collection: She welcomed her guests to the Ritz dressed as a Dior fiancée. The dress code was "Full moon or la-di-da." In July 2007 the *Bal des Artistes* collection designed by John Galliano was shown at the Orangerie at Versailles. "The house of Christian Dior is a vast ball that invites you to take part in the magic, to wear party clothes and make your party come true."[8]

---

[1] Christian Dior, *Dior by Dior* (London: V&A Publishing, 2012), 31.
[2] *Dior by Dior*.
[3] *Dior by Dior*.
[4] Carole Weisweiller, *Je l'appelais Monsieur Cocteau* (Monaco: éditions du Rocher, 2003).
[5] Jacqueline de Ribes in the preface to *Dior by Avedon* (New York: Rizzoli, 2015).
[6] *Elle*, 1949.
[7] Catherine Örmen, *Un siècle de mode* (Paris: éditions Larousse, 2012).
[8] John Galliano in the preface to *Le Grand Bal de Dior* (Paris: Artlys, 2010).

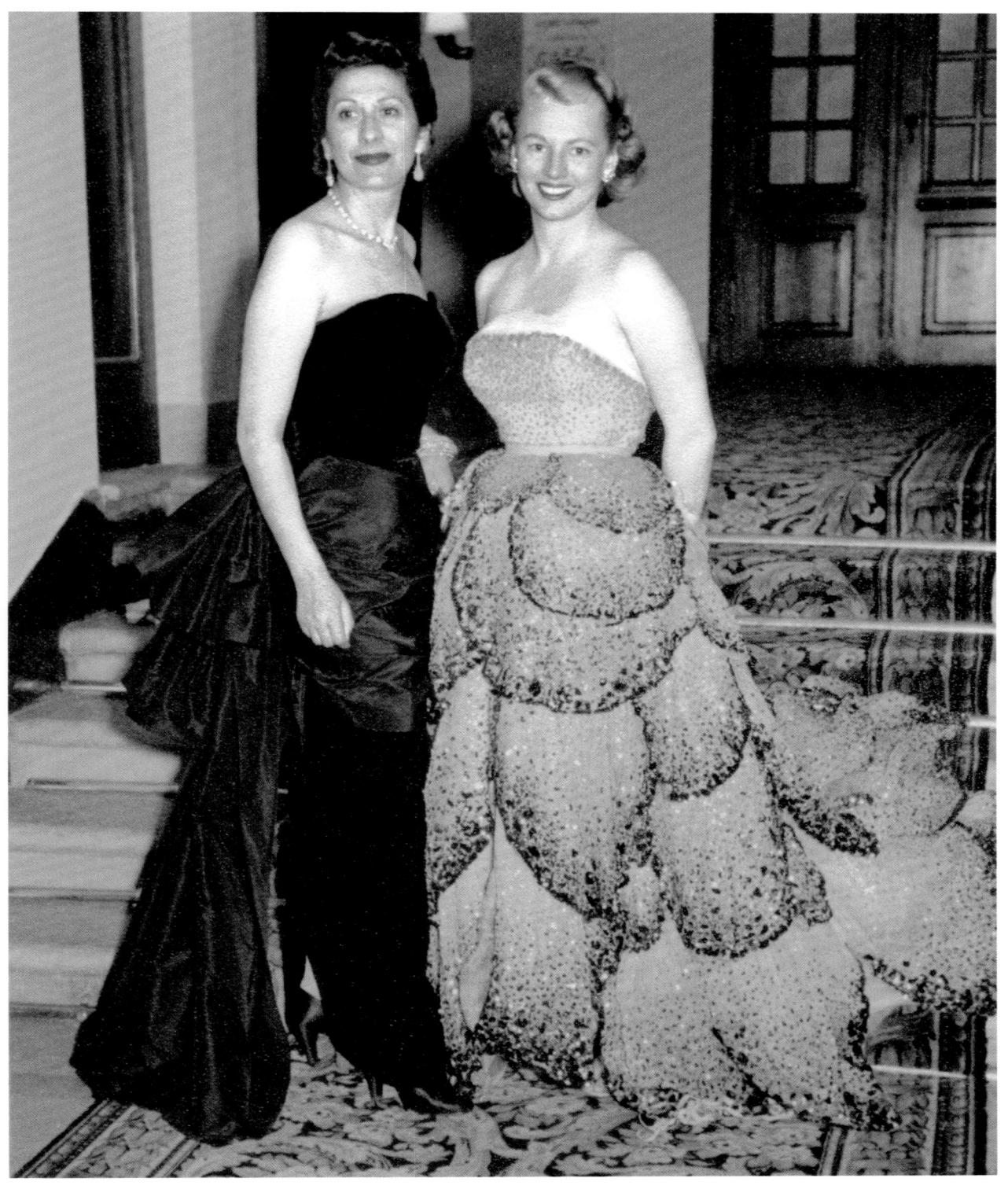

The wife of industrialist Robert Newman, Claire Poe Newman (right) poses next to Countess Clara de Zara during a gala soirée. She wears the *Junon* dress, Autumn-Winter 1949 haute couture collection, *Milieu du siècle* line.

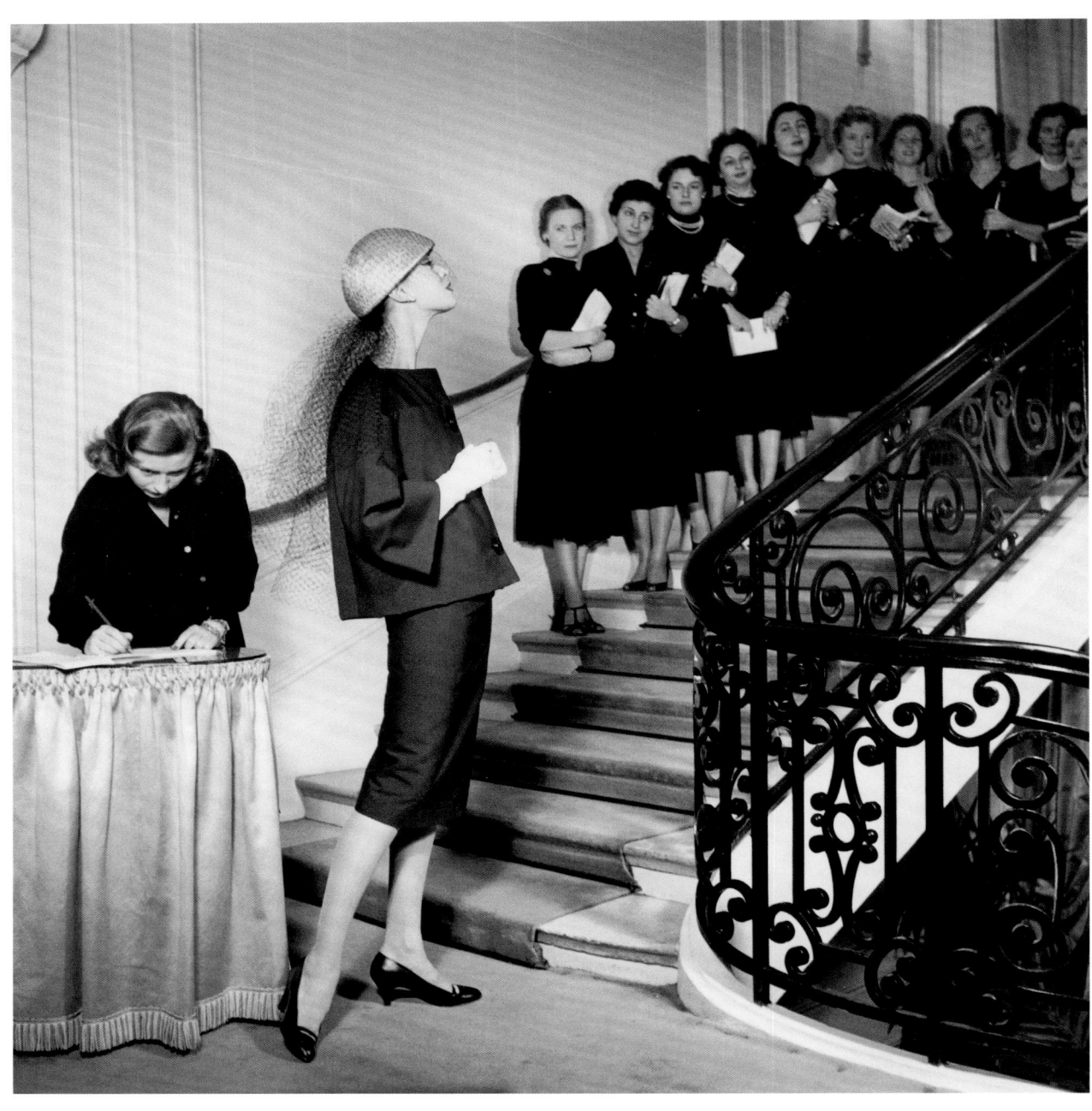

PREVIOUS PAGE Order notebooks from the house of Dior showing the name of the design, client, and couturière as well as the price and date.

ABOVE The cover girl Barbara Mullen poses in the house of Dior's famous staircase next to haute couture saleswomen dressed in black. Photograph by Louise Dahl-Wolfe for *Harper's Bazaar* magazine, March 1956.

Dior Clients and the Sense of Perfection

*"How can I express my feelings about fêtes?
In an age when it is fashionable to affect to despise luxury
and grand entertainments, I will not disguise the fact that
they are a memory which I am proud to possess."*

Christian Dior

Some dresses are their very own invitation to travel, to live moments representing the "ideal of civilized happiness" as defined by Christian Dior. The inventor of the New Look was the first couturier to magnify the newfound joy of the postwar years with a panache that had Café Society jostling to be dressed by him. "It was true that I was a Parisian couturier, but I had to understand the needs of elegant women all over the world as well as my fellow countrywomen . . . in an effort to give women of different ways of life the clothes they wanted," wrote Dior.[1]

At the time, clients would meet in Paris twice a year, in January and July, to discover the great couturiers' collections and choose their designs during the presentations in the salons. Orders for different garments became part of a return to fancy kingdoms, glittering extravaganzas, society balls, and a desire to flaunt splendor. From New York to Rio, Dior knew that he made his couture house "an established Parisian attraction, like the Eiffel Tower or the Cancan," loved by fans of parties and cruises.[2] Dior took part in this endless celebration of taste in which couturiers, decorators, and clients shared their affinities. But this celebration was a reality that would turn his couture house into an empire associated with Paris, the City of Light. He evoked the "year of grace, 1947": "As if possessed by a frenzy, everybody wanted to give their ball for a particular project or friends, in Paris, in the country, on the Eiffel Tower, on a boat on the Seine, anywhere where it was a novelty to dance. As our friends from abroad poured in to visit us, Paris became cosmopolitan once more."[3]

Flitting from parties to cruise ships, Café Society became the enchanted screen masking the irreparable wounds of World War II. Francine Weisweiller became Jean Cocteau's patron and in 1949 let the poet use her Parisian mansion as the location for

I

HIGH SOCIETY

Mme Dinztagle

Mme Marlène Dietrich   35000 ah a bât   11/8/5...

Mme agnès de Puthod   70 000

Mrs William H Dodge   70 000

Mme Bricard   bon blanc   Hél...

Mme Bricard   bon blanc   Hélène

Hage   40.000   Martino

roi Stein   70.000   Pascale

70.000   Hélène   9 septem...

Maud   2...

J.C. Servan Schreiber

INTRODUCTION

Dior is like the "school for women." The mannequins' dressing room was at its heart. "Like a theater dressing room, it has a chair, lamps, and mirrors. Like a dressing room, it is only inhabited by fairies," the couturier said. Dior worked in the wings with his close circle: Raymonde Zehnacker, Marguerite Carré, Mitzah Bricard, known as "the woman who dresses the dresses," Carmen Colle, and Suzanne Luling. Trianon gray salons, stucco *médaillons*, saleswomen dressed in black: a Parisian world as structured and controlled as a *grain-de-poudre* jacket—yet never cold nor fixed. Dior is a kingdom within a city, where outfits are never taken anywhere without their chaste white cotton-canvas cases, shrouded in the privacy that befits their status. Then shown and revealed, unique to the world. "When I opened my house, I told M. Boussac that I only wanted to dress the most elegant women from the most elegant ranks of society. I have watched the clientele I desired build up, little by little, by the most natural means. It is for them that I am working all the time: It is they who answered my appeal."[8]

[1] Christian Dior, *Dior by Dior* (London: V&A Publishing, 2012), 36.
[2] Ibid., 22–23.
[3] Ibid., 34–35.
[4] Ibid., 57.
[5] Ibid., 110.
[6] *Vogue*, August 2012.
[7] *Le Figaro*, September 7, 2013, http://www.lefigaro.fr/.
[8] *Dior by Dior*, 139.

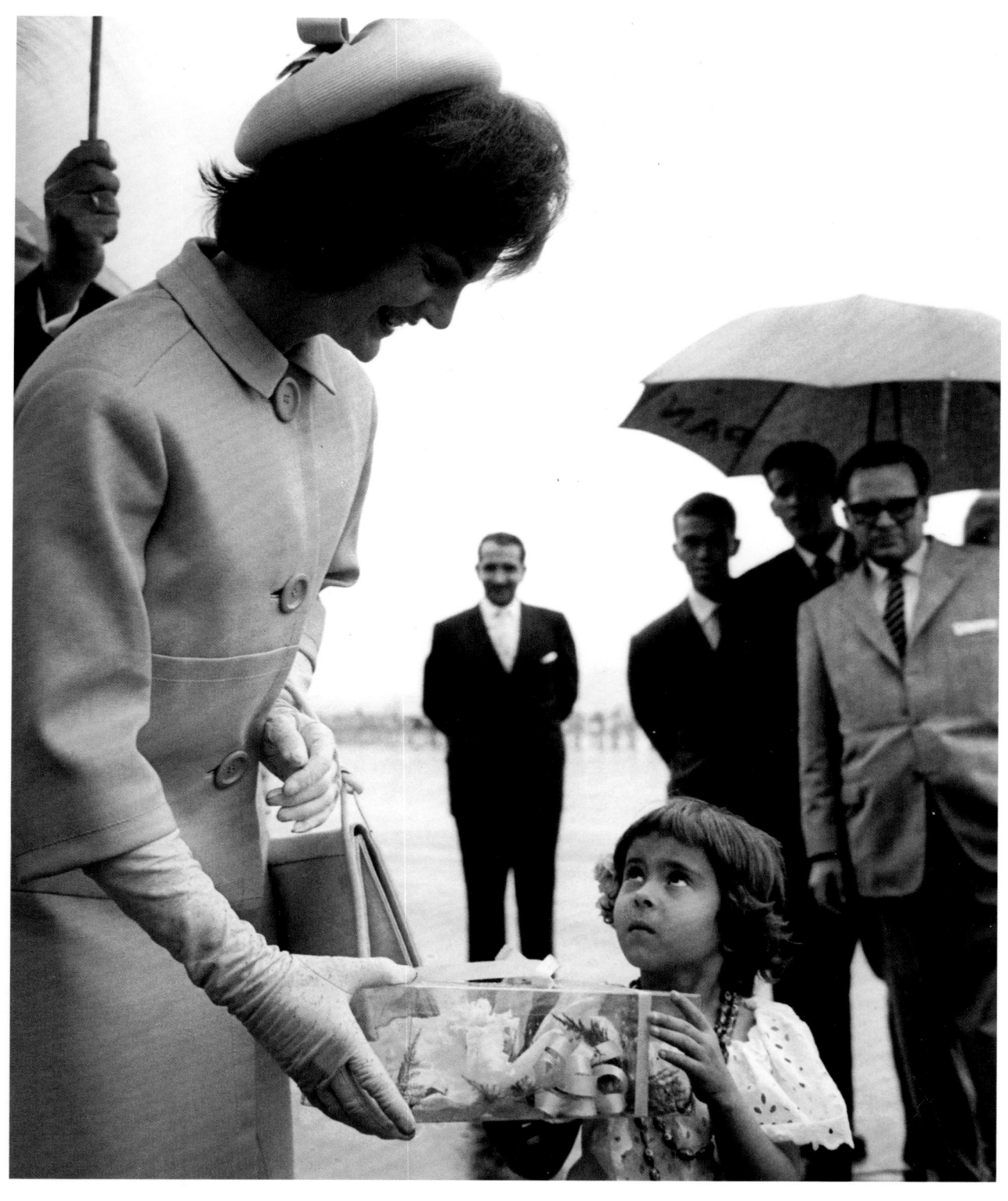

Jackie Kennedy during an official trip to Caracas, Venezuela, in December 1961. She wears the *La Vie en rose* jacket, Spring–Summer 1961 haute couture collection.

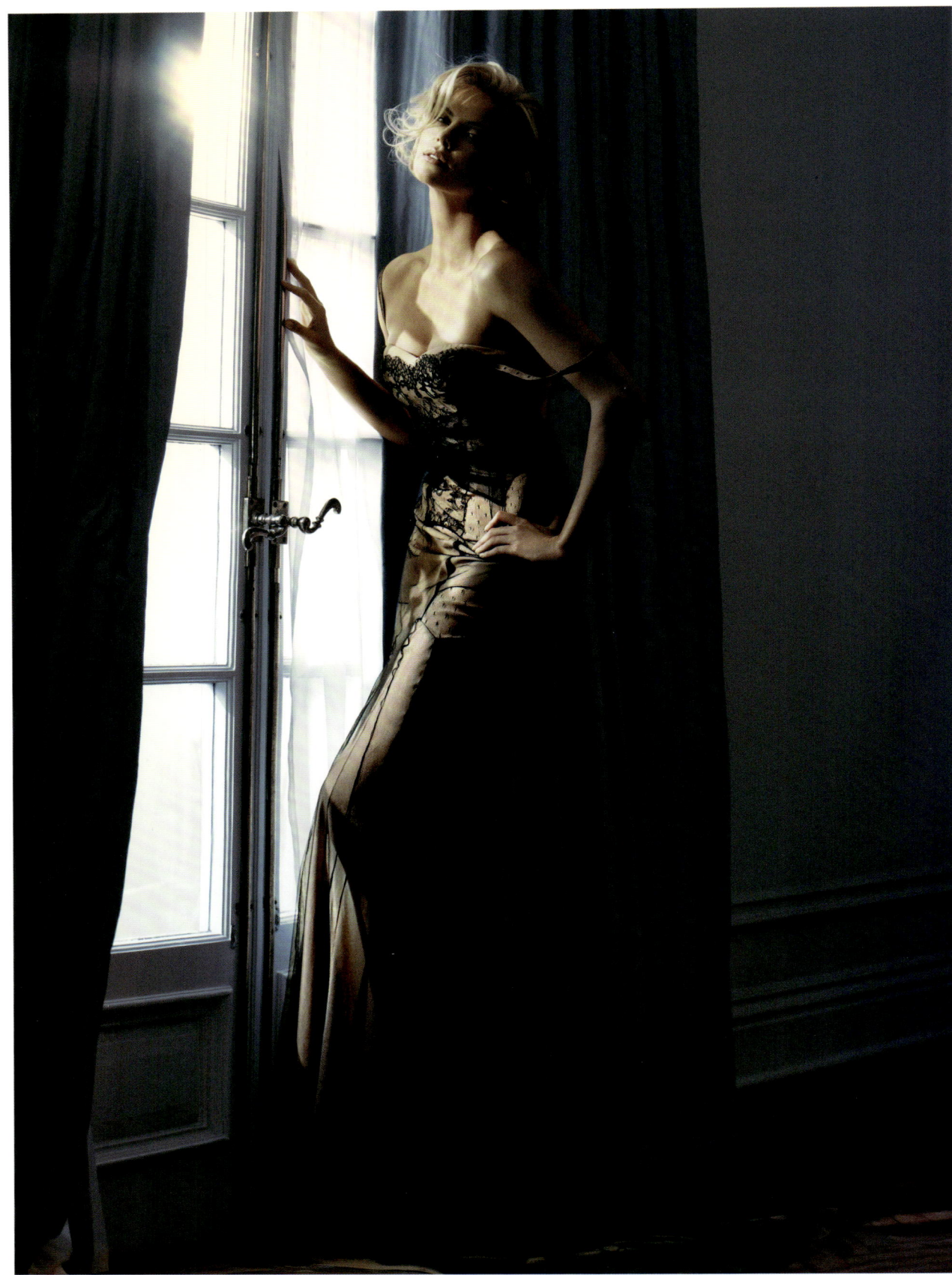

INTRODUCTION

Held at 3:30 p.m. in the salons, the daily couture show ceased for good in the 1980s. The new clients lived fast-paced lives, practiced sports, traveled, and worked. Less time may have been spent, but the rituals remained the same. In 2016 an American client took the luxury of sending one of her chambermaids to Dior to learn how to iron chiffon. Eschewing "look at me" dresses, haute couture customers prefer the absolute discretion of couture made to measure and to match their lifestyle. A Middle Eastern client, for example, regularly orders suits for the meetings she presides: official outfits and power dresses—it's all a matter of confidence and self-assurance. "Dior is about structure." Say no more. Haute couture is a "style." A promise. With no recipes, rather principles approved by Jacqueline de Ribes, the "last queen of Paris," and by all the women at the fashion shows who represent the last patrons of couture savoir-faire.

What unites Cecil Beaton's photo of Daisy Fellowes in her lyre feather headdress at the Palazzo Labia (1951) and Bert Stern's pictures of Marilyn Monroe at her "last sitting" (1962)? Or Mathilde of Belgium—who chose to wear a very French sky blue Dior crepe suit by Raf Simons (a compatriot) on her first visit to France (2014)—and Marion Cotillard, who introduced John Cameron Mitchell to the house of Dior to shoot the first *Lady Dior* commercial? The Oscar-winning French actress says that Dior "woke me up to a world I did not know.... Dior gave me my fashion education."[6] Certain gestures, a style, a way of embodying a role, plus everything the "Dior dress" implies in terms of standards and creative discipline: The primary responsibility of a woman on stage, whether an actress or a First Lady, is to be believed, to not pretend nor imitate reality, but to truly become the personality they embody. Which is why Natalie Portman, the face of *Miss Dior*, could honestly state: "You see me dressed, my hair styled, adorned in jewelry, but it's not reality. It's like a super-hero movie: In the evening I'm transformed, but during the daytime I'm invisible."[7] A certain amount of discipline is required to wear a Dior dress. With nothing that slumps or is falsely natural: Be it straight-grain or evanescent, the fabric always holds, determining the ultimate exercise in style. It is the starting point for the construction of any Dior dress, dictating the language of the neckline, the arms, the cherished ladylike poise.

By bringing wasp waists, narrow busts, and swirls of silk back into fashion, Christian Dior did much more than dress his era: He offered it the keys to a secret garden, a city whose very name could open up the gates of enchantment: "The Duchess adores Paris because Paris is not far from Dior," the Duke of Windsor used to say about Wallis... "The Duchess always arrived in the salon looking as though she had stepped out of one of our clothes boxes," recalls Sophie Gins, Dior haute couture saleswoman at the time. In December 1965 the house of Dior gave the Duchess a silk scarf on which the following words were calligraphed on color blocks: *"Amitié"* (Friendship), *"Bonheur"* (Happiness), *"Amour"* (Love), *"Avenue Montaigne," "Chance," "Fortune."*

the embroidered midnight blue wool *Bar* coat (Spring-Summer 2016 haute couture collection), the Dior line lends itself to a thousand and one desires, moods, whims, feelings, and head-over-heels moments.

Dior is the large white salon murmuring with secrets, where "women suddenly remember that they are there to be looked at."[5] The Dior story is replete with meetings that rapidly turned a name into a label, with the creation of Parfums Christian Dior (1947), then a subsidiary in New York (1948), and the first licences, starting with the commercialization of a line of stockings (1949) for which Marlene Dietrich would become the ambassador in 1955, and the opening of the *Grande Boutique* on the corner of Avenue Montaigne and Rue François 1er, also in 1955. Women the world over became Dior clients well before the globalization of the twenty-first century—as though between the fairy tale and the rigor, the society balls and the signature suits, Dior had defined the essential joy: "My mannequins are the life of my dresses, and I want my dresses to be happy," the couturier famously said. His couture house fast became the backdrop people would stand before to have their photograph taken, "like the Eiffel Tower." It was linked to a certain notion of France.

Dior—"that magical name that combines God (*Dieu*) and gold (*or*)," to quote Jean Cocteau—reveals very singular identities, from Rihanna, the pop music icon with fifty-five million followers, to Jacqueline de Ribes, who, beginning in 1956, was considered one of the best dressed women in the globe. They seem worlds apart, yet are so very close. To start with, women in Dior are personalities. Within this cosmopolitan yet cozy kaleidoscope Dior is the realm of every possibility, where reality seems like a fairy tale. "The sky is the limit," the haute couture saleswomen were told. "We do our job with passion: It's our task to guide the client in her dream." Times have changed, of course. Long gone are the days when wealthy American women would take up residence in Paris for fifteen days to choose their outfits, or when certain clients, such as Baroness Thyssen, thought nothing of ordering a leopard-skin coat for her dog, designed to match her own. A request that was duly refused… The Brazilian Elisa Morera would turn up with her jewelry box, and Rose Kennedy with a Louis Vuitton vanity case filled with swatches of fabric. "You will never marry my son," she declared to Arlette, a saleswoman whom Kennedy's son had a crush on, reducing her to tears. Up until the 1960s, the house of Dior employed around forty first and second saleswomen. They would be summoned to "the little telephone cabins" to ensure diplomatic relations and uphold different protocols, juggling the constraints of etiquette or social standing with the most outlandish requests: In the 1950s, for example, Baroness de Montesquiou demanded chiffon fabrics in the "color of delphiniums at sunset"—the exact shade that matched her eyes.

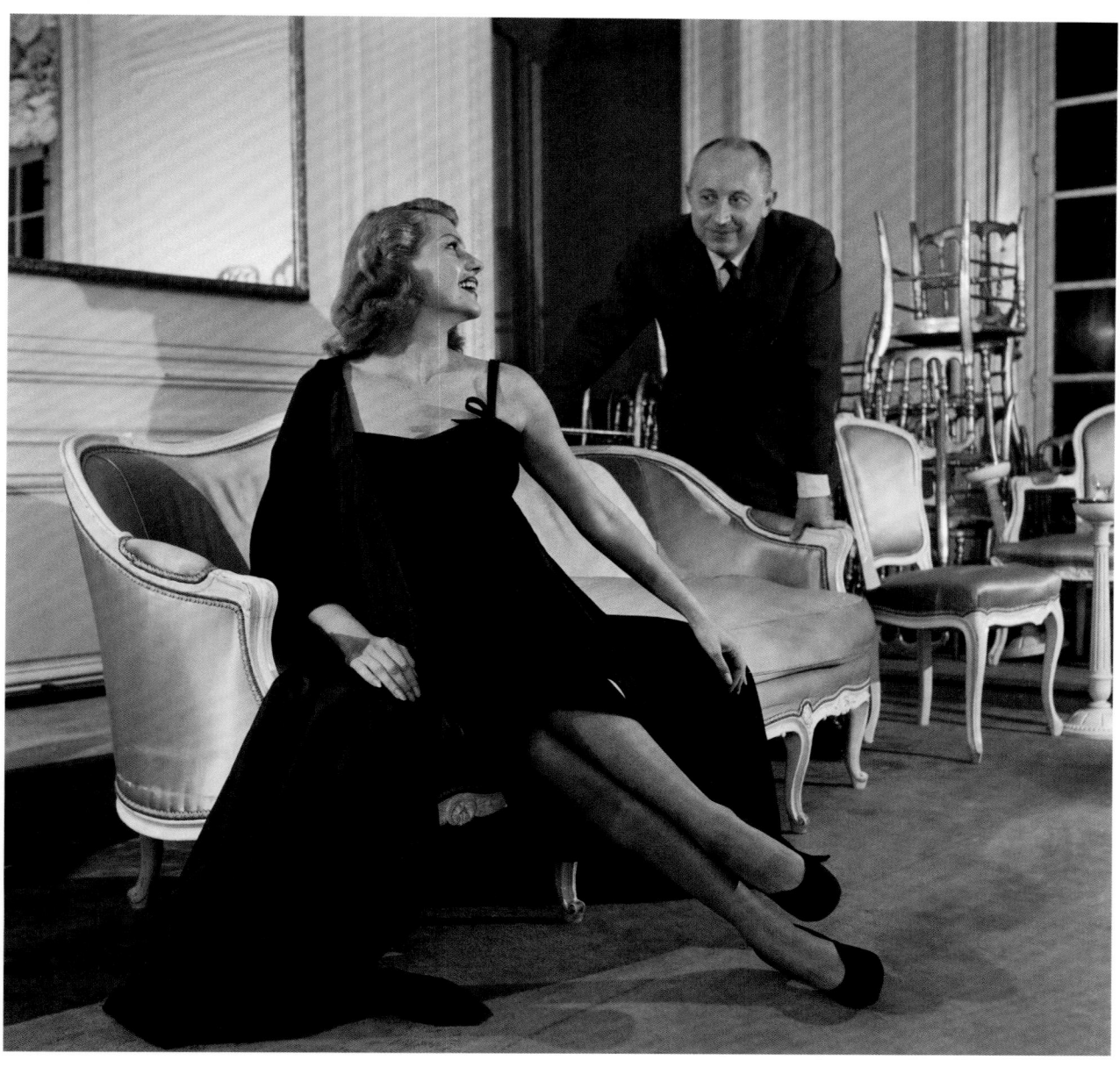

ABOVE Rita Hayworth accompanied by Christian Dior during a private presentation in the couture house's large salon on Avenue Montaigne, October 1952.

FOLLOWING PAGE Charlize Theron photographed in 2010 by Patrick Demarchelier. She wears a Dior design that was specially created for the *J'adore* campaign.

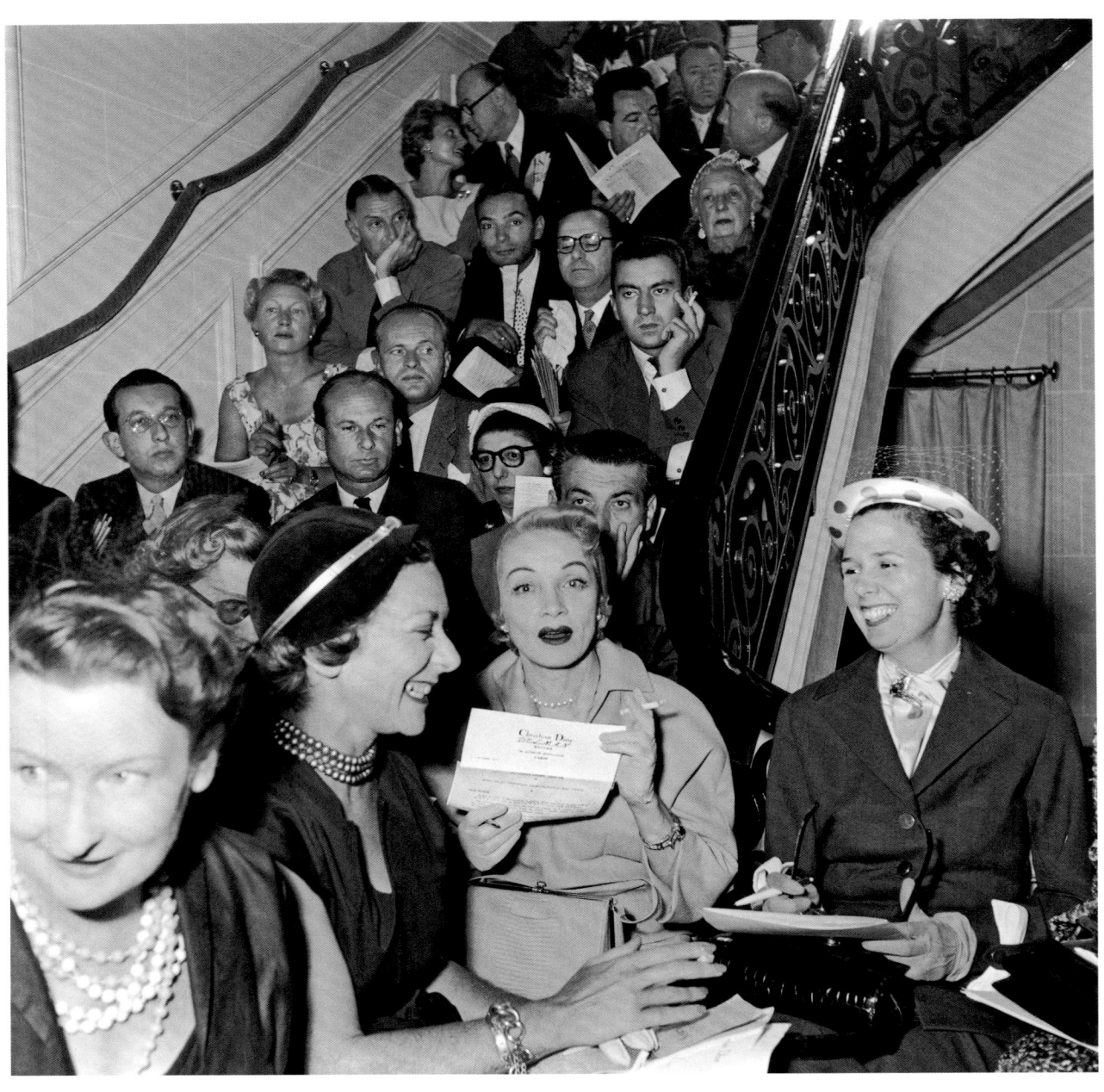

Marlene Dietrich in the front row
of a Christian Dior fashion show
in the early 1950s.

Introduction

"Women have instinctively understood that I dream of making them not only more beautiful, but also happier. That is why they have rewarded me with their patronage."[1] With these words, Christian Dior offered the best definition not only of himself, but of a profession whose history he embodied and whose aura he restored to the full. With Dior, every woman became a favorite, and every man her king. Dior offered an extra occasion to state one's difference. What do the twenty-two outfits that Dior designed for Yvonne Printemps in the film *La Valse de Paris* by Marcel Achard (1950) have in common with *Pompadour*, *Du Barry*, *Fête à Versailles*, *Bal Romantique*, and *Fêtes Galantes*—dresses that featured in the programs of his collections? What do *Bar*, *Chérie*, and *Passe Partout*, the first silhouettes from Spring-Summer 1947 that were "made to enhance the wearer" share with all the other dresses that followed? They were all "a thousand fleeting images" in which "long-forgotten techniques" could be felt.[2] And beyond this they were overriding desires, the kind of longing that made *Bonbon*, a "simple afternoon dress," into a best seller: A design from the second collection (Autumn-Winter 1947), it was sold 121 times (known in-house as 121 "*répétitions*"). Lana Turner was one of the clients who succumbed to its charms. "This dress created a sensation, partly because it was so pretty, but also, and more to the point, because a mistake had been made in working out the price, and it was fixed at a figure which was considerably less than what it cost us to make."[3] From the very start Dior set out to conquer the world and women who would wear his "*chimères apprivoisés*" passing "from the world of my dreams into the world of practical utility."[4]

By setting the tone for haute couture of the postwar years, Christian Dior recomposed the alphabet of seduction, restored confidence in imagination, and gave the body the armour of its dreams—an armour that has considerably softened today to suit modern comforts. He was the creator of the "new you," the first "couturier-architect" of the twentieth century. He was a maestro of the full dancing skirt, composing a score whose silhouettes prolonged a new yet familiar air every season: the Dior line. Clean and curvaceous. Structured. Lined with percale or taffeta from the very start, to give the garments more "hold." What were the advantages of the *Corolle* dress? It "disguises hips that are a bit wide. Flatters the legs. Looks 'young,' and 'men like it,'" noted *Elle* magazine in March 1947. From the *Bar* suit (1947) to

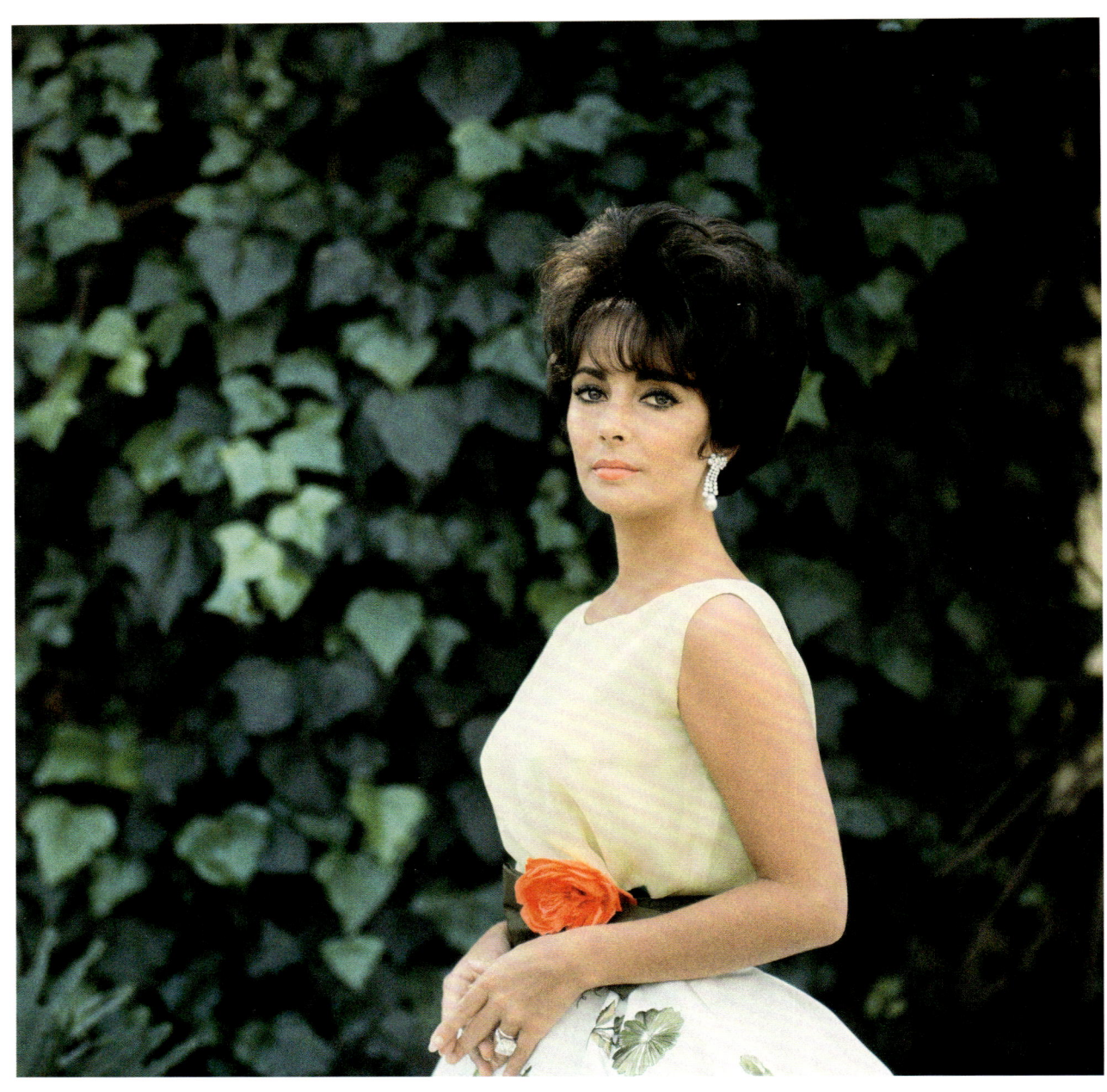

Elizabeth Taylor wearing the *Soirée à Rio* dress, Spring-Summer 1961 haute couture collection.

such as Marilyn Monroe or Liz Taylor, Leonor Fini or Marion Cotillard; society figures, such as the Countess of Chambrun or Francine Weisweller; or Christian Dior's close circle, such as Mitzah Bricard or Suzanne Luling, his childhood friend from Granville. Created by Dior, chosen during the salon presentation, and then cut and fitted to match the client's exact measurements, a dress left the couturier's world to enter the client's private history. Each dress was not simply the fruit of his imagination: When his designs were embodied by a unique woman, the couturier's creation became a completed work. The dress took on the density of real life. When preserved with care, it tells a story of desires, joys, passions, and sorrows just like a private diary. When it is taken out of its archive box, traces of the woman who wore it reappear.

In the exhibition *Women in Dior*, ninety dresses are presented alongside photo portraits, paintings, drawings, and souvenirs to evoke the elegance of women in Dior. From the sobriety of daywear to the extravagance of gala gowns, the selection of pieces illustrates all the aspects of a life dressed in Dior. Keepsakes, anecdotes, and family pictures help to highlight the singularity of each ensemble. Different themes imagine these figures from the perspective of moments in the day or year. When a whole wardrobe has been preserved, the image of its owner transpires, a portrait of her tastes, habits, and lifestyle. The visit is punctuated by five such wardrobes—entire sets of clothes, accessories, and lingerie items belonging to the same person. The exhibition ends with the apotheosis of refinement and elegance: bridal gowns and red carpet outfits.

All these different ensembles and images illustrate the ways in which a woman has chosen to express her personality through Dior's style and demonstrate her contemporaneousness through a love of creativity beyond the trends. They also show that each lady has known how to portray her own unique temperament with a consistency of taste, colors, shapes, or forms. These women in Dior are all different, yet all share one thing in common: In Dior they found a style that suited them magnificently. Christian Dior's dearest wish came true, to "make women not just more beautiful, but also happier."

Foreword

Florence Müller
Curator of the exhibition *Women in Dior*

After a series of exhibitions evoking Dior's relations with the art world and the origins of Dior's style, the Musée Christian Dior in Granville pays tribute to the women, famous or anonymous, without whom a couture house could never exist. Following *Dior Impressions* and associated for the second time with the Normandy Impressionist Festival—this year devoted to portraits—the museum presents a modern, sensitive, impressionistic "haute couture" gallery of over forty personalities dressed in Dior from 1947 to 2016.

The Impressionists preferred to depict female grace highlighted by all of fashion's artifices and captured in snapshots of modern life. Their paintings portray women in the privacy of their homes or bringing life to the streets, theaters, and fashionable boulevards of Paris with their crinoline or bustle-clad silhouettes. By showing them adorned in the latest novelties, the Impressionists managed to implicitly represent their models' characters in a fully sociological and psychological dimension. The clothes, accessories, hairstyles, and makeup tell us how each woman saw herself and liked to be admired. A woman's finery completed the definition of the personality, which language or social behavior outlined in a much more symbolic way. Through her clothing, a woman revealed silent information about herself that was far more legible than an identity certificate.

In the exhibition *Women in Dior*, dresses and accessories play a role in revealing the personalities who wore them. With Dior as their couturier, figures of elegance take shape from France and abroad, the worlds of aristocracy, the bourgeoisie, the media, entertainment, stage, or screen. Christian Dior and his successors imagined haute couture as an art form for everyday life in which every moment counts, be it the simplicity of daytime or the sumptuousness of gala evenings. The couture house offered designs adapted to life's different occasions and conceived them for the day's key moments or throughout a seasonal calendar.

In the wealth of garments the couturier proposed, a host of personalities found what they needed to express their individuality. Each case is different, from Princess Grace of Monaco to the Duchess of Windsor or Lady Diana; actresses or artists,

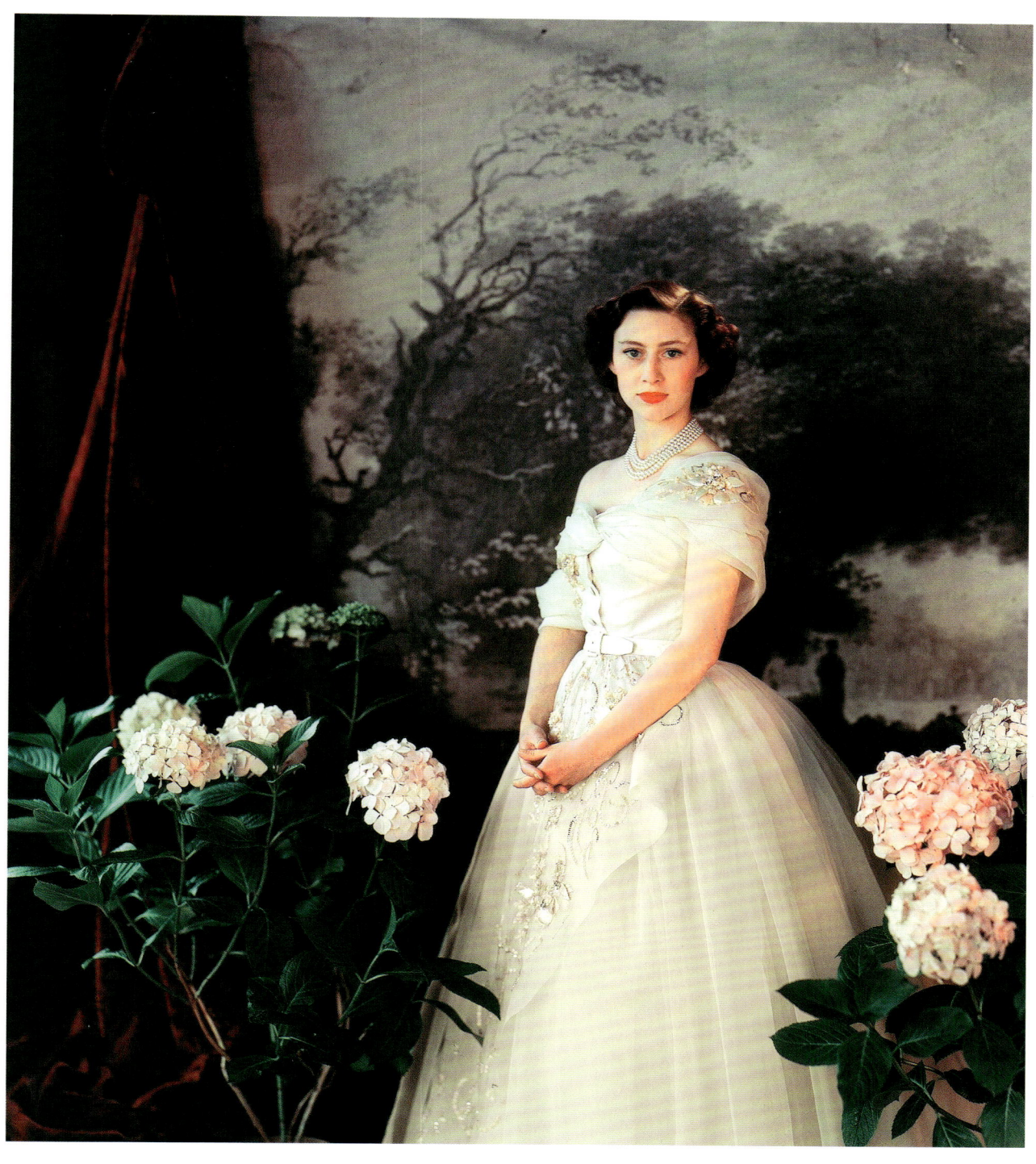

Official portrait of Princess Margaret photographed by Cecil Beaton in 1951 for her twenty-first birthday. She wears a special Christian Dior design.

CONTENTS

Foreword
6–9

Introduction
10–17

I
HIGH SOCIETY
18–49

Dior Clients and
the Sense of Perfection
20–45

Society Balls
46–49

II
THE CLOSE CIRCLE
50–81

Queens of
30 Avenue Montaigne
52–77

The Dior Models: La Cabine
78–81

III
OFFICIAL EVENTS
82–111

Wardrobes and Protocol
84–103

The Grimaldi Family
104–107

Grand Weddings
108–111

IX
RED CARPET
112–149

Divine Apparitions
114–141

Dior Perfumes the Stars
142–145

Special Creations
146–149